AFTER GUN VIOLENCE

EDITED BY CHERYL GLENN AND STEPHEN BROWNE
THE PENNSYLVANIA STATE UNIVERSITY

Cofounding Editor: J. Michael Hogan

Rhetoric and Democratic Deliberation focuses on the interplay of public discourse, politics, and democratic action. Engaging with diverse theoretical, cultural, and critical perspectives, books published in this series offer fresh perspectives on rhetoric as it relates to education, social movements, and governments throughout the world.

A complete list of books in this series is located at the back of this volume.

AFTER GUN VIOLENCE

DELIBERATION AND MEMORY IN AN AGE OF POLITICAL GRIDLOCK

CRAIG ROOD

The Pennsylvania State University Press | University Park, Pennsylvania

Library of Congress Cataloging-in-Publication Data
Names: Rood, Craig, 1985– author.
Title: After gun violence : deliberation and memory in an age of political gridlock / Craig Rood.
Other titles: Rhetoric and democratic deliberation.
Description: University Park, Pennsylvania : The Pennsylvania State University Press, [2019] | Series: Rhetoric and democratic deliberation | Includes bibliographical references and index.
Summary: "A rhetorical study of the American political debate on gun violence and gun policy. Examines the role of public memory in shaping this discourse and its eventual policy outcomes"—Provided by publisher.
Identifiers: LCCN 2019005851 | ISBN 9780271083834 (cloth : alk. paper)
Subjects: LCSH: Firearms and crime—United States. | Violent crimes—United States. | Mass shootings—United States. | Firearms—Government policy—United States. | Collective memory—United States. | Rhetoric—United States.
Classification: LCC HV7436.R66 2019 | DDC 364.150973—dc23
LC record available at: https://lccn.loc.gov/2019005851

Printed in the United States of America
Published by The Pennsylvania State University Press, University Park, PA 16802-1003

The Pennsylvania State University Press is a member of the Association of University Presses.

It is the policy of The Pennsylvania State University Press to use acid-free paper. Publications on uncoated stock satisfy the minimum requirements of American National Standard for Information Sciences—Permanence of Paper for Printed Library Material, ANSI Z39.48-1992.

focus too on all the planes that do not crash
all the spaces that are indeed safe
all the vehicles that do not collide
all the hugs exchanged
all the love that does indeed pass between persons

remember that because "it can happen anywhere" doesn't mean it is going to happen anywhere in particular—where you and your loved ones are—at any particular time

love and reason
and a steady hand

—ROSA A. EBERLY, *TOWERS OF RHETORIC*

CONTENTS

ACKNOWLEDGMENTS

I gratefully acknowledge permission to use revised versions of two previously published essays. Chapter 3 has been adapted from "'Our Tears Are Not Enough': The Warrant of the Dead in the Rhetoric of Gun Control," *Quarterly Journal of Speech* 104, no. 1 (2018): 47–70. This essay is reprinted by permission of Taylor and Francis Ltd. (http://www.tandfonline.com) on behalf of the National Communication Association. Chapter 4 has been adapted from "The Racial Politics of Gun Violence: A Brief Rhetorical History," in *Was Blind but Now I See: Rhetoric, Race, Religion, and the Charleston Shootings*, ed. Sean Patrick O'Rourke and Melody Lehn (Lanham, MD: Lexington, forthcoming).

Crafting this book has been a long process, and I am grateful to the many people who have helped at different stages. Thanks to everyone involved with the Rhetoric and Democratic Deliberation series at Pennsylvania State University Press, including press editors Kendra Boileau and Ryan Peterson, series editors Cheryl Glenn and Stephen Browne, and the two peer reviewers (who elected to disclose their names), Robert Asen and Kendall Phillips. Their thoughtful readings and encouragement have helped make this a better book. Thanks as well to the team at Scribe Inc. for their excellent work during the final stages of preparing this manuscript (copyediting, proofreading, creating an index).

Thanks to everyone in the Department of English and Program in Speech Communication at Iowa State University. Ben Crosby (now at Brigham Young University) helped me get this project off the ground. During our periodic lunches around Ames, we puzzled through the process of writing *any* book, and he helped me test out ideas for how to write this one. Near the end of this process, Lori Peterson, editor extraordinaire, provided a close reading of the entire manuscript. And throughout the process, I have been inspired by my colleagues and buoyed by their questions, suggestions, and encouragement. Special thanks to Lesley Bartlett, Barbara Ching, Abby Dubisar, Sean Grass, Charlie Kostelnick, Anne Kretsinger-Harries (and Mark!), Maggie LaWare, Prashant Rajan, Brandon Sams, Matt Sivils, and Jeremy Withers. Finally, the department, college, and university deserve praise for their efforts to support and mentor junior faculty. In particular, the College of Liberal Arts and Sciences's Humanities Scholarship Enhancement Initiative freed up time in fall

2016 to make progress on this project. And the Iowa State University Publication Endowment Fund (ISU Foundation) provided a subvention grant to support the publication of this book.

Outside of Iowa State, several people have provided valuable feedback and encouragement on various pieces of this book, even though they might not recognize its current form. Thanks to Brian Amsden, Earl Brooks, Mark Hlavacik, Mike Hogan, Bill Keith, Melody Lehn, Andrew Mara, Sean Patrick O'Rourke, Sam Perry, Billy Saas, Jack Selzer, Brad Serber, Mary Stuckey, Kirt Wilson, and David Zarefsky.

Since this is my first book, I feel like I need to thank every single teacher who has helped me up to this point. Three of them deserve special recognition for inspiring me with their intense intelligence and unparalleled generosity. Lee Kruger introduced me to rhetoric in a composition class during my first year of college (and read my first essay on the gun debate). Amy Rupiper Taggart, who died far too young, encouraged me to go to graduate school, taught me how to teach, and then advised me through my master's program. Rosa Eberly advised me through my doctoral program. I have learned much from her about gun violence and rhetoric. On and off the page, Rosa's example provides a regular reminder of Wayne Booth's claim that "the quality of our lives, moment by moment, depends upon the quality of our rhetoric."

Thanks to all my family. Special thanks to my parents, Brenda and Rodney, whose love and support have been constant. Without your encouragement, I sincerely doubt whether I would have ever gone to college, let alone graduate school. As a teenager growing up in North Dakota, I spent many weekends with my dad shooting at targets and hunting gophers, ducks, and deer. Although I have since chosen not to own or use guns, I value the time we spent together, and I think those early experiences have helped me write a better book. Thank you both for everything. Thanks also to Laura's family—especially her parents, Keith Brown and Martha Branson—for your questions about my research and for welcoming me into your family.

And then there is my favorite person—Laura Michael Brown. Without you, this book would not exist. You've been there every day, optimistic when I needed it most (and critical when I did not realize that's what I needed). Thanks for reading all those drafts and for all our conversations. Thanks, too, for reminding me that there is life outside of my office. I am so grateful that you sent me that Kenneth Burke article all those years ago and that we have gotten to spend our lives together.

Finally, thanks to our two cats, Hank and Harriet, who have been regular writing companions and supportive in their own ways.

INTRODUCTION: DELIBERATING GUN VIOLENCE

December 14, 2012, started as a day of excitement and promise for many families in Newtown, Connecticut. Reporter Matthew Lysiak notes that "for parents, the chaotic hustle and bustle of getting their children out the door for school on the morning of December 14 was amplified for two reasons: it was a Friday and Christmas vacation was fast approaching."[1] Jesse, a six-year-old, had spent the prior evening purchasing gifts "for friends, family members, and his beloved first-grade teacher."[2] He was spending that Friday morning eating breakfast at a local deli with his father before the school day started. Charlotte argued with her mother about whether she could wear a new dress to school rather than save it for the holidays. Josephine was anticipating her birthday party the next day, and her family was "busy planning an indoor pool party with all of her classmates."[3] None of the children knew Adam Lanza nor had any reason to suspect that the twenty-year-old would come to Sandy Hook Elementary School that morning. Lanza shot and killed twenty children and six adults at the school; if you count him killing his mother and himself—which people rarely do—the total killed was twenty-eight.

News broke, and the nation watched. Aerial images showed first responders outside the school while ground images showed adults escorting a group of confused children out of the school in single file. Reporters noted that "as many as [varying numbers]" had been murdered.[4] Commentators tried to explain what had happened. At 3:15 p.m., President Barack Obama spoke from the White House: "Our hearts are broken today. . . . We have been through this too many times." He continued, "We're going to have to come together and take meaningful action to prevent more tragedies like this, regardless of the politics."[5] In the days that followed, we heard the names and saw the faces of all who had been murdered. And more often, we heard the name and saw the face of the murderer. The persisting questions were Why? What now?

Almost everyone had an explanation for what had happened.[6] The shooter was to blame—he was evil or mentally ill or a loner longing for fame. Or perhaps those closest to him were to blame—they did not get him the help he needed, did not notice his odd behavior before the shooting, or did not teach him right from wrong. Or the location of the violence was to blame—there should have been better security, maybe even armed guards or armed teachers. Or society was to blame—the entertainment industry and news media give airtime to ghastly violence and make mass murderers famous, cultural norms teach boys and men to be violent, we fail to provide adequate support to address mental illness, or we make it too easy for anyone to get an assault weapon. X is to blame; X is not to blame.

President Obama had responded to previous mass shootings: he spoke in Fort Hood in 2009, Tucson in 2011, and Aurora and Oak Creek in 2012. But this shooting marked a turning point. Speaking at a press conference on December 19, 2012, Obama stated, "We know this is a complex issue that stirs deeply held passions and political divides." "But," he argued, "the fact that this problem is complex can no longer be an excuse for doing nothing. The fact that we can't prevent every act of violence doesn't mean we can't steadily reduce the violence, and prevent the very worst violence."[7] He announced that Vice President Biden would lead a task force to "come up with a set of concrete proposals no later than January."[8] Then, on January 16, 2013, the White House released a plan—"Now Is the Time: The President's Plan to Protect Our Children and Our Communities by Reducing Gun Violence"—which consisted of four parts:

1. Closing background-check loopholes to keep guns out of dangerous hands
2. Banning military-style assault weapons and high-capacity magazines and taking other common-sense steps to reduce gun violence
3. Making schools safer
4. Increasing access to mental health services[9]

To help make a case for this plan, Obama appeared alongside Biden on its release day, and both men spoke. Obama focused on the first two items of the plan: background checks and the ban on assault weapons and high-capacity magazines. From January until April, Obama continued to emphasize these gun-control measures in speeches delivered in Chicago, Colorado, Connecticut, and Washington, DC. On April 17, 2013, the Senate voted on the White

House's gun-control proposals. All of them failed to reach the necessary sixty votes.

Gun-control advocates saw the vote as a failure, while many (though not all) gun-rights advocates saw the vote as a victory. Regardless of one's politics, however, the vote suggested that Americans might never be able to agree about how to address the problem of gun violence in America. In response to subsequent mass shootings, Obama would wonder aloud if Americans had given up hope and begun to accept mass shootings as a normal part of American life. On September 16, 2013, a gunman at the Washington Navy Yard killed twelve people before committing suicide. Commentators revisited the usual topics—guns, mental illness, and security—but the debate seemed especially routine and empty. At a memorial service on September 22, 2013, Obama stated that "after the round-of-clock coverage on cable news, after the heartbreaking interviews with families, after all the speeches and all the punditry and all the commentary, nothing happens. Alongside the anguish of these American families, alongside the accumulated outrage so many of us feel, sometimes I fear there's a creeping resignation that these tragedies are just somehow the way it is, that this is somehow the new normal."[10] By October 1, 2015, after a shooting at Umpqua Community College, Obama had become less patient: "Somehow this has become routine. The reporting is routine. My response here at this podium ends up being routine. The conversation in the aftermath of it. We've become numb to this."[11]

Some readers might dismiss Obama by claiming that mass shootings are an exaggerated problem. And there are disagreements about how often mass shootings happen. These disagreements boil down to different definitions of the term *mass shooting*.[12] A 2015 Congressional Research Service report offers one of the more restrictive definitions, in which a *public mass shooting* refers to a "multiple homicide incident in which four or more victims are murdered with firearms, within one event, in at least one or more public locations, such as, a workplace, school, restaurant, house of worship, neighborhood, or other public setting." According to this definition, public mass shootings are relatively rare: from 1999 through 2013, "offenders committed 66 mass public shootings, murdering 446 victims and non-fatally wounding another 329 victims."[13] Yet others challenge this definition, claiming that it is "arbitrary to distinguish between a death and an injury." For instance, "some shootings that injure a dozen or more people but don't kill four people would not be considered a mass shooting under the more restrictive definition."[14] The Gun Violence Archive offers a far more expansive definition that includes the injured in the tally as well as violence that occurs in nonpublic settings such as the home: "Four or more shot and/or killed in a single event, at the same general time and location, not including the shooter." According to this definition, mass shootings are a far more serious problem; there were 253 mass shootings in the United States in 2013, 270 in 2014, 335 in 2015, and 382 in 2016.[15]

But even if we accept the more restrictive definition—which suggests that mass shootings are relatively rare—mass shootings remain worthy of public and scholarly attention for several reasons. First, regardless of how frequently mass shootings happen, even a single mass shooting has devastating and enduring consequences. Those consequences matter. Those lives matter. Second, mass shootings are a distinctly American problem. One study found that the United States "makes up less than 5% of the world's population, but holds 31% of global mass shooters."[16] We should consider how American life might enable—and perhaps even encourage—such horrific violence. And third, mass shootings are typically the moments of gun violence that capture national attention and are remembered. Some of these shootings function as "focusing events" that initiate national debates and mobilize people to enact change.[17] While these focusing events are important on their own, they also encourage us to consider why our national debates focus on *mass* shootings and how this choice influences how we imagine gun violence and debate gun policy.

Our collective inaction in response to high-profile mass shootings suggests that we would be even less likely to address the more common forms of gun violence that happen daily yet fail to gain national resolve or even attention. This daily gun violence comes in numerous forms, including domestic violence, armed robbery, gang violence, suicide, and so on. Although gun-homicide rates have decreased since the early 1990s, there are still over 10,000 gun homicides a year in the United States. In 2014, for instance, 11,008 of the total 15,872 homicides were committed with a firearm; in 2015, 12,979 of the total 17,793 homicides were committed with a firearm.[18] Firearms are used in nearly half of all suicides. In 2014, for instance, firearms were used in 21,386 suicides;[19] in 2015, firearms were used in 22,018 suicides.[20] And "over 67,000 persons are injured by firearms each year."[21]

Compared to other high-income countries, this much gun violence is atypical. Based on an analysis of 2010 mortality data from the World Health Organization, Erin Grinshteyn and David Hemenway found that "US homicide rates were 7.0 times higher than other high-income countries, driven by a gun homicide rate that was 25.2 times higher."[22] A 2017 study found that per one million people, Australia has 1.4 homicides by firearm, Germany has 1.9, Canada has 5.1, and the United States has 29.7.[23]

These numbers are staggering, but they do not tell the full story. They do not capture all the potential lost. They do not quantify the number of hours that families struggle to figure out how to live without their loved ones or the number of hours that the injured must spend rehabilitating. Nor can any number represent the strains placed on individuals, families, and communities directly affected by gun violence. Nor can the numbers represent the strains placed on all Americans who have become fearful of one another and of being together in public spaces, including places designed for education, work, worship, and entertainment. Regardless of one's political perspective, it is undeniable that gun violence has a profound effect on American life. Gun violence is everyone's problem, even if some individuals and communities feel it more directly and urgently than do others.

While the toll of gun violence is devastating, our debates about it are baffling. "The political pattern typifying the gun debate," Robert J. Spitzer writes, "is one in which repetitive political scenarios play themselves out with great fury but astonishing little effect."[24] If a mass shooting or another form of gun violence captures national attention, public debate follows a familiar routine: cast blame, pick sides, and move on. Our dysfunctional debates about gun violence—and in turn, about gun policy—often consist of talking points and talking past one another. Such talk fails to address the problem while only seeming to drive Americans further and further apart. Many choose to disengage and keep silent, sensing that nothing will change and that our deliberative dysfunction is simply the new normal. How did we get to this point? And what hope is there, if any, for breaking the cycle of violence and gridlock?

After Gun Violence is a book about America's long-standing debates about gun violence and gun policy. But it also speaks to any public debate marked by gridlock. It is a search to understand why. And it is a search for how we might do better.

My Stance

I believe that debates about gun violence could use more honesty and directness. So I want to be forthright about where I stand: throughout the process of writing this book, I have come to support the kind of reforms that the Obama White House proposed after the Sandy Hook Elementary School shooting. The fact that I have a personal stance should be unsurprising (indeed, I think that I would be embarrassed if I spent years studying a topic without arriving at any opinions). Yet in our current cultural climate, disclosing my personal stance feels risky for at least two reasons.

First, I have studied the gun debate long enough to know where things might go from here. Some readers might conclude that I am not on their side and stop reading. Other readers might conclude that I am on their side and eagerly anticipate my biting critique of the opposition. We all regularly divide—and are divided—into "them" and "us." But as much as possible, we need to resist the "us versus them" mentality. Whether we are debating gun violence and policy or some other divisive issue, we must find ways to talk and listen across our differences without dismissing or dehumanizing one another. Sometimes that is easier said than done. But if we are unwilling to try, then there is little hope for change.

Second, some readers might expect a scholar to be wholly neutral—they might expect that a scholar should either not have a point of view or hide it if they do. I understand this desire, but I ultimately do not think that any scholar can be entirely neutral. Indeed, my very decision to write about gun violence reveals human judgment from the outset; after all, I could have decided to write about something else. Nor do I think that "balance" is an automatic virtue.[25] If someone says something untrue or potentially dangerous, then scholars should call it as they see it. Saying this does not permit me to find fault only with gun-rights advocates and to pretend that gun-control advocates are perfect. However, the test is not whether I spend an equal number of paragraphs on gun-control advocates or gun-rights advocates but whether I present both positions fairly and accurately and offer analyses of those positions that can withstand critical scrutiny. Put differently, scholars should exercise their judgment to help readers improve their own judgment—even if they do not ultimately agree with one another.

Disclosing my personal stance is important. But I also do not want readers to miss the point of this book. I did not write this book in order to advocate for or against any specific policies. Experts in public policy are better qualified for that sort of work. Instead, I want to take a step back to consider how Americans—scholars, citizens, activists, media commentators, public leaders, and so on—communicate about gun violence and gun policy. Why is common ground so elusive and division so persistent? Why do seemingly good arguments fall on unreceptive ears?

A Rhetorical Perspective on Gun Violence and Gun Policy

The problems of gun violence and our gridlocked debates about it are multifaceted and require the insights of many stakeholders and researchers. The problems concern the broad public—those directly affected by the violence as well as journalists, politicians, advocacy-group members, school and community leaders, security experts, and everyday citizens. Among researchers, gun violence and gun policy have attracted the attention of scholars in communication, criminology, history, law, media studies, philosophy, political science, public health, psychology, sociology, and other fields.[26] This book complements existing research on gun violence, including works that detail specific mass shootings,[27] the psychology of mass shooters,[28] and the social contexts in which violence occurs.[29] It also complements existing research on gun policy, including works that examine the history of the Second Amendment,[30] the power of the gun industry and lobby,[31] the efficacy of various policy proposals,[32] and various social movements committed to gun control and gun rights.[33]

Drawing this research together, I consider the relationships between gun violence and gun policy rather than one to the exclusion of the other. Some readers might object that it does not make sense to talk about gun policy and gun violence together, and I examine different variations of this argument in subsequent chapters. But it is hard to deny that guns and gun policy are commonly debated in the aftermath of high-profile acts of gun violence. For better or worse, gun violence is a dominant catalyst and context for talking about gun policy. This is true for both sides of the gun debate. Proponents of gun control argue that limited restrictions can help keep guns out of the "wrong hands" and keep all Americans safe, whereas proponents of gun rights argue that the best defense against a criminal or mass murderer is to be armed and ready to return fire.

I draw from diverse bodies of literature, but I do not seek to duplicate them. By offering a rhetorical perspective, this book focuses on the communication dimensions of debates about gun violence and gun policy in order to clarify why public deliberation is often so dysfunctional. By adopting a rhetorical perspective, I can explore how people and institutions communicate, why, and to what effect. Rhetorical scholars remind us that we are born into a social world in which language already exists, so we will never have complete control over our words or world. Sometimes we use language to express ourselves, and sometimes language does our thinking for us. Invoking Kenneth Burke, Krista Ratcliffe explains that "rhetoric is the study of how we use language and how language uses us."[34]

At the outset, a rhetorical perspective encourages us to see that disagreement is not necessarily bad. Indeed, disagreement is a central component of democratic life. As David Zarefsky explains, rhetoric and democracy are both based on the fact of human fallibility and thus our need to "make collective decisions under conditions of uncertainty."[35] If humans were unerring or if all our problems could be easily solved, we would have no need to argue or vote. But that is not us or our world. Since we must live with one another—more or less—we are bound to disagree, sometimes quite passionately. Our disagreements can be a sign that our democracy is healthy and that we care about the future. The goal, then, is not to eliminate disagreement or to seek some kind of utopian harmony. Instead, the goal is to make sure that we have good reasons for disagreeing—that our disagreements are rooted in understanding and accuracy rather than demonization or distortion.

Commentators and scholars without training in rhetoric sometimes assume that the strongest argument should and will win—that if we do the right study and get the facts right, then debates about gun violence and gun policy will change and perhaps end. To be clear, facts matter, and I support further empirical research on gun violence. For over two decades, Congress has blocked the Center for Disease Control and Prevention from researching gun violence.[36] But while we need reliable empirical data to make informed decisions, data alone are not enough. As Dan M. Kahan puts it, "The hope that the gun control debate can be made less contentious by confining it to empirical arguments is in fact an idle one."[37] For better or worse, political debate is not reducible to cogent arguments, and arguments are not reducible to facts. For starters, our debates about the sources and potential solutions to gun violence are intertwined with our "beliefs and values, hopes and fears." They are predicated on our "different senses of agency, rights, and the role of government." And they are often struggles over "our past, present, and future—about who 'we' are individually and collectively."[38] To account for these debates, let alone change them, we must study them as complex rhetorical phenomena.

Within the field of rhetorical studies, scholars "have done significant work on the gun debate, but that work is narrowly focused and episodic."[39] Such scholars have perhaps given the most sustained attention to the 2011 mass shooting in Tucson, Arizona, since that shooting spurred debates about the relationship between gun violence and vitriolic rhetoric.[40] They also have started examining the rhetoric of gun-rights advocates[41] but have given little attention to the rhetoric of gun-control advocates.[42] To appreciate the complexity of public deliberation about gun violence and gun policy, we must see key moments in relation to one another as well as key players in relation to one another. Current rhetorical scholarship on gun violence suffers from the same problem as the public discussion of gun violence: both lack a broad historical perspective, thus keeping us from seeing how disparate moments of debate are related to one another and face recurring challenges. As J. Michael Hogan and I have outlined, what is needed is a rhetorical history that offers a "coherent narrative of how we arrived at today's deliberative impasse" and explains how we might move forward. Hogan and I explained that such a rhetorical would identify and trace the "key players, important policy texts, and transformative moments in debates over guns and gun control policies."[43] Given the gridlock of the gun debate and persistent inaction at the national level, I now realize that such a rhetorical history must also examine the absences, exclusions, and failures: Who has not been a key player in the gun debate, and why not? Why were policies proposed in response to some violent events but not others? And why were some moments transformative while others were not?[44]

As a rhetorical critic and theorist, I cannot offer any unique expertise about why gun violence *really* happens, nor can I offer a plan for preventing it. And that is not my goal here. What I can offer is insight about our public talk. Rhetorical studies—as a discipline with a history—offers a vocabulary and unique insights for understanding how public argument and deliberation work or do not work.

A Brief Rhetorical History

As a methodology, a rhetorical history traces how arguments and appeals in a given debate or disagreement have developed—or failed to develop—across time.[45] A rhetorical history oscillates between two needs: specificity and generality. On the one hand, a critic examines "how, and how well, people deployed rhetorical resources in a historical moment that called for them." On the other hand, by looking at several historical moments, a critic seeks to generalize about "patterns and variations in rhetorical exigencies and responses."[46] Among the benefits of rhetorical history is the recognition that arguments expressed in a particular moment typically have a history, and those arguments are shaped, for better or worse, by that history.

Rather than write history for history's sake, I write a history that can help us understand contemporary deliberation about gun violence and gun policy. My emphasis is on President Obama's second term. In subsequent chapters,

I offer thematic histories focused on three of the most divisive contemporary debates related to gun violence and gun policy: the Second Amendment (chapter 2), our obligations to the dead (chapter 3), and racism (chapter 4). Each of these thematic histories draws from key moments throughout U.S. history to help explain how these debates became so dysfunctional. I regularly return to the 1990s and 1960s to help explain our current predicament. At times, I trace our contemporary debates even further back, including the Civil War and America's founding.

Although my emphasis in this book is on our post–Sandy Hook world, it is useful to start by taking a step back. To provide additional context for the thematic histories offered in subsequent chapters, I want to briefly describe three transformative years in debates over gun violence and gun policy: 1966, 1994, and 1999.

1966

In the early morning of August 1, 1966, Charles Joseph Whitman murdered his mother and his wife. After writing several notes trying to explain his actions, he spent several hours organizing an arsenal of weapons and supplies. Then, around 11:00 a.m., he headed to the University of Texas at Austin. He shot and killed three people as he made his way to the twenty-eighth floor of the clock tower. Perched atop the observation deck, he looked below to unknown people walking across campus and on the adjacent streets. He continued shooting.[47]

Although this was not the first mass shooting in the United States, it appears to be the first one on a college campus.[48] In 1966, this act had no clear precedent other than in fiction.[49] There was no history of school shootings to make sense of what Whitman was doing. Reporters did not have a script to recite. Students and law enforcement had no active-shooter protocols to follow. Local police and citizens tried shooting Whitman from the ground, but he was effectively barricaded. The shooting spree lasted for over an hour and a half. By the time Whitman was killed, he had killed sixteen and injured thirty-one. In America's perverse ranking system, the shooting marked what was then the "largest simultaneous mass murder [committed by a lone gunman] in American history."[50]

Of course, gun violence did not begin in the 1960s. But it was then that Americans began to experience such violence and its aftermath through television. Reports "aired locally and nationally on network news."[51] On the evening of the shooting, KTBC, a local station in Austin, aired a special report.

The anchorman began, "Good evening. One of history's worst mass murders occurred here in Austin today." After describing the sequence of what had happened, the broadcast then turned to video footage from the shooting. The camera starts by focusing on the clock tower, allowing viewers to see and hear Whitman's gunshots. Then viewers are shown dead people on the ground, people rushing to help the injured, and people running for safety.[52]

After the shooting, the search began to understand why this had happened. Brutal mass violence had happened before, but this was not wartime. Nor could this be fit into a narrative of revenge. The people that Whitman shot on campus were strangers. For some commentators, the explanation was simple: Whitman alone was to blame. He was "mean as hell" or just simply crazy. Others pointed to Whitman's personal circumstances: the tumor found in his brain, domestic abuse in his family, and his marine training. Still others blamed society, including violence in the media and easy gun access.[53] This blaming of society was succinctly captured in Walter Cronkite's broadcast shortly after the tragedy. Mentioning social unrest within the United States and war abroad, Cronkite claimed that Whitman was not the only one to blame: "It seems likely that Charles Joseph Whitman's crime was society's crime."[54]

Americans have continued to disagree about *what* to blame in the aftermath of mass shootings—whether the shooter, guns, mental illness, the media, norms of masculinity (since mass shootings have been committed almost exclusively by men),[55] or something else. But these disagreements are often predicated on different choices about *how* to blame. Researchers emphasize that trying to understand a specific mass shooting—let alone mass shootings or gun violence in general—requires a "multiperspectivist interpretation" because a "constellation of specific factors" are typically at work.[56] But public discourse in response to mass shootings tends to be governed by an either-or logic that often coalesces around just one or two factors: it was the gun *or* it was the shooter; it was *X* or *Y*, not both.[57] As we see again and again, Americans explicitly and implicitly disagree about the scope of blame—that is, whether blame is localized or expansive. *Localized blame,* in its purest form, suggests that the shooting was an isolated act, that the shooter bears exclusive or at least primary responsibility, or that the cause of violence is relatively simple. *Expansive blame,* by contrast, suggests that a particular shooting is part of a larger pattern of gun violence, that some aspect of society bears at least some responsibility, or that the causes of violence are relatively complex.

The Austin shooting was used to help make the case for what would become the Gun Control Act of 1968. The day after the violence, President

Lyndon Johnson issued a statement on "the need for firearms control legislation." He insisted that "we must press urgently for the legislation now pending in Congress to help prevent the wrong persons from obtaining firearms." While the bill "would not prevent all such tragedies," it promised to "reduce the unrestricted sale of firearms to those who cannot be trusted in their use of possession." The bill has "been under consideration in Congress for many months," and "the time has come for action before further loss of life that might be prevented by its passage."[58] Notably, the shooting in Austin did not initiate this legislation: the bill was created after President John F. Kennedy was assassinated on November 22, 1963. And while the Austin shooting was used to help justify gun control, other events were also important, including the assassinations of Martin Luther King Jr. and Robert F. Kennedy in 1968, as well as urban riots (which I describe more in chapter 4).

The Gun Control Act of 1968 restricted the interstate sale of firearms, including the type of mail-order rifle that was used to kill President Kennedy. It also sought to keep guns away from felons, people convicted of a domestic-violence crime, drug abusers, and the "mentally defective."[59] Upon signing the act, Johnson noted that "we have made much progress—but not nearly enough." Johnson had called on Congress to require "the national registration of all guns and the licensing of those who carry those guns," but there was not enough support. "The voices that blocked these safeguards were not the voices of an aroused nation," Johnson explained. Instead, they were the "the voices of a powerful lobby, a gun lobby, that has prevailed for the moment in an election year."[60]

Although the gun lobby of 1968 was strong, it was not nearly as strong as it is today. Indeed, the Gun Control Act of 1968 was instrumental in transforming the National Rifle Association (NRA) because it "exacerbated a split between the sportsmen and the politicos in the organization."[61] In 1977, at the NRA's annual meeting in Cincinnati, the politicos took control over the organization. Chapter 2 will explain more about this transformation, but for now, what is important is that the "Cincinnati Revolt" of 1977 "completed the organization's evolution into a politically active gun lobby."[62] This evolution would come to have a profound effect on gun politics in America.

1994

In 1994, two important changes took place in American gun policy. The 1993 Brady Handgun Violence Prevention Act went into effect, requiring firearm purchasers to undergo a federal background check. And the 1994 assault-weapons ban (formally known as the Public Safety and Recreational Firearms Use Protection Act) was passed. But 1994 also represented a turning point in American gun politics. Since 1994, the gun debate has become exceptionally polarized.

After its change in leadership in 1977, the NRA gained cultural prominence and political influence. For politicians, one's stance on guns was becoming a litmus test. The NRA's endorsement of Ronald Reagan during the 1980 presidential election marked "the first time in the gun organization's 109-year history that it had backed a candidate for the nation's top office." In May 1983, Reagan spoke at the NRA's annual meeting, becoming the "first sitting president" to do so.[63] The occasion was significant, but so were Reagan's words. Two years earlier, a gunman had shot Reagan and nearly killed him. But in his speech to the NRA, Reagan suggested that the problem was not with guns but with criminals: "Guns don't make criminals. Hard-core criminals use guns. And locking them up, the hard-core criminals up, and throwing away the key is the best gun-control law we could ever have." Endorsing America's war on crime, Reagan suggested that "longer prison sentences and tougher treatment" were the best solutions for reducing crime. "But there's one thing we do not want: We will never disarm any American who seeks to protect his or her family from fear and harm." He praised NRA members for never backing down "one inch from defending the constitutional freedoms that are every American's birthright."[64]

While Reagan offered a clear defense of the Second Amendment, he also maintained that gun rights and gun control were not mutually exclusive. On March 29, 1991—the eve of the ten-year anniversary of when he was shot—Reagan published "Why I'm for the Brady Bill" in the *New York Times*. The bill was named after Reagan's press secretary, James Brady. (The Brady Campaign to Prevent Gun Violence—one of the most prominent groups advocating for gun reforms today—is also named after him.) The gunman who shot Reagan in 1981 also shot Brady in the head. Reagan noted that although Brady recovered, he had to live with "physical pain every day and spend much of his time in a wheelchair." Reagan continued, "This nightmare might never have happened if legislation that is before Congress now—the Brady bill—had been law back in 1981." He explained that the Gun Control Act of 1968 "prohibits the sale of firearms to felons, fugitives, drug addicts, and the mentally ill," but it "has no enforcement mechanism and basically works on the honor system, with the purchaser filling out a statement that the gun dealer sticks in a drawer." With the Brady Bill in place, handgun dealers would be required to "provide a copy of the prospective purchaser's sworn statement to local law enforcement authorities so that background checks could be made." Furthermore, "since many handguns are acquired in the heat of passion (to settle a quarrel, for example) or at times of depression brought on by potential suicide, the Brady bill would provide a cooling-off period that would certainly have the effect of reducing the number of handgun deaths."[65] Thus Reagan made the case for a seven-day waiting period; when the bill passed in 1993, it included just a five-day waiting period, "but that ended with the implementation of an instant 'phone in' background check system in 1998."[66]

Reagan also publicly expressed support for the 1994 assault-weapons ban. An assault weapon, Philip J. Cook and Kristin A. Goss explain, is "most commonly defined as a semiautomatic firearm with some of the features of a military firearm." Today, one of the "most popular assault weapons is the AR-15, the civilian (semiautomatic) version of the US military's M16." Although the National Firearms Act of 1934 regulated civilian use of fully automatic firearms (firearms that discharge more than one bullet if the trigger is held), it did not regulate semiautomatic firearms (firearms that discharge a bullet each time the trigger is pulled). Whereas a hunting rifle typically requires a person to move a bolt action to load and then discard a bullet, semiautomatic weapons fire quickly, making them exceptionally deadly. The 1994 assault-weapons ban described assault weapons as semiautomatic firearms possessing "features of certain military weapons such as a pistol grip, a folding stock, a bayonet mount, or a flash suppressor."[67] Harry L. Wilson, a political scientist, claims that the 1994 ban would have been a much clearer policy if it had focused on all semiautomatic firearms. Describing assault weapons according to their cosmetic features offered the "path of least political resistance," but it also "left many copycats on the market as well as many guns that function identically but appear slightly different than a banned gun."[68]

The 1994 assault-weapons ban originated from a January 17, 1989, mass shooting in Stockton, California, where a twenty-four-year-old man opened fire with a semiautomatic rifle on an elementary school playground. Five children were killed. In response, President George H. W. Bush "banned imports of semiautomatic assault rifles."[69] But legislators argued that the bill was insufficient and that something also needed to be done about domestically manufactured semiautomatic firearms. On October 16, 1991, a man crashed his pickup into a Luby's Cafeteria in Killeen, Texas. He then drew two semiautomatic pistols. By the end, he had killed twenty-three people.[70]

Once President Bill Clinton was in office, he called for a more comprehensive ban, which drew broad support. By 1993, polls showed that 77 percent of Americans supported "a ban on the manufacture, sale, and possession of what were known as semiautomatic assault weapons."[71] On May 3, 1994, Presidents Reagan, Carter, and Ford issued a joint letter calling on members of the U.S. House of Representatives to support a "ban on the domestic manufacture of military-style assault weapons." They concluded, "While we recognize that assault weapon legislation will not stop all assault weapon crime, statistics prove that we can dry up the supply of these guns, making them less accessible to criminals. We urge you to listen to the American public and to the law enforcement community and support a ban on further manufacture of these weapons."[72] On September 13, 1994, President Clinton signed the bill into law. It went into effect for ten years, expiring in 2004.

The 1994 midterm election seemed to represent political backlash, as Republicans took control of the House and Senate. The NRA and its members had sought to retaliate against elected officials who supported the bill. While there is debate about how much influence recent gun-control legislation actually had on the election, many politicians who saw their colleagues voted out of office concluded that talking about—let alone supporting—gun control meant political suicide. And President Clinton pointed to the NRA's influence after the 1994 midterm election when he claimed, "The NRA is the reason the Republicans control the House."[73]

For the NRA, the election suggested its strength, while the recent legislation suggested that the NRA needed support more than it ever had. In the NRA's telling, gun control was a slippery slope that would lead to more gun control and ultimately the loss of freedom. At times, this rhetoric became extreme. In 1995, for instance, NRA leader Wayne LaPierre solicited money from NRA members by comparing federal agents to storm troopers from Nazi Germany and referring to them as "jack-booted government thugs" out to "attack law-abiding citizens."[74] For some members, the NRA's rhetoric had gone too far. Former President George H. W. Bush, for instance, wrote a public letter retracting his lifetime NRA membership.[75] But other members stayed, believing that the NRA was committed to defending the Second Amendment. With the help of Charlton Heston—the actor turned NRA president—the NRA would fine-tune its message and grow its membership, as I explore further in chapter 2.

1999

On April 20, 1999, Eric Harris and Dylan Klebold entered Columbine High School in Littleton, Colorado, with plans to cause mass destruction. The two high school seniors walked into the cafeteria and set down duffel bags with homemade bombs made of propane tanks. The bombs were set to go off at 11:17 a.m., when the cafeteria would be bustling with students. Harris and Klebold expected that hundreds would be killed in the explosion. They strategically positioned themselves in the school parking lot to shoot the remaining students who fled after the explosion. They had also rigged their cars with bombs, set to go off later in the day, when the scene would be filled with first responders and reporters. Altogether, they hoped to kill five hundred people.

The bombs did not detonate. Harris and Klebold walked from the parking lot toward their school and started shooting. They entered through the cafeteria doors, wandered the halls, and then ended their rampage in the library. Along the way, they threw pipe bombs and joked. They taunted and shot peers both from afar and at point-blank range. At 12:08—with police and SWAT teams surrounding the school—Harris and Klebold committed suicide.[76] They left twelve peers and a teacher dead, twenty-one others injured, and thousands of others traumatized, heartbroken, angry, and fearful. They left a nation searching for answers, captured succinctly by the *Newsweek* cover: "Why?"[77]

There had been several other mass shootings in the 1990s, including school shootings, but none seemed to shock the nation like the Columbine shooting did. It is hard to know precisely why. Perhaps it was the magnitude of the violence (thirteen were killed); perhaps it was the location (a high school in a suburb of Denver); perhaps it was the shooters themselves (two white, relatively well-off kids just weeks away from graduation, thus challenging common racist and classist stereotypes about which youth were dangerous and which communities were prone to violence); perhaps it was the viciousness of their attack (the months they spent planning it seemed to amplify their callousness); perhaps it was the media coverage (live news coverage featured images of students running and being pulled from the school, and media coverage continued long after the shooting); perhaps it was a combination of these factors or something else.

What happened at Columbine High School was unprecedented and yet familiar. The day after the shooting, an article in the *New York Times* began, "Once again a routine school day was interrupted by blasts of gunfire,"[78] while another article inaccurately began, "In the deadliest school massacre in the nation's history."[79] The rhetoric of accumulation ("once again") and magnitude ("deadliest") compounded to make Columbine seem to be a tipping point. As President Clinton expressed on the day of the tragedy, "Perhaps now America would wake up to the dimensions of this challenge" and work to "prevent anything like this from happening again."[80] But what were the "dimensions of this challenge"?

For some, the shooters were simply "sick people"[81] and "evil bastard[s]" who would "burn in hell." What is striking, however, is how frequently these perpetrators were depicted not as outsiders but as insiders gone astray—not as "them" but as one of "us." A makeshift memorial erected after the tragedy included thirteen crosses for the victims, and briefly, there were two crosses for the perpetrators. Before getting torn down, the two crosses for the killers lasted long enough for people to write things like "Sorry we all failed you" and "No one is to blame."[82] Appearing on *The Oprah Winfrey Show*, Gavin DeBecker, a security expert, declared, "These boys give us all the opportunity to look at ourselves."[83] As one of Klebold's friends wrote, "I knew Dylan long enough to know that he didn't start out as a monster. He became one. And that's what makes his fate so scary."[84] For those who identified Eric Harris and Dylan Klebold as normal kids gone astray—rather than as radically evil—the shooting seemed to indict different parts of U.S. culture. Dave Cullen suggests that Harris and Klebold were perceived as "just kids," so commentators reasoned that "something or someone must have led them astray." (As I explore in chapter 4, the fact that these murderers were able to garner empathy was a privilege not just of their age but also of their whiteness.) Many blamed the shooters' parents, though blame reached far beyond them: "National polls taken shortly after the attack would identify all sorts of culprits contributing to the tragedy: violent movies, video games, Goth culture, gun laws, bullies, and Satan."[85]

On April 29, 1999, a reporter asked First Lady Hillary Clinton what she thought "needs to be done to address the problem of youth violence." Acknowledging that there is not "one single strategy that will answer this problem" and that what was needed was a "unified approach," she went on to discuss the need to work together to create a national campaign against youth violence, to improve mental health services, and to reduce children's access to guns. Yet she also challenged Americans to change the "culture of violence," calling on the "entertainment and media industry" to be more responsible and not create "the kind of video games that these young men played" or the "kind of horrible movies that they watched." Further, she challenged media consumers and parents to exercise "more responsibility" by "turning off the television sets, not buying or letting your kids use those video games." More fundamentally, she challenged everyone—"everybody has to search his or her heart about how we take care of children." She continued, "What kind of time do you spend with your kids? How much do we really listen to them?" Parents needed to "really get back into our children's lives," even if it required rearranging schedules or foregoing "some material possessions."[86]

The Clinton administration also pushed for gun control—specifically, legislation that would close the gun-show loophole. Although the 1993 Brady Bill required federally licensed dealers to conduct a background check before selling a gun, there was an exception for private sellers, such as those who sold guns at gun shows. Harris and Klebold were underage when they purchased three of their four guns from a gun show, so they had a friend purchase their guns for them (what is called a straw purchase). In her deposition after the shooting, the friend explained, "Eric and Dylan were walking around the floor asking sellers if they were private or licensed. They wanted to buy their guns from someone who was private, so there would be no paperwork or background check." She further explained that "I would not have bought a gun for Eric or Dylan if I had had to give any personal information or submit to any kind of check."[87] For gun-control advocates, then, the Columbine shooting exemplified a much larger problem in U.S. gun policy. An amendment was proposed after the shooting to close this loophole. Vice President Al Gore broke a tie vote in favor of the amendment in the Senate, but it was later voted down in the House of Representatives.

Although the legislation failed, the NRA nonetheless sought revenge against Gore, who became the Democrat nominee for president, and other gun-control supporters by spending $20 million in the 2000 election.[88] The election seemed to reinforce the lesson drawn from the 1994 midterm election: supporting or even talking about gun control was politically dangerous. Democratic strategists Paul Begala and James Carville reflected on this conundrum: "Democrats risk inflaming and alienating millions of voters who might otherwise be open to voting Democratic. But once guns are in the mix, once someone believes his gun rights are threatened, he shuts down."[89]

Throughout President George W. Bush's two terms in office, there was no serious attempt to close the gun-show loophole. But some progress was made on improving background checks after the 2007 shooting at Virginia Tech. The shooter had passed a background check before acquiring his guns, but he should have failed. The problem was that his mental health records were not in the federal database. Following the shooting, Congress passed the NICS (National Instant Criminal Background Check System) Improvement Act of 2007 "to incentivize states to enter mental-health and other records into the federal database of people barred from purchasing a gun."[90] Bush's unwillingness to do more to expand background checks revealed his belief that responsibility rested primarily with the shooter, not guns or gun sellers. The contrast between Bush and the two previous Republican presidents (H. W. Bush and Reagan) also revealed how partisan gun politics had become.

There was also no serious attempt to close the gun-show loophole or otherwise expand background checks during the first term of Obama's presidency. Obama's unwillingness to engage in the gun debate suggested that Democrats had learned their lesson about the difficulty and risk of gun-control politics. But that changed during Obama's second term. The shooting at Sandy Hook Elementary School happened a month after Obama's reelection. Although expanded background checks would not have stopped this specific mass shooter (but an assault-weapons ban might have), for many Americans, this shooting highlighted the much broader problem of gun violence occurring throughout the country. Ignoring the holes in our background-check system had not made them go away. By 2013, estimates suggested that "40 percent of all gun purchases occur through private sales at gun shows, at flea markets, through classified advertisements, or among friends with no background check."[91]

Public Deliberation

Understanding the network of forces that contribute to a single mass shooting—let alone mass shootings or gun violence in general—does "not lead to straightforward solutions or policies whose effectiveness is guaranteed." Sociologist Katherine S. Newman explains that "in almost all cases, interventions that might make a positive difference have negative consequences that may be intolerable." Because of this uncertainty and need to weigh different proposals and values, "it is up to our society—students, parents, teachers, administrators, politicians, and citizens at large—to weigh the pluses and minuses."[92] Responding to gun violence, then, requires more than careful reporting or rigorous analysis, more than empirical data or disciplinary expertise. It requires nonexperts to engage questions about causes, values, and priorities. What is required, in short, is public deliberation.

As a starting place, I prefer this relatively expansive definition of public deliberation: "the discursive process through which people in a democracy articulate, explain, and justify their political opinions and policy preferences to their fellow citizens."[93] Scholars study deliberation from a variety of disciplinary perspectives, including communication,[94] political science,[95] political philosophy,[96] and rhetoric.[97] What unites these scholars is a belief that healthy democracies and healthy deliberation are codependent. To paraphrase Wayne Booth, the quality of our lives—individually and collectively—depends on the quality of our communication.[98]

Scholars of deliberation disagree about what kind of talk counts as deliberation, much less "good" deliberation. Some scholars subscribe to an aspirational view of deliberation, in which participants engage in reasoned and respectful debate designed to reach consensus. They hope that, ideally, "no force except that of the better argument is exercised."[99] Critics charge that this idealized deliberation mistakenly ignores power imbalances, assumes that the norms of reasoned discourse are universal, and implies that communication that defaults from these norms should be dismissed.[100] While critics charge that this idealized form of deliberation is exclusionary and impractical, defenders maintain that these criticisms can be overcome to achieve inclusive and effective decision-making. That debate is a lively one.

Those interested in creating a more deliberative democracy often express this hope: "Through the sharing of information and knowledge, and careful listening to people's personal narratives and perspectives, public deliberation can transform individuals' understanding and grasp of complex problems and allow them to see elements of an issue they had not considered previously."[101] I too share this hope, and I want to transform deliberation that wrongly demonizes others, distorts issues, and keeps people from addressing significant public problems. Yet for the sake of analysis, I do not want to limit myself only to the "best" deliberation. First, to do so would require me to ignore a large part of the gun debate. But second, deliberation that falls short of the ideal can teach us something valuable. If and when people are unwilling to share knowledge, listen to others, perceive problems as complex, and so on, we should respond carefully and ask, Why? What might this purported failure teach us? What goals might the breakdown be achieving and for whom? What structural and rhetorical forces made it possible for—and perhaps encouraged—people to avoid sharing knowledge, listening, or searching for complex understandings?

By approaching the study of deliberation from a rhetorical perspective, I do not assume that participants should—or even can—be devoid of emotion, self-interest, or strategy. As Robert Ivie explains, "Rhetorical deliberation is often a rowdy affair, just as politics is typically messy."[102] I use the term *deliberation* here to encompass dialogue as well as advocacy, stories as well as arguments, and invitations as well as exclusions. Those who engage in actually existing public deliberation can be reasonable or not, respectful or not, emotional or not, self-interested or not, and strategic or not. Deliberation includes not only the careful weighing of "various perspectives and proposals"[103] but also words that are careless or inflammatory. Deliberation can lead to harmonious consensus, rhetorical war, or some place in between.

What's Next

After Gun Violence offers a rhetorical history focused on the interplay of public deliberation and public memory. Whatever kind of deliberation we are talking about—whether it is aspirational or descriptive, whether it is the talk among a small group on a single morning or the talk among the nation across decades—scholars and citizens alike can benefit from exploring the concept of public memory. Put negatively, the failure to account for the relationships between public memory and public deliberation has impoverished scholarly theories and analyses of public deliberation, our advice to deliberators, and our own practice as participants in public deliberation. The chapters ahead will explore the implications of this basic claim.

The fact that memory and deliberation shape one another is perhaps unsurprising for some scholars trained in rhetoric and hermeneutics, given that classical rhetoricians saw a clear link between memory and the creation of arguments. Yet contemporary scholars of deliberation—outside and even inside of rhetorical studies—have too often ignored memory's role in shaping deliberation. In the following chapters, I strengthen this link by examining public deliberation about gun violence; I assess how memory and deliberation shape one another, why, and to what effect; and I identify three prominent relationships between public memory and public deliberation.

Chapter 1 explains the concept of public memory and begins to explore how public deliberation and public memory shape and misshape one another. The subsequent three chapters examine three distinct relationships between memory and deliberation: the weight of the past (how arguments can accrue meaning and significance throughout their use in public debate—chapter 2), the fleeting past (how willful or accidental forgetting shortens and simplifies public deliberation—chapter 3), and the implicit past (how unchecked assumptions shape what we see and do not see, say and do not say—chapter 4). My concluding chapter then draws together my claims by considering memory's potential to help move deliberation beyond gridlock.

1

DELIBERATION AND MEMORY

For at least fifty years, the word that has regularly come to mind to describe mass shootings is *senseless*. On July 12, 2016, President Barack Obama spoke at a memorial service in Dallas, Texas, for five police officers who had been murdered. He remarked that his responses to mass shootings had become routine and that "too many families" have "lost a loved one to senseless violence."[1] But the routine was not unique to Obama. On August 2, 1966, President Lyndon Johnson issued a statement about a mass shooting that had happened the day before at the University of Texas at Austin. Again, the word that came to mind was *senseless*: "The shocking tragedy of yesterday's event in Austin is heightened because it was so senseless." The word *senseless* highlights that such violence was unjustified—that it was unnecessary and cruel. But it would be wrong to conclude that this violence was without meaning. Johnson continued, "While senseless, however, what happened is not without a lesson: that we must press urgently for the legislation now pending in Congress to help prevent the wrong persons from obtaining firearms."[2] Obama drew a similar lesson about the need to reform gun laws. The important point, however, is that both presidents made sense out of seemingly senseless violence. Indeed, this is something that we all do.

On its own, a violent act does not communicate meaning or offer lessons. Humans impose meaning and lessons, often pretending to extract or stumble upon such lessons. Collectively and individually, we decide which violent events justify our attention, concern, and response—and at least implicitly, which violent events do not. This is a thoroughly social process. As individuals, we can be more or less active, though never completely in control: we draw attention, and our attention is drawn. When we focus on a specific act of gun violence, we cannot possibly know all the details about the shooting and its social context. But even if we could know everything, our need for judgment remains. Since there is an overwhelming abundance of information that is at least potentially relevant, we need to decide which details are most important—and at least implicitly, which ones are of less or no importance. For instance, we might choose to focus on a conversation that the shooter had with a friend three days before the shooting rather than the conversation that happened four days before, or we might decide that these recent conversations are less important than what happened in the shooter's childhood, or we might decide that the shooter's personal life is less important than the fact that this shooting happened in a particular place. We might decide that all of this is relevant or that none of it is.

Once we have selected which details to focus on, our work continues; after all, details do not speak for themselves. We must decide how to interpret those details. A conversation happened—what, if anything, is to be made of that? The shooter wore a trench coat—what, if anything, is to be made of that? The shooting happened in a particular place—what, if anything, is to be made of that? The shooter used a semiautomatic rifle—what, if anything, is to be made of that? Sometimes we weigh evidence before drawing conclusions, but sometimes reasoning works the other way: we have our conclusion and simply seek out evidence that supports it and ignore what does not.[3]

We can be more or less thoughtful and rigorous when interpreting and deliberating about gun violence. But we—both collectively and individually—cannot escape our own role in the process of meaning making, no matter how hard we try. The concept of public memory can help illuminate this process of meaning making by highlighting what we bring to—and what we take from—debates about gun violence and gun policy.

This chapter proceeds in four steps. In the first section, I make two basic claims: deliberation shapes memory, and memory shapes deliberation. The rest of the chapter then illustrates and extends these two claims by focusing on deliberation about gun violence and gun policy. The second section examines how rhetors use particular public memories to interpret and argue about the source of and solutions to mass gun violence. In the third section, I discuss potential consequences of public deliberation in the aftermath of mass gun violence, even in the absence of policy talk. Specifically, I consider how the purported lessons drawn from and remembered about specific acts of gun violence can shape daily living, distort how mental illness and the mentally ill are perceived, and influence copycats. Finally, I shift my emphasis from gun violence to gun policy. I urge rhetors to reengage in public deliberation by breaking the mold of routine policy arguments; at the same time, I use the concept of public memory to point out why breaking the mold is often so difficult.

Deliberation ← → Memory

The study of public memory—what some prefer to call collective memory—is undertaken from a variety of disciplinary perspectives, including history, philosophy, rhetoric, and sociology.[4] What unites these scholars across their disciplinary divides is the belief that what people remember about the past is never neutral. Since we cannot remember everything, then what we choose to remember—and what we choose or allow ourselves to forget—can be significant and consequential. Sometimes we explicitly deliberate about how or even whether to remember the past, and at other times, we simply assert a particular representation of the past as a direct, obvious, and unvarnished truth. In any case, what and how a public remembers often says as much about their present needs and goals as it does about the past and what "really happened." As Stephen H. Browne puts it, public memories are "formed in the crucible of ideology and the politics of identity."[5] And since public memory is "partial, partisan, and thus often contested," public-memory scholars are interested in which accounts of the past get highlighted (and which get downplayed or forgotten), why, and to what effect.[6]

Memory lives in individual minds and bodies, but it also dwells publicly in monuments, books, news reports, myths, speeches, stories, and so on. In a sense, all memory is public because individuals remember even the most personal of experiences within social contexts, including socially constructed narratives, genres, words, and feelings. Yet as Edward Casey explains, scholars tend to use the phrase *public memory* "to contrast such memory with anything that takes place privately—that is to say, offstage, in the *idios cosmos* [private world] of one's home or club, or indeed just by oneself (whether physically sequestered or not). 'Public' signifies out in the open, in the *koinos cosmos* [shared world] where discussion with others is possible."[7] As Browne explains, public memory can be provisionally understood as "a shared sense of the past, fashioned from the symbolic resources of community and subject to its particular history, hierarchies, and aspirations."[8]

In subsequent chapters, I explore several distinct relationships between public memory and public deliberation. But let me start with two basic relationships. First, public deliberation shapes public memory; in other words, we deliberate about how to remember. What, for instance, is the legacy of the Second Amendment today? What lessons, if any, should we remember from the Columbine shooting? Second, public memory shapes public deliberation. Put simply, our deliberations about gun violence and gun policy are influenced by memory—by the purported lessons we remember from previous acts of gun violence as well as by basic assumptions about violence, human motives, and responsibility. Public memory shapes what we see (and do not see) when interpreting violence as well as what we say (and do not say) when debating how, if at all, guns contributed to that violence. Taking these two claims together, we can see that the relationships are often reciprocal: we draw from memory when deliberating, and when we deliberate, we repeat or refashion memory, thus offering a potential resource for subsequent deliberation.

Public-memory scholars tend to focus on that first relationship—we deliberate about what and how to remember. But I want to focus here on the second relationship—how public memory shapes and misshapes deliberation—because it is key for understanding public deliberation and why it is so often dysfunctional. Classical rhetoricians offer a useful starting place.

Within classical rhetoric, memory is one of the five canons of rhetoric—it is one step in the process of preparing and delivering a speech. In public-speaking classrooms today, the five canons are often taught as a linear sequence: first, find or create arguments (invention); second, organize that material effectively (arrangement); third, choose words carefully, using metaphors and other devices to make a speech appealing (style); fourth, use mnemonic devices and practice to remember one's speech (memory); and fifth, use the voice and body to communicate effectively (delivery). Yet this contemporary sequence oversimplifies the five canons, particularly that of memory. Mary Carruthers reminds us that in Greek legend, "memory, or Mnemosyne, is the mother of the Muses. That story places memory at the beginning, as the matrix of invention for all human arts, of all human making, including the making of ideas."[9] Rather than seeing memory simply as rehearsing one's already crafted speech, then, classical rhetorical theorists saw a relationship between memory and invention. "Memory was not only a system of recollection," Sharon Crowley explains, but it was also "a means of invention."[10] According to Lisa Ede, Cheryl Glenn, and Andrea Lunsford, memory serves as a kind of storehouse for arguments that, when tapped, "ignites the process of invention."[11] And as Mark T. Williams and Theresa Enos point out, a "rhetor sorts knowledge into places of the mind and draws on this information when the occasion demands."[12]

Contemporary speakers are perhaps less disciplined about training and organizing their memories than speakers in ancient Rome were, but the important point is that all speakers rely on memory to interpret, argue, and deliberate.[13] And so do audiences. Aristotle teaches that speakers do not need to state all their premises or claims outright. If the speaker and audience share a premise in common, then audience members will be able to supply this missing premise in their own minds as they listen. Aristotle calls this an *enthymeme*—an abbreviated form of reasoning that counts on knowledge shared between a speaker and an audience. In formal logic, one might reason, "All men are mortal. Socrates is a man. Therefore, Socrates is mortal." Yet since audiences will already know and accept the major premise that "all humans are mortal," a speaker can simply state, "Socrates is human and is therefore mortal." And if an audience knows that Socrates is a man rather than a rock, then a speaker could simply state, "Socrates is mortal."[14] Memory, then, is the means by which missing premises are supplied. As David Zarefsky explains, memory refers to the "storehouse of common knowledge and beliefs about history that forms the premises for arguments and appeals."[15]

Of course, public deliberation typically centers on more controversial matters than whether humans are mortal. But the same process is at work when we deliberate about probable matters, in which the best option is uncertain, and there are both benefits and drawbacks. For instance, should a city raise taxes to build a new school? A person might try to convince a friend that the current school should be remodeled because that is the cheapest option. The unstated assumption, then, is that the cheapest option is the best one. If the friend shares this assumption (and determines that that assumption fits this particular situation), then she might support plans to remodel the school or respond that another plan is cheaper. If the assumption is not shared, the friends will need to address the assumption directly by negotiating what qualities are most important for addressing the problem (e.g., the best learning environment), or they will risk talking past one another.

Although memory can be a helpful resource, it can also get us into trouble. We do not want to be continually surprised by the world, with everything appearing new and incomprehensible. Beliefs and values already accepted and held in common—what classical thinkers called *sensus communis*, or what we might call common sense—are necessary for getting on with life. These beliefs and values facilitate judgment and argument. Most of us do not want to listen to a drawn-out speech for hours upon hours, especially if what the speaker says is obvious. But common sense can also lead us astray, particularly if the premises that rhetors draw from and audiences supply are untrue or if what appears to be meaning shared in common is actually not. At times, then, we should pause to reflect on the relationship between public memory and public deliberation. Doing so is particularly urgent for our contemporary gun debate.

When interpreting, arguing, and deliberating, there is no beginning point or space of pure neutrality. We are always in the middle, always *after* gun violence. "In the case of memory," Casey explains, "we are always already in the thick of things." He continues, "Memory itself is already in the advance position. Not only because remembering is at all times presupposed, but also because it is always at work."[16] And to greater or lesser degrees, rhetorical invention depends on the memory of what has come prior. Debra Hawhee's phrase "invention-in-the-middle" clarifies memory's relationship with invention and deliberation: "This mode of invention is not a beginning, as the first canon is often articulated, but a middle, an in-between, a simultaneously interruptive and connective hooking-in to circulating discourses."[17] Even if we are young or new to politics, we inherit language that predates us and that works to do our thinking for us. This is generally true of all language use, but it is particularly urgent for trying to understand debates about gun violence and gun policy. To disrupt this cycle, we need to understand it.

Using Memory to Interpret Gun Violence

The resources of public memory are nearly limitless. Because of this, a comprehensive analysis is impossible, and I will not even attempt it. Instead, I make two general claims about how we use public memories to interpret gun violence: First, we interpret acts of gun violence by relying on the purported lessons drawn and remembered from some previous acts of gun violence. Second, we interpret acts of gun violence by relying on a broader set of beliefs, narratives, and values. In making these claims, I hope to illustrate the broader point that we rely on a range of public memories to interpret and deliberate about the sources of and solutions to gun violence.

Lessons Learned from Previous Shootings

The blaming that happens after mass shootings can serve as a resource and a constraint for interpreting and deliberating about subsequent mass shootings. Blaming the "culture of violence" after the Columbine shooting included blaming movies and video games because the shooters had enjoyed movies focused on violence and played first-person shooter games, such as *Doom*.[18] To be clear, anxiety about video games ran much wider and deeper than the Columbine shooting. But Columbine helped make blaming video games a default response. That purported lesson from Columbine resurfaced again on April 16, 2007, as people tried to make sense of the mass shooting at Virginia Tech. MSNBC host Chris Matthews conducted a live interview with Virginia Tech student Karan Grewal. Although Grewal was not friends with the shooter, Seung-Hui Cho, he shared a dorm suite with him and therefore had unique access to Cho's habits and personality. Matthews asked about the shooter's media consumption: "What did he watch?" According to Grewal, Cho watched professional wrestling and game shows. This answer did not fit the narrative that Matthews expected, so he went to his next question: "Let me get into the video game thing. Do you know anything about *Counter-Strike*, as a video game?" Grewal said that he was personally familiar with the game but that he never saw Cho playing that game or any video game. Instead, he was usually watching television or typing into a Word document on his laptop. Matthews returned to the topic a few questions later, asking if there was a subculture of video games at Virginia Tech.[19] Given that Grewal had just stated that he never saw Cho play video games, asking if there was a subculture of video games at Virginia Tech seemed an irrelevant and forced question. Matthews's failure to listen makes the interview painful to watch.

My point, however, is not simply to critique Matthews. The script that Matthews relied on was a cultural one, a script existing in public memory that was used even when the evidence did not support its use.[20] Drawing from the past can lead us astray, as it did in Matthews's case, or it can be an asset to make sense of the world. For good or ill, we all regularly draw from the past, even if implicitly. Public memory shapes how we understand gun violence. Public memory shapes which questions are asked (and not), what evidence is considered relevant (and not), and which explanations are offered (and not).

A Broader Set of Beliefs, Narratives, and Values

The resources of public memory are not limited to the purported lessons from previous mass shootings. When interpreting gun violence, people also draw from a broader set of beliefs, narratives, and values. Public memory is "activated by concerns, issues, or anxieties of the present," and in turn, particular public memories are selected and marshaled to address concerns, issues, and anxieties of the present.[21] For some—but not all—audiences, the violence at Columbine represented the absence of religion in American life, including prayer in schools. One narrative suggested that the shooters sought to persecute Christian students; a related narrative suggested that the violence represented Christianity's absence and the need for its presence in American life. Both narratives depended on audiences' preexisting beliefs, narratives, and values.

The narrative of religious persecution was not new. But the fact that the Columbine shooting happened in Littleton and at the end of the 1990s—a decade marked by culture war—gave this narrative added force and, in turn, shaped how the violence in Columbine was understood. Ralph W. Larkin suggests that responses to the Columbine shooting cannot adequately be understood apart from the "political and cultural conservatism of Southern Jefferson County." He claimed that "Columbine became a battleground in the American culture wars as the religious and cultural right defined the massacre as the outcome of a liberal, crime-tolerating, secular, anti-Christian society that fails to teach the children right from wrong, prevents children from praying in school, and refuses to display the Ten Commandments in public schools."[22] Some audiences, then, were primed to focus on religion. For evangelicals and culture warriors, among others, the existence of an evil act was a sign of Christianity's absence and the need for its presence.

Early news reports claimed that before Eric Harris killed seventeen-year-old student Cassie Bernall, he looked under the table where she was hiding and asked her a question: "Do you believe in God?" Her response was an unequivocal yes. Whether this exchange actually happened has been highly disputed, with the strongest evidence suggesting that it was in fact another student, Valeen Schnurr, who was asked the question, answered yes, and yet was not killed. Regardless of what happened, the story became a powerful one for Christian proselytizing.[23] Bruce Porter, a Littleton evangelical minister, captures this view most concisely: "It matters little in the end whether or not Cassie was quoted correctly in this circumstance. The fact that so many who knew her instantly accepted the initial reports that she said 'yes' is a clear indication that, without any doubt whatsoever, she would have said it!"[24] The story was used not only to illustrate religious courage in the face of evil; it was used to ascribe a motive to the killers and a mission for the living: the killers' immoral rampage was a consequence of a religious vacuum; they were waging a war against Christianity; to restore order and goodness required embracing Christianity.

This example highlights that the details of the case were in some sense less important than those who interpreted them. The (apocryphal) story about Cassie Bernall's martyrdom did not speak on its own. To amplify or downplay that story was a choice shaped by the beliefs, narratives, and values of some interpreters and audiences. Erika Doss points out that Bernall became "Columbine's most visible martyr" because of her "recent conversion to evangelical Christianity, by the bestselling book her mother wrote shortly after her death (*She Said Yes: The Unlikely Martyrdom of Cassie Bernall*), by the many references to her in Columbine's temporary memorial, and by the comments of her pastor at her funeral service." The pastor declared that "Cassie died a martyr's death. She went to the martyr's hall of fame."[25]

The narrative of religion's absence became a lens for seeing the Columbine shooting. The lens magnified data that reinforced the narrative. But that lens also minimized, hid, or discounted data that did not match the narrative. For example, the parents of another victim, Rachel Scott, claimed that the "ultimate issue" was the "ongoing battle between the forces of good and evil."[26] They claimed, "We must recapture our nation's great spiritual inheritance of Judeo-Christian values."[27] Given this narrative, policy solutions like gun control were viewed as distractions—mere "legislative Band-Aids on our country's gaping social and spiritual wounds."[28]

The Hold of Memory

Dave Cullen reported on the Columbine shooting in 1999, and he spent the next ten years researching and writing his book *Columbine*. Shortly after the Sandy Hook shooting in 2012, Cullen appeared on *CBS This Morning*. He noted that reporters covering Columbine had depicted the shooters as loners who were part of the trench-coat mafia and engaged in destruction to retaliate against jocks who had bullied them. None of this was true, Cullen claimed. Yet those interpretations still stuck because they were the immediate ones offered. Since the media spotlight will always fade—even from the most horrific tragedy—and turn to the next big story, these immediate interpretations are most often the ones that constitute public memory. In his *CBS This Morning* appearance, Cullen's warning was simple: "This week, whatever we leave the public with, is going to be with them forever."[29]

Cullen overstates his point. Indeed, his very attempt to correct how we remember the Columbine shooting highlights that public memory is not necessarily static. But he also gets at an important truth: how we talk about mass shootings matters, even in the absence of policy change or talk. Since I will focus on policy talk in subsequent chapters, it is worthwhile here to describe some of the other ways that public deliberation and public memory can be consequential. Specifically, I examine how the purported lessons that are drawn and remembered from high-profile acts of gun violence can shape daily living, distort how mental illness and the mentally ill are perceived, and influence copycats. This list is by no means exhaustive, yet it helps us see the broader potential consequences of public deliberation and public memory.

Deliberation and Memory Shape Daily Living

The purported lessons drawn from acts of gun violence can influence how people perceive, feel, interpret, think, talk, and act. For example, after the Columbine shooting, the Clinton administration urged Americans to remake U.S. culture—in Vice President Al Gore's words, to "replace a culture of violence with one of values and meaning." On April 25, 1999, Gore traveled to Colorado to speak at a memorial service. He insisted that laws could make it more difficult for "a young child to get a gun" but that we must also change a culture that constantly exposes children to "lessons in how to use one." Changing the culture required "more discipline and character in our schools, and more alternatives to crime and drugs." It required looking out for children who show the "earliest signs of trouble" and teaching them to "resolve their differences with reason and conscience, not with flashes of passion." Most generally, it required living up to the promise of America by creating "a community of goodness, of reason, of moral strength." In Gore's telling, the culture of violence—and thus the Columbine massacre—resulted from the failure to care for one another and the lack of moral guidance and discipline. According to Gore, the Columbine shooting illustrated a cultural problem; in turn, "all adults in this nation must take on the challenge of creating in all of God's children a clean heart, and a right spirit within."[30]

On May 20, 1999, President Clinton, along with First Lady Hillary Clinton, traveled to Colorado to speak at a relatively small, indoor gathering of Columbine students, parents, and community members. It was now a month after the tragedy and just two days before graduation. Like Gore had done, the Clintons claimed that this violence represented larger spiritual, moral, and civic challenges. Bill Clinton imagined a future "where parents and children are more fully involved in each other's lives," "where students respect each other even if they all belong to different groups," "where schools and houses of worship and communities are literally connected to all our children," and "where society guards our children better against violent influences and weapons that can break the dam of decency." This future of engagement, respect, and goodness could only be brought about if individuals changed their attitudes and practices. It was a large responsibility—potentially empowering and potentially overwhelming and unfocused. Yet it was a responsibility that depended on each individual's daily acts, not government action. Following a series of "you" and beginning a series of "you can," Clinton explained, "You can give us a culture of values instead of a culture of violence."[31]

Blame of the culture of violence seemed to indict a variety of institutions—schools, local communities, the entertainment industry, and so on—yet it also suggests that some battles were to be won or lost in the home. In her April 29, 1999, press conference, Hillary Clinton claimed that "everybody has to search his or her heart about how we take care of children." She asked, "What kind of time do you spend with your kids? How much do we really listen to them?" And she claimed that parents needed to "really get back into our children's lives" even if it required rearranging schedules or foregoing "some material possessions."[32] If the conclusion that we draw and remember from a specific shooting is that it could have been prevented if parents had only searched their child's room, then that lesson can serve as justification for other parents to monitor their children.

Of course, these suggestions did not emerge from nowhere. During the 1990s, crime prevention was a national priority. Concern about youth violence coexisted with long-standing anxieties about media consumption, parenting, and the status of the family. Hillary Clinton's 1996 book *It Takes a Village* invoked an African proverb: "It takes a village to raise a child."[33] The very phrase *culture of violence* had long been in use. For instance, in 1988, as part of her larger push to get music and movie producers to provide warning labels on their products, Tipper Gore claimed that America's entertainment industry celebrated "the most gruesome violence," arguing that we must "protect children from the culture of violence."[34] Although these concerns about media consumption and family life were not new, expressing them after the Columbine shooting was nonetheless significant because doing so represented attempts to explain why gun violence happens and to recommend daily actions that were allegedly necessary to prevent future acts of gun violence.

Drawing lessons for daily living can be empowering and, in some cases, might help prevent gun violence. But these lessons also come with potential dangers. First, our daily actions might actually cause harm. Monitoring one's children can be valuable but not if it violates their privacy and breeds mistrust. Second, isolated actions might be insufficient. Although not writing specifically about responses to gun violence, Dana L. Cloud critiques talk that locates responsibility for social change solely in the individual, as well as talk that emphasizes "individual adaptation rather than social change." Isolated actions might make individuals feel good, but according to Cloud, the danger of such feel-good politics is that there is little hope of redressing underlying social problems without "structural critique and collective action."[35]

Deliberation and Memory Distort How Mental Illness Is Perceived

Perpetrators of mass gun violence are regularly described as lone wolves, deranged, or simply evil. It is worth asking what such labels accomplish.[36] Michel Foucault's work on the historical construction of "madness"[37] and Kenneth Burke's work on the rhetorics of identification and division[38] help formulate several key questions: What does labeling individuals as mentally ill do? What does it do to "them," and what does it do for those who are purportedly divided from "them"? How do such labels shape how we understand gun violence? And how do such labels shape how we understand mental illness? To help answer these questions, I briefly examine responses to the 2007 Virginia Tech shooting and the 2011 Tucson shooting.

On April 16, 2007, reporters gathered in the White House for their daily press briefing. News of the Virginia Tech shooting was still unfolding, but reporters wanted to know whether President Bush and his administration intended to do anything to prevent future tragedies. A reporter asked, "What more does this White House think needs to be done as it relates to gun issues?" Dana Perino, the acting White House press secretary, responded, "The President believes that there is a right for people to bear arms, but that all laws must be followed."[39] Another reporter pushed back, implying that current policies were not working: "Columbine, Amish school shooting, now this, and a whole host of other gun issues brought into schools—that's not including guns on the streets in many urban areas and rural areas. Does there need to be some more restrictions? Does there need to be gun control in this country?"[40] Perino responded that she would update the press if the administration's policy changed. For now, however, their policy consisted of "enforcing all of the gun laws that we have on the books and making sure that they're prosecuted to the fullest extent of the law."[41]

On April 17, 2007, President Bush spoke at a memorial service in Blacksburg, Virginia. Bush's speech focused on individual and communal grief rather than national policy. He claimed that "it's impossible to make sense of such violence and suffering." Those who died "were simply in the wrong place at the wrong time." Addressing the "grieving families, and grieving classmates, and a grieving nation," he suggested that the first priority during this difficult time was to "look for sources of strength to sustain us," including prayer and the support of loved ones.[42]

In subsequent days, Bush and Perino veered from the claim that it is "impossible to make sense of such violence" by directing blame solely to the shooter. They referred to the shooter as evil and mentally ill, and at times, these two descriptors became synonymous. When the press gathered on April 18, 2007, reporters again asked about gun policy, including the president's stance on weapons-free school zones. Perino shifted her attention to the shooter's mental state as a way to deflect blame from guns. A reporter asked about gun policy, and Perino responded, "I'm not going to comment about—obviously, the investigation is ongoing on Virginia Tech." Asked again, she responded, "I think that what the President thinks is that, in this time of mourning and grieving and thinking about the aftermath of one individual's actions, that it's only natural that you think about what led to such a tragedy and how to prevent one in the future." The phrase "in this time of mourning and grieving" appealed to a sense of decorum and suggested that deliberation about policy questions should be deferred to a more appropriate time. By characterizing the tragedy as "one individual's actions" rather than as representative of a larger trend in gun violence, she localized blame, suggesting that the shooter at Virginia Tech was an outlier and that federal policy should not be based on outliers. When asked about guns yet a third time in the same briefing, Perino further displaced blame from guns to the shooter:

> As I said yesterday, I think that there's going to be a debate. The President said there's going to be a debate, and it's one that we have in our country about the right to bear arms, as well as gun control policies. In addition to that, I think one of the things that we're learning out of this investigation, as we have from many of the others, is that there *are some individuals who are disaffected in society, lonely*, and we have to figure out as a society how to identify those individuals and get them help prior to them having—going on a rampage and killing all this innocent life.[43]

Even though Perino had refrained from commenting about guns and said that she did so because the investigation was ongoing, she did not refrain from commenting on the shooter's mental state and social status, of which little information was known at the time. In addition to shifting blame away from guns to the shooter, Perino shifted blame away from society to the individual by relying on rhetorics of identification and division. The shooter was "disaffected in society" and "lonely." He was apart from us—those who were presumably not disaffected in society and lonely—so there was no reason for us to change. Since he was "other," he—and he alone—was to blame.

By April 19, 2007, no reporters in the briefing room asked questions about guns. They had turned to the topic of mental illness—partly because the shooter, Seung-Hui Cho, had mailed a package to NBC with "pictures of himself holding weapons, an 1,800-word rambling diatribe, and video clips in which he expresses rage, resentment, and a desire to get even with his oppressors."[44] NBC decided to broadcast these materials. In his diatribe, Cho claimed that his peers were immoral and oppressive and that they deserved his destruction: "You forced me into a corner and gave me only one option."[45] His specific claims, however, became less important than what his texts seemed to reveal about his mental state.

Asked about the materials that NBC had broadcast, Perino said that she did not know if the president had seen them, but she offered her own reaction on his behalf. She began by reiterating that the investigation was ongoing, and she ended by acknowledging the families who "are having a very difficult time in the days following this event." Yet between making these two points, she discussed the shooter's mental state: "There was, unfortunately, a very disturbed and deranged individual who was a loner on campus and who needed help for his own mental health, and that did not happen in time to prevent a tragedy." In fact, the shooter had repeatedly sought help for his own mental health but did not receive adequate care—a fact that was not yet public knowledge. So in the press briefing, Perino suggested that "as a society, we're going to have to continue to think about . . . how do you recognize the signs of somebody who is so disturbed that they would take 32 innocent lives, and then take their own?"[46] Perino's characterization of the shooter as "a very disturbed and deranged individual" rightly indicated that his actions were horrific. Yet this characterization also undermined her call to deliberate about mental health and how to recognize the warning signs of mental illness. Her very language—"disturbed," "deranged," "loner"—worked to stigmatize mental illness and further ostracize those who have a mental illness.

On April 20, 2007, Bush spoke about mental illness in his weekly radio address. He acknowledged, "We can never fully understand what would cause a student to take the lives of 32 innocent people." He continued, "What we do know is that this was a deeply troubled young man—and there were many warning signs. Our society continues to wrestle with the question of how to handle individuals whose mental health problems can make them a danger to themselves and to others." Bush began with a call for inquiry and a debate about "questions of how to handle individuals whose mental health problems can make them a danger to themselves and to others." However, by the time he had concluded his address, he had implied that mental illness was synonymous with evil. For example, Bush approvingly cited a letter written by a Virginia Tech graduate: "Evil can never succeed, not while there are . . . men and women like the people of Virginia Tech who reach every day for success, and endeavor for the improvement of the human condition across the planet."[47]

Calling a shooter evil might make us feel better and work to restore our sense of moral order, but as Rosa A. Eberly explains, the use of the word *evil* often has "dysfunctional consequences for deliberative discourse" because "such claims conceal causes and obscure possible solutions."[48] Moreover, the slippage between using the word *evil* and using the words *mental illness* or *mentally ill* has significant implications that extend far beyond our understanding of a single shooting.

On January 8, 2011, U.S. Congresswoman Gabrielle Giffords organized a Congress on Your Corner event in the parking lot of a Tucson supermarket. Jared Lee Loughner showed up and started shooting. Giffords survived but suffered brain damage as a result of the shooting. Six others died. In the aftermath, the debate about blame for the shooting focused on two main topics: divisive political rhetoric and mental illness.

Some commentators suggested that political rhetoric—among other forces—created a context that enabled violent acts such as the one in Tucson. In a nationally televised news conference, Pima County Sheriff Clarence W. Dupnik railed against divisive political rhetoric. Commenting on Dupnik's speech, Jeremy Engels writes, "For Dupnik, the angry, polarizing, take-no-prisoners, violent talk of the Republican Right—its 'vitriolic rhetoric'—was the primary cause of the shooting. Americans searching for an explanation for Loughner's act needed to look no further than talk radio, Fox News, campaign ads decorated with gun sights, and warlike speeches."[49] As Dupnik stated, "To try to inflame the public on a daily basis, 24 hours a day, seven days a week, has impact on people, especially those who are unbalanced personalities to begin with." He continued, "It's time that this country take a little introspective look at the crap that comes out on radio and TV."[50]

Sarah Palin—former Alaska governor and 2008 vice presidential candidate—had been singled out for her over-the-top rhetoric. For example, during the 2010 midterm elections, "one of her slogans was 'Don't Retreat, Reload'; another urged supporters to 'Take Up Arms,' and she posted a now-infamous map on her PAC website that marked seventeen winnable congressional districts held by Democrats with gun sights—including Giffords's district in Arizona."[51] After the Tucson shooting, the map was removed, and Palin released a video-recorded speech on her Facebook page. In opposition to Dupnik and others who had blamed political rhetoric for the violence in Tucson, Palin claimed that no rhetoric—not hers or anyone else's—bore any responsibility for the shooting. To help make her case, she quoted Ronald Reagan:

> President Reagan said, "We must reject the idea that every time a law's broken, society is guilty rather than the lawbreaker. It is time to restore the American precept that each individual is accountable for his actions." Acts of monstrous criminality stand on their own. They begin and end with the criminals who commit them, not collectively with the citizens of the state, not with those who listen to talk radio, not with maps of swing districts used by both sides of the aisle, not with law-abiding citizens who respectfully exercise their First Amendment rights at campaign rallies, not with those who proudly voted in the last election.[52]

Palin thus engaged in localized blame, arguing that blame should be placed on the shooter and only the shooter. She reasoned that blaming political rhetoric or society or anything other than the shooter misdiagnoses the source of violence and that expansive blame punishes the innocent (including herself) and excuses the guilty (the shooter).

Whether it was sincere, strategic, or a bit of both, blaming the shooter became politically useful. Blaming the shooter—especially his mental state—attempted to rebut critics who charged that divisive rhetoric from Palin and others might have in some way encouraged the shooter in Tucson. Such blaming also suggested that the government could do little to address the problem of gun violence. Francesca Marie Smith and Thomas A. Hollihan observed that Palin, among numerous other conservative commentators after the Tucson shooting, engaged in "an almost surgical isolation or localization of blame" that reduced the act to a "single event." Localizing blame disconnected the Tucson shooting from others and thus separated it from any larger problem. And by depicting the shooter as "deranged," commentators were suggesting that "we could not and should not attempt to make sense of his motives," that the shooter's "motivations were either unknowable or inscrutable."[53] Similarly, Jeremy Engels highlights that Palin's speech after Tucson suggests that "violence is not social or political but instead solely the product of deranged individuals." He reads this localized blame as representing and perpetuating neoliberal politics: "Palin models the neoliberal privatization of responsibility by denying this particular act had any context outside of Loughner's evil mind."[54] Such localized blame fails to acknowledge the relationship between violent events that happen again and again. Moreover, such blame fails to acknowledge the large and complex forces that sustain gun violence, including the "lack of mental health care," "deregulation of the gun market," and "violent political rhetoric that frames politics as 'war' and talks about 'targeting' rival politicians."[55]

Not only does blame focused on the shooter's mental state impoverish our understanding of gun violence and thus thwart productive action; it can also harm innocent Americans. Some public responses to the Tucson shooting depicted mental illness and the mentally ill in general as dangerous. Katie Rose Guest Pryal claimed that "news reports and opinion pieces create an in-group of the 'sane' and then divide the 'insane.'" She acknowledges that mass shooters such as the one in Tucson are "guilty of horrible crimes and deserve to be punished," yet she urges us to consider the additional harm caused by how we talk about gun violence and its perpetrators: "The public rhetoric surrounding these events shifts focus from the *crimes* of a single perpetrator to focus on the *mental illness* of the perpetrator, and, from there, the mental illness of *anyone* with a psychiatric disability."[56] In turn, "this division allows for rhetorical aggression"[57] toward anyone with a mental illness yet assuages "popular guilt over the lack of care our society provides to the mentally ill."[58] If we conclude—as the NRA's executive vice president Wayne LaPierre did after the Sandy Hook shooting—that the perpetrators of violence are "so deranged, so evil, so possessed by voices and driven by demons that no sane person can possibly ever comprehend them,"[59] then we might wrongly conclude that everyone who is violent is mentally ill or that everyone who is mentally ill is violent. Such misjudgment distorts our understanding of mental illness and stigmatizes the mentally ill.

There is a mental health crisis in the United States. And if we are sincerely concerned with this crisis, then we need to make sure that we understand it and act in ways that will address it. The crisis, in short, is that people are not getting the help that they need to live good lives. The crisis pertains to stigma about mental illness and inadequate resources for mental health. Furthermore, the crisis pertains to America putting the severely mentally ill in jails and prisons rather than providing actual treatment.[60]

Although mental illness is repeatedly blamed for gun homicides, little evidence backs up that claim. (Though I should add this caution: *clinical* diagnosis of a mental illness is by no means simple or neutral. And as I will describe in chapter 4, *public* diagnosis of a mental illness is a complex rhetorical act shaped by implicit and explicit racism, among other factors.) The shooters in some high-profile mass shootings were severely mentally ill, but these high-profile mass shootings are not representative of all mass shootings, much less gun violence in general. Jonathan M. Metzl and Kenneth T. MacLeish point out that "fewer than 5% of the 120,000 gun-related killings in the United States between 2001 and 2010 were perpetrated by people diagnosed with mental illness" and that "the percentage of crimes that involve guns are lower [for the mentally ill] than the national average for persons not diagnosed with mental illness."[61] Cook and Goss highlight that while mentally ill people rarely commit acts of violence, they are "disproportionately likely to be victims of violent death." Furthermore, the greater danger is not that a mentally ill person with a gun will harm others—but that they will harm themselves. Cook and Goss remind us that "suicides in the United States outnumber homicides by more than two to one, with depression, substance abuse, or other psychiatric disorders estimated to be a factor in some 80% to 90% of self-inflicted death."[62]

The most prominent responses to the Virginia Tech and Tucson shootings—similar to the responses to other shootings—included no such careful discussion of America's mental health crisis.[63] Mental illness had become something to blame and then move on from rather than to study and address. Indeed, "mental illness" was functionally equivalent to "evil." Demonizing the mentally ill and mental illness is a common response, but it does not help us reduce gun violence. In fact, it only seems to ensure that those who might benefit from treatment will be more afraid to seek help—and that for those who do seek help, there will be fewer systems of support. We must do better. We ought to cultivate public deliberation about mental illness that does not stigmatize mental illness and scapegoat the mentally ill but instead seeks the best ways to support Americans in living openly and effectively with mental illness.

Deliberation and Memory Influence Copycats

After the Sandy Hook Elementary School shooting, investigators searched Adam Lanza's computer and found "a list of mass murders broken down into categories by number of victims killed."[64] They also found a chart in his room. Matthew Lysiak explained that "the seven-by-four-foot-long chart discovered in Adam's room that listed the names, numbers of kills, and weapons used by the most brutal mass killers throughout history was likely a scorecard that he was hoping to top with his name."[65] Mary Ellen O'Toole, a criminal profiler for the FBI, claimed that "Adam was on almost a military-like mission to kill as many people as possible." According to this interpretation, Lanza seemed to target an elementary school because young children were especially vulnerable and defenseless. As O'Toole puts it, "Killing one or two people doesn't get you the attention anymore. He chose something as terrible and awful as possible to ensure he would get maximum publicity."[66]

Lanza amassed a large number of kills in a perverse attempt to "top" previous mass shootings. But he was also interested in details about previous mass shootings and shooters. Lysiak notes that "between August 2009 and February 2010, Adam spent hours poring over entries about mass killers on Wikipedia. . . . Adam went into the communal encyclopedia, obsessively correcting small details of the killers' lives."[67] He was especially interested in the Columbine shooting. Investigators found "hundreds of documents, images, videos pertaining to the Columbine H.S. massacre including what appears to be a complete copy of the investigation."[68]

Lanza was not the first shooter to identify with the Columbine shooters. The Virginia Tech shooter, Seung-Hui Cho, was in eighth grade when the Columbine shooting happened. In his school writing assignments shortly after, he "expressed generalized thoughts of suicide and homicide, indicating that 'he wanted to repeat Columbine.'"[69] His parents were informed, and he was sent to a psychiatrist. But his interest in Columbine continued. In the diatribe that he sent to NBC, Cho threatens, "Generation after generation, we martyrs, like Eric and Dylan, will sacrifice our lives to fuck you thousand folds for what you Apostles of Sin have done to us."[70] His use of the word *martyr* indicates that he interpreted the destruction at Columbine as noble, while his use of *we* indicates that he identified with the Columbine killers. There are numerous problems with how Cho remembers Columbine. He identified with the killers and assumed a special bond with them even though this bond had no basis in reality. More important, Cho remembered Harris and Klebold as the downtrodden rising up against their oppressors, but in truth, they were cruel killers, not martyrs or heroes.

But no matter how wrong Cho was, he took inspiration from the Columbine shooting. In addition to referencing the shooting, he also followed the Columbine killers' lead by leaving behind writings, images of himself with guns, and recording a video of himself for reporters and investigators to puzzle through. Cho was not alone in taking inspiration from Columbine. Ralph W. Larkin notes that of the "12 documented school rampage shootings in the United States between Columbine in 1999 and the end of 2007, eight (66.7%) of the rampagers directly referred to Columbine."[71]

Columbine shooters Harris and Klebold, however, claimed not to have been influenced by other mass shootings (although that very claim suggests otherwise). In one of their home-recorded videos, Harris says, "Do not think we're trying to copy anyone." He distinguishes between their planned shooting and the recent shootings in Jonesboro, Arkansas, where the shooters were "only trying to be accepted by others."[72] Harris and Klebold instead saw their destruction in the tradition of the April 19, 1995, Oklahoma City bombing. Indeed, the date they selected for their attack marked the four-year anniversary of the Oklahoma City bombing (and that bombing, in turn, marked the two-year anniversary of law enforcement sieging the Branch Davidians' compound in Waco, Texas). They also saw their destruction in the tradition of Nazi genocide; April 20 was Adolf Hitler's birthday.

The Columbine shooters, then, had learned an unfortunate lesson from recent history, a lesson made all the more true by the logic of commercial mass media: to get noticed, their destruction had to be large scale. Although their plan to bomb their high school and shoot their peers two weeks before graduation was enough to capture the nation's attention, the killers wanted to make sure that attention was sustained even if they would not live to enjoy the fame. "Directors will be fighting over this story," Klebold said. Together they considered whether Steven Spielberg or Quentin Tarantino should direct the script.[73] Having lived in an age of relentless news coverage of the O. J. Simpson trial, the search to find the killer of child beauty queen JonBenét Ramsey, and so on, Harris and Klebold knew of America's obsession with violence and the media's ability to glorify it.

The Columbine killers wanted their destruction "to create flashbacks" and "drive [survivors] insane," and the Virginia Tech killer predicted that survivors would always live in fear: "You will never be able to go to school or work or rest or sleep. Your heart will always pound nonstop." In short, they wanted reports and images from the day of the shooting to be etched into public memory and to have ongoing influence. With the help of the media, this fear has become a reality. And this fear extends beyond the communities that mass shooters directly targeted. According to one poll, becoming a victim of a mass or random shooting is now among Americans' top-five fears.[74]

When the shooters leave behind images and videos of themselves, journals, and other materials, then reporters and investigators latch on to these materials. The information seems key to understanding the shooters' motives and to preventing future mass shootings. But it is also a trap. The search to understand why offers seemingly endless answers—which means continued attention on the killers.

Implications

Given that media coverage of mass shootings often exacerbates fears of violence without helping reduce them, distorts the public understanding of mental illness and the mentally ill, and inspires copycats, I sometimes wonder if we would be better off without even paying attention to mass shootings. What if a mass shooting happened and it was met with utter silence rather than a swarm of cameras and commentators? What if we did not show the faces or say the names of shooters? What if we did not tally up the dead?

But silence will not make the problem go away. Given the magnitude of mass gun violence and that mass gun violence often reveals much deeper problems in American life, it seems both unlikely and unwise that mass gun violence can be ignored. Another option, then, is to encourage more careful coverage and thoughtful deliberation. How do media organizations cover this violence, and how do politicians, opinion leaders, and everyday citizens talk about it? How does this violence get represented in social media feeds? Do our representations of the killers grant them rhetorical power? Are our discussions about the sources and potential solutions to violence accurate and helpful? What are the potential implications of our talk? When we attempt to make sense of violence, what public memories are we relying on, and which ones are we perpetuating or refashioning?

Part of the challenge in improving our talk is that the aftermath of gun violence seems to require two levels of commentary and analysis—specificity and generality. These two levels can be either complementary or at odds. For survivors, families, and the community directly affected by gun violence, the specific act of gun violence, not gun violence in general, has upturned their lives and is probably what matters most. Moreover, jumping to conclusions too quickly can also lead us to ignore important details that might make a specific case different from others. But there are also dangers in focusing on a specific shooting or shooter. For survivors, families, and the community directly affected by gun violence, obsessive media coverage can prolong trauma and interrupt the grieving process. Moreover, such a narrow focus on a specific shooting can inspire copycats and keep the American public from acting to reduce violence. Charles W. Collier ridicules journalists who obsess over the details and potential motives of specific shooters. He claims that the journalistic genre of "gun-murder reportage has evolved" so that the "suspect's life history is studiously explored, as if it held clues to a solemn mystery."[75] Collier insists that this "individualist paradigm" blinds us from understanding the broader pattern of gun violence.[76] And the search for a motive may ultimately be futile: there might be nothing deeper and more illuminating than the brutal fact that a gunman wanted to kill as many unknown people as possible and that he had the means of doing so.

Since April 20, 1999, Sue Klebold has sought to understand why her son Dylan did what he did. "When tragedies like Columbine or Virginia Tech or Sandy Hook happen," she writes, "the first question everyone asks is always 'Why?' Perhaps this is the wrong question. I have come to believe the better question is 'How?'" She continues, "Asking 'how' instead of 'why' allows us to frame the descent into self-destructive behavior as the process that it is. How does someone progress along a path toward hurting oneself or others?"[77] The question "Why?" often focuses on specific shooters and wrongly assumes that by trying to get into their heads or into their pasts, we will uncover satisfying answers. By instead asking "How?" or "What made this violence possible?" we can gain more resources for understanding and potentially reducing gun violence.

Routine Policy Arguments

I have made the case that deliberation matters, even apart from policy talk. But let me now focus on policy. Here too we can see public memory at work. At times, Americans are too reliant on memory: we recite clichés, fall back into familiar grooves, and talk past one another. Such routines signal a need to reengage. Those committed to creating more honest and productive deliberation need to forge new patterns of public talk. Yet the concept of public memory also highlights why it can be so difficult to break old argumentative routines.

Debates about gun policy have routinely centered on this question: To what extent, if any, are guns responsible for gun violence? For decades, gun-rights advocates have insisted that guns don't kill people, people do. This argument has a commonsense appeal because millions of Americans own guns, yet most do not use them to harm themselves or others. But this argument wrongly forces an either-or choice: either individuals are wholly to blame or guns are. Our debates about gun violence and gun policy can improve if we abandon this false dichotomy—a dichotomy that caricatures both the gun-control and gun-rights positions while it undermines the possibility for advocates on either side to talk with rather than just past each other.

Guns, of course, do not crawl out of a drawer, load themselves, and then start attacking people. At the same time, individuals who intend to cause havoc are powerless if they do not have some means to undertake violence. While guns are not the only means of undertaking violence, they are a particularly convenient and powerful means. Gun-rights advocates will sometimes extend their argument that "guns don't kill people, people do" by claiming that guns are neutral tools that can be used for good or bad. They say that a person set to do harm will find a way to do so, even without a gun. Yet research on gun violence offers a more complicated picture. While more guns do not equal more crime, more guns do increase the chances that the crime that does happen will be deadly. Moreover, having a gun in the home increases the chances that suicide attempts and domestic abuse will end in death.[78] Guns are not autonomous or independent agents, of course, but that does not mean that they do not possess some agency. In fact, they confer enormous power. After all, that's why gun-control advocates want restrictions and why gun owners and gun-rights advocates want guns for hunting and self-defense. It is why someone who is hunting a bear or a moose brings a rifle, not a stick or a hammer.

To ask "Are guns to blame or are people?" is the wrong question. As Philip J. Cook and Kristin A. Goss point out, gun violence depends on two factors: guns and someone who uses them to undertake violence.[79] It is possible to hold both accountable. Individuals who undertake gun violence should be held responsible, but that does not mean that the search for responsibility should necessarily end there. Put differently, to consider how guns enable gun violence does not mean that individual actors should not also be held accountable.

A more productive starting point, then, is to focus on the substantive disagreement: What, if anything, should we do about the fact that guns give people such enormous power to undertake deadly violence? As a country, we have already established restrictions on certain types of people (e.g., felons cannot own guns) and on certain types of weapons (e.g., machine guns). But what more, if anything, should we do? Nothing is one answer. Greater gun access is another. Greater restrictions are a third answer. A hybrid approach—greater gun access for the majority of Americans, with greater restrictions on certain people or weapons or spaces—is also possible. Whatever answer wins out, the debate will be more honest if all sides in the debate acknowledge that agency or power does not rest wholly in individuals or guns; it rests between and beyond them (e.g., specific contexts can make committing gun violence easier or more difficult).

The concept of public memory helps us understand not only why Americans regularly fall into old argumentative grooves but also why they find it so difficult to get out of these grooves. Arguments get recycled because they seem effective or seem to reveal something of value. Moreover, how one ascribes responsibility for gun violence is hardly a simple matter. Since our judgments rely on memory, trying to change our minds or someone else's can be incredibly difficult. If you are asking people to reassess their experiences, narratives, and values, you might be asking them to risk their senses of order and their very senses of self. Such a transformation cannot be expected to happen quickly or easily.

Although we regularly draw from memory when interpreting gun violence and deliberating gun policy, I should be clear: memory is not destiny, nor are all memories equally embedded in one's sense of self. Individually and collectively, we have at least some freedom to choose which memories to activate and which to ignore. While individuals might have preexisting beliefs about the sources of violence and the role of government, these beliefs coexist with their other beliefs and desires, as well as the beliefs and desires expressed by other people. Depending on the situation, beliefs about the cause of violence, for instance, might be amplified, downplayed, or ignored outright. Moreover, commitment to consistent beliefs about what or who is to blame for gun violence can be less important than doing what seems necessary to win. For example, if individuals worry about impending gun restrictions, they might shift blame to the individual act by dismissing the shooter as evil; if they worry about terrorism, they might shift blame from the individual act to some broader aspect of society, such as an entire religion (which happened after the 2015 shooting in San Bernardino). Assigning blame relies on previous forms of blaming stored in memory, but like all rhetorical acts, blaming is a complex and malleable process.

Gun-rights advocates regularly claim that guns are not to blame for gun violence; indeed, they argue that a heavily armed citizenry is the best way to prevent such violence. But the debate over gun policy extends far beyond the topic of blame. For some gun-rights advocates, assigning blame does not ultimately matter, nor does the cost-benefit analysis of various policies. Instead, the standard is whether or not we honor our constitutionally protected right to keep and bear arms. The next chapter therefore turns to the Second Amendment. By continuing to focus on the relationship between public deliberation and public memory, we can see that how the Second Amendment gets imagined and invoked is by no means simple or unproblematic.

The Relationship Between Memory and Deliberation

In the chapters ahead, I further theorize the interplay of deliberation and memory by focusing on three relationships: the relationship between memory and the weight of the past (chapter 2), the fleeting past (chapter 3), and the implicit past (chapter 4). Chapter 2 illustrates the weight of the past by examining the relationship between memory and the Second Amendment. Contemporary debates about the Second Amendment are not reducible to the twenty-seven words ratified in 1791. Instead, the meanings of the Second Amendment have been subject to over 225 years of history, culture, and politics. To understand current debates about the Second Amendment and why it is so difficult to argue productively requires considering these broader accumulated meanings. Although advocates of gun rights invoke the Founding Fathers to establish a sense of immediacy with them, thereby instilling a patriotic obligation to defend and preserve tradition, their assumption of immediacy is problematic. I claim that the Second Amendment has been made to matter in distinct ways throughout its use in public deliberation. It bears the weight of its rhetorical history—of its use and repurposing across time. To support this claim, I focus on the NRA's rhetoric, particularly over the last forty years. In particular, I trace how the Second Amendment became symbolically intertwined with absolutism and cultural war.

Chapter 3 illustrates the fleeting past by examining the relationship between memory and our purported obligations to the dead. Whereas gun-rights advocates make their case by appealing to rights (i.e., the Second Amendment), gun-control advocates increasingly make their case by appealing to responsibility (i.e., our purported obligation to honor the dead victims of gun violence). Yet leaders in the gun-control movement have also identified a challenge within their own ranks: feeling moved and then moving on.[80] The fleeting past and fleeting engagement reinforce one another. To address this problem, they have attempted to extend, expand, and intensify memories of gun-violence victims and thus develop a sustained commitment to gun control. Gun-rights advocates, in turn, charge that any talk of gun policy in the aftermath of a national tragedy is manipulative. Both sides, then, disagree about our obligations to the dead and how best to honor their memory. To illustrate these claims, I focus on responses to the shooting at Sandy Hook Elementary School, particularly President Obama's rhetoric.

Chapter 4 illustrates the implicit past by examining the relationship between memory and racism. The conjunction of racism and gun violence in the 2015 Emanuel African Methodist Episcopal (AME) Church shooting in Charleston, South Carolina, illuminates the much larger role that racism has implicitly—and often explicitly—played in debates about gun violence and policy throughout U.S. history. America's history of white supremacy functions as a lens or filter that sorts and distorts interpretation and deliberation as well as perception (including what is and is not seen and heard). Since America's founding, racist fears have been activated and exacerbated by those arguing for and against gun control. Today, racist assumptions continue to shape who can and who cannot freely exercise their Second Amendment right, with people of color (especially black men) often rendered a threat. Moreover, racist assumptions shape which victims of gun violence are perceived as innocent and which are not, as well as which victims and forms of violence warrant pushes in federal policy. To understand—let alone change—public debates about gun violence and gun policy, we need to acknowledge and then challenge the ideology of white supremacy. In fundamental ways, the problems of racism and gun violence are inseparable.

As the next chapters will demonstrate, the interplay of memory and deliberation is neither simply a passive process nor a deterministic one in which we are doomed to repeat what was previously said. Seeing the canons of invention and memory together can help us recognize that while we draw from memory when interpreting and deliberating, we are not required to accept or perpetuate past ways of seeing and arguing. We have the capacity for rhetorical invention—to pursue different ways of seeing and talking and perhaps even create new ones. We have at least some agency to change the conversation, and that is why critical analysis and reflection are so important. The ways that we interpret gun violence and deliberate about its sources and solutions could be different—which means that they could be better. In that basic truth, there is hope.

2

THE WEIGHT OF THE PAST: MEMORY AND THE SECOND AMENDMENT

A well regulated Militia, being necessary to the security of a free State, the right of the people to keep and bear Arms, shall not be infringed.

—SECOND AMENDMENT, BILL OF RIGHTS, 1791

Unlike the Ten Commandments, the Bill of Rights wasn't cut into stone tablets. But the text surely has that same righteous feel to it. It's as if you can sense the unseen hand of the Almighty God guiding the sweep of a goose quill pen, while some rebellious old white guys sweated out the birth of a nation.

—CHARLTON HESTON, JANUARY 27, 1998

When Americans talk about gun policy, they regularly talk about the Second Amendment. Such was the case after the shooting at Sandy Hook Elementary School on December 14, 2012. A month after the shooting, the White House proposed expanding background checks, banning assault weapons, and limiting magazine capacity to ten rounds. In making the case for these proposals, President Obama attempted to challenge the presumption that debates about gun policy should only be about the Second Amendment. He claimed that this right, while crucially important, should not be allowed to infringe on other rights, such as free speech and the right to life. He also claimed that rights must coexist with responsibilities (a claim that I describe further in chapter 3). But Obama also addressed the Second Amendment head on, declaring, "Like most Americans, I believe the Second Amendment guarantees an individual right to bear arms." He continued, "I also believe most gun owners agree that we can respect the Second Amendment while keeping an irresponsible, law-breaking few from inflicting harm on a massive scale."[1] Meanwhile, Wayne LaPierre, executive vice president of the NRA, insisted that there could be no middle ground: any regulation, no matter how large or small, undermined the Second Amendment. "I've got news for the president," LaPierre declared. "Absolutes do exist. Words do have specific meaning, in language and in law."[2] Announcing the NRA's "four-year communications and resistance movement," he warned that "the enemies of the Second Amendment will be met with unprecedented defiance, commitment and determination. We will Stand and Fight."[3]

When the Senate voted down the White House's gun-control proposals on April 17, 2013, reporters and commentators searched to understand why this had happened. Robert Draper chronicled the NRA's hand in the process. Draper noted that the NRA initially seemed open to working with Congress on expanding background checks. Senator Joe Manchin, who cosponsored the legislation, met Chris Cox and Jim Baker of the NRA in early March. Manchin reportedly "knew that the lobbyists were never going to embrace universal background checks. His hope was simply that they would not fight him." But when word of the negotiations between senators and the NRA leaked, other gun-rights groups, such as the Gun Owners of America, sent out emails disparaging any potential compromise and blasting the NRA. The NRA felt the backlash from its "most-activist members." Within a few days, "Cox and Baker stopped communicating with Manchin's office." When Manchin spoke to Baker on the phone, Baker announced that the NRA was now totally opposed to the bill: "We're going to be fighting it with all we have." And the NRA did. Senate office phone lines got flooded with calls. Staff members heard over and over again "the distinct and fevered outcry of a single-issue constituency with every intention of echoing its wrath at the ballot box."[4]

Draper's chronicle offers a behind-the-scenes look at the legislative process in the spring of 2013, shedding light on the NRA's enduring political power, backed by its ability to organize and mobilize members to donate money and pressure representatives. Yet Draper ignores several key questions: How has the NRA acquired and sustained such a wide and passionate following? What kind of worldview does it offer to its supporters? And how does it characterize America's gun debate, particularly debates over the Second Amendment? To answer those questions, we need to examine the NRA's rhetoric to its members and to the broader public.

The fight over the meaning and significance of the Second Amendment is rhetorically complex. Obama's speech on the day of the Senate vote begins to illuminate this complexity. Obama charged, "The gun lobby and its allies willfully lied about the bill. They claimed that it would create some sort of 'big brother' gun registry, even though the bill did the opposite. This legislation, in fact, outlawed any registry. Plain and simple, right there in the text. But that didn't matter."[5] Obama was telling the truth. The White House plan and the proposed legislation included no mention of a registry, yet the NRA warned that Obama "wants to put every private, personal transaction under the thumb of the federal government, and he wants to keep all those names in a massive federal registry. There are only two reasons for that federal list of gun owners—to tax them or take them."[6] Lies do matter; among other reasons, they undermine the common ground necessary for productive deliberation. Yet even if inadvertently, Obama's comment highlights something else important about public deliberation. Whether we are deliberating specific legislation or the Second Amendment more generally, what is "right there in the text" matters—but it is not all that matters. The rhetorical struggle is not simply a textual one.

The battle over the Second Amendment is not confined to its twenty-seven words ratified in 1791. And although appeals to the Second Amendment can represent a legal argument, the amendment's meaning and rhetorical power extend far beyond the law. The Second Amendment has been subject to over 225 years of history, culture, and politics. It bears the weight of its past. Through its own rhetorical history—how it has been invoked and repurposed across time—the Second Amendment has been infused with meaning and made to matter in distinct ways.

"Rhetoric," Thomas B. Farrell explains, "is the art, the fine and useful art, of making things matter." Farrell urges rhetorical scholars to examine "how our largely unstudied conceptions of 'worth' are themselves created, enhanced, and reaffirmed."[7] To focus on the weight of rhetoric requires that we examine how certain ideas or values are "made to matter and why."[8] The simple act of mentioning the Second Amendment—and doing so again and again—suggests its magnitude. But its weight is also established by *how* it is used, particularly in public talk. To understand current debates about the Second Amendment and why it is so difficult to debate productively requires that we examine these accumulated meanings.

This chapter proceeds in four steps. First, I describe America's gun culture and note that it is sustained by a variety of forces, most notably stories about who "we" are individually and as Americans. Second, I identify how gun-rights advocates regularly invoke the Second Amendment as if it were a direct, unvarnished inheritance from America's Founding Fathers. Yet this assumption of immediacy is problematic. Third, I trace how the NRA has helped recast the Second Amendment as an absolute right and entangled it with America's culture war. In so doing, the NRA has changed the meaning and significance of the Second Amendment. And in the final section, I draw the two previous claims together to contend that it is inaccurate to depict the Second Amendment as a self-evident truth rather than as an argument. But this argument depends on public memories largely built and sustained by gun-rights advocates. Consequently, if there is any chance for productive deliberation about the Second Amendment, gun-control advocates and gun-rights advocates alike must recognize that the gun debate is not simply about the Second Amendment that is etched into the Bill of Rights; it is also about the Second Amendment that lives, grows, and changes in public memory.

America's Gun Culture

Guns loom large in the American imagination. Although the attention we give to guns might be taken for granted, this development was not inevitable. As Spitzer asks, "Why do relatively simple metal-and-wood objects that do nothing more than propel metal at high speeds evoke such strong feelings?" One answer is relatively simple: guns evoke such strong feelings because they can kill and wound so easily. A second answer, however, is more complicated: guns evoke such strong feelings because they have played a central role in American life throughout history—or they are at least remembered as having done so.[9] In the words of historian Richard Hofstadter, America has created and maintained a unique "gun culture."[10]

America's gun culture today is sustained by the gun industry and gun-advocacy groups. But gun owners also sustain it: approximately 30 percent of Americans own at least one gun,[11] and estimates suggest that these Americans own between two hundred and three hundred million guns.[12] The gun culture is also sustained by products (hunting gear, targets, movies, books, magazines, video games, toys, etc.), as well as institutions (e.g., the military), events (e.g., gun shows), places (e.g., shooting ranges), education (e.g., hunter safety courses and more informal modes of instruction), relationships (e.g., family and friends), and so on. Gun culture covers a variety of practices—harmless ones, such as collecting guns or shooting clay pigeons, and harmful ones, such as shooting people—and thus includes moments of joy as well as moments of horror. Above all, though, gun culture is animated by stories—whether accurate or not—about who "we" are individually and as Americans.

In America's beginning, there were guns—first to fight the British and then to claim the West: "Moving westward in the post-Revolutionary period, American frontiersman required firearms to hunt, ward off threatening wildlife, and vanquish Native Americans, cattle rustlers, and pugnacious troublemakers in mining camps and other untamed surroundings. In areas with little if any organized law enforcement, private individuals relied on themselves for protection."[13] Cook and Goss explain that the gun culture of today "has its roots in lived experience." Yet "mass marketing and media" have also embellished the role of guns in American life.[14] Spitzer notes that "although gun ownership dates to America's beginnings, it was far less prevalent in or important to colonial and early federal life than popular impressions and mythology suggest." There are numerous reasons: "Guns were expensive, cumbersome, difficult to operate, unreliable, and made from materials (mostly iron) that deteriorated rapidly even with regular maintenance." Moreover, "subsistence agriculture, including the raising of crops and animals, was the main source of sustenance for most Americans, not the hunting of wild game."[15]

Guns gained prominence in American life after the Civil War due to technological advances that made guns "cheaper, more reliable, easier to use, and more durable." But they also gained prominence because gun manufacturers such as Samuel Colt "developed advertising campaigns that deliberately romanticized the attachment to guns."[16] America's gun culture, Pamela Haag reminds us, is largely a business that "developed out of an unexceptional, perpetual quest for new and larger markets."[17]

Historians describe a large gap between frontier myth and reality. While Americans then and now might imagine the 1800s as a time of "western-style shoot-outs," such violence was actually quite rare, even in the "most violent cow towns of the old West—Abilene, Caldwell, Dodge City, Ellsworth, and Witchita."[18] As Richard Shenkman puts it, "The truth is many more people have died in Hollywood westerns than ever died on the real frontier."[19] And while Americans might imagine that everyone in frontier towns was armed, gun control was actually quite common. Adam Winkler explains that "almost everyone carried firearms in the untamed wilderness," but in frontier towns, "where people lived and businesses operated, the law often forbade people from toting their guns around." For example, during the 1870s, a sign in Wichita read "Leave Your Revolvers at Police Headquarters, and Get a Check." In Dodge City, a billboard read, "The carrying of firearms strictly prohibited." Winkler explains that "frontier towns handled guns the way a Boston restaurant today handles overcoats in winter. New arrivals were required to turn in their guns to authorities in exchange for something like a metal token."[20]

It is important, of course, to strive for an accurate historical record and to correct inaccuracies, as I have tried to do here. Yet accuracy is not the only value that guides storytelling and remembering. What stories a group tells and remembers is shaped in part by their present needs and goals. Haag notes, for instance, that the "emotional and political affinity for the gun was perhaps a post-frontier phenomenon of the twentieth century talking about the nineteenth."[21] The stories told about the role of guns in American life came from many sources, including "entrepreneurial fiction writers, movie makers, showmen, political advocates, and even gun makers."[22] And this storytelling has continued throughout the twentieth century to today and become even more rhetorically complex.

Whether accurate or not, the stories that Americans tell and remember about themselves are key to understanding America's gun culture—and gun debate. In what follows, I examine the stories that the NRA tells about who "we" are individually and as Americans and, in turn, consider how these stories have shaped public deliberation about guns and the Second Amendment.

Appealing to the Founding Fathers

In 1999, the NRA's annual convention was scheduled to take place less than two weeks after the Columbine shooting. As fate would have it, the convention was planned to take place in Denver, about fifteen miles away from Columbine High School.[23] The mayor of Denver requested that the convention be canceled. On May 1, 1999, approximately three thousand protestors "encircled the site," singing songs and carrying signs, including ones that read "We Shall Overcome" and "Shame on the NRA."[24] The next day, approximately eight thousand protestors gathered a few blocks away on the front lawn of the capitol building.[25] Tom Mauser, whose son Daniel was killed in the shooting, spoke to the crowd, "It is time we own up to the fact that we have a violence problem in this society. Something is wrong in this country when a child can grab a gun so easily and shoot a bullet in the middle of a child's face, as my son experienced."[26]

Inside the convention center, NRA members and leaders gathered for an "abbreviated annual gathering."[27] NRA President Charlton Heston expressed shock and horror about the recent shooting, yet he rejected the implication that the NRA, its members, or guns bore any responsibility for what had happened: "We have the same right as all other citizens to be here," he explained in his opening remarks to the convention.[28] In his closing remarks, he insisted that "America must stop this predictable pattern of reaction, when an isolated, terrible event occurs, our phones ring, demanding that the NRA explain the inexplicable."[29] Heston nonetheless offers a partial explanation for the shooting by blaming the media, balkanization, immorality, and so on. But his primary focus was not to explain why mass gun violence happens or identify potential solutions to address it. Instead, Heston focused on defending the NRA, its members, and the right to own guns. "The individual right to bear arms," Heston argued, "is freedom's insurance policy."[30] Guns were not just about self-protection; guns were about protecting the rights that make America possible. Heston stated, "If you like your freedoms of speech and of religion, freedom from search and seizure, freedom of the press and of privacy, to assemble, and to redress grievances, then you'd better give them that eternal bodyguard called the Second Amendment."[31]

Gun-rights advocates, of course, regularly invoke the Second Amendment—that's not surprising. What's interesting is the justification they give. Heston, for instance, argues that the Second Amendment fulfills our present and future needs for self-defense. Yet he also suggests that we have a sacred obligation to the past—particularly to the Founding Fathers—to defend the Second Amendment: "We cannot, we must not, let tragedy lay waste to the most rare and hard-won human right in history."[32] Gun-rights advocates regularly invoke the Second Amendment as if it were a direct, unvarnished inheritance from America's Founding Fathers. I ultimately think that this assumption of immediacy is false. But before developing that claim, I first want to further illustrate how the NRA appeals to the Founding Fathers and assess how those appeals function rhetorically.

Our Obligation to the Founding Fathers

Heston's rhetoric—both before and after his 1999 appearance in Denver—is worth examining more closely. The actor-turned-activist joined forces with the NRA in the early 1980s when he appeared in its "I'm the NRA" ad campaign.[33] In 1996, Heston "campaigned for more than fifty candidates who supported gun rights."[34] In 1997, NRA leaders convinced him that his celebrity would give increased visibility to the organization.[35] He was elected vice president of the NRA that year and became president in 1998, serving as NRA president until 2003. Heston explained that he wanted to "bring the NRA back to the table of mainstream political debate."[36] He accomplished this in part through his celebrity—even those who had not seen him in movies such as *Planet of the Apes* (1968) and *The Ten Commandments* (1956), in which he played Moses, were struck by his square jaw and deep voice. Yet his celebrity alone does not explain how he helped bring the NRA into the mainstream of political debate. To help us understand how he did so, we must look at his arguments, particularly his appeal to the legacy of America's Founding Fathers.

Speaking to the Conservative Political Action Committee on January 27, 1998, Heston stated, "Our ancestors were armed with pride, and bequeathed it to us—I can prove it. If you want to feel the warm breath of freedom upon your neck . . . if you want to touch the proud pulse of liberty that beat in our Founding Fathers in its purest form, you can do so through the majesty of the Second Amendment right to keep and bear arms."[37] Heston's vivid description—"warm breath of freedom upon your neck," "proud pulse of liberty"—suggests that the founders are not entirely dead. Instead, America's founders come to life whenever we use guns or defend the Second Amendment. By implication, those who do not use guns or actively defend the Second Amendment are disconnected from the Founding Fathers.

In Heston's telling, the Second Amendment is not simply a law but an inheritance that imposes a sacred and urgent obligation. Speaking at the NRA's annual meeting on May 22, 1998, Heston begins by noting the significance of the meeting being held in Philadelphia: "This is where it all started, isn't it? Right here in Philadelphia. Two and a quarter centuries ago, a bunch of amazing guys traveled here. They had freedom's business to tend to."[38] Heston ends by returning to that theme, claiming that like "those great men that travelled here two and a quarter centuries ago, because of them, we have freedom's business to tend to."[39] In short, the cause of the founders and the cause of the NRA become one and the same. Heston suggests that this mandate comes from the founders themselves: "I think Jefferson and Paine, Adams, Madison, Mason, Franklin, I think they're looking down right now at us. I think they understand what we're trying to do, what we strive to do. I came here to help make them proud of us."[40] With the founders looking down on them, NRA members should be brave and proud. Even small acts matter: "Never again will you think twice before saying you're an NRA member, or think twice about putting that NRA decal on your car."[41]

Although Heston maintains that the Second Amendment is a direct inheritance from the Founding Fathers, he also suggests that this inheritance has been passed down from one generation to the next. Speaking before the National Press Club on September 1, 1997, Heston insists that the

Bill of Rights, including the Second Amendment, "must be delivered into the 21st century as pure and meaningful as they came to us at the beginning of this century." He continues, "I believe the freedoms that provided my generation with so much opportunity must remain the birthright of each generation that carries the torch forward." The torch metaphor suggests urgency, since torches can grow dim or dark. Carrying a torch forward emphasizes the obligation between generations and suggests continuity (i.e., the Second Amendment is the same as it has always been). Placing himself within the lineage of the Founding Fathers, Heston suggests that he is passing the torch directly from the founders to tomorrow's gun-rights advocates: "Traditionally the passing of that torch is from a gnarled, old hand down to an eager, young one. So now, at 72, I offer my gnarled, old hand."[42]

Although Heston's careful attention to metaphor is largely distinct to him, the same basic argument has appeared long after his time in the NRA. That is, the NRA continues to invoke the Second Amendment as if it were a direct, unvarnished inheritance from America's Founding Fathers. In 2007, LaPierre of the NRA published *The Essential Second Amendment Guide*. The book cover features a painting entitled *Stand Your Ground—Battle of Lexington Green*. Even though the painting is from the perspective of a contemporary artist, Don Troiani, it seems like an authentic account of being on the battlefields of the American Revolution. The painting depicts a ragtag group of armed colonists in the foreground defending themselves against British soldiers in the background. The painting's contrast is stark: the bottom left is dark, and the top right is bright; a large musket is featured in the painting's center, pointing the way from darkness to light, from fear and oppression to confidence and freedom. In this depiction, the cause of the Founding Fathers becomes not merely similar to but synonymous with the cause of the NRA. The American Revolution is thus imagined as a war fought exclusively for the Bill of Rights, especially the Second Amendment.

Within this book, LaPierre addresses his readers as "Fellow Americans." He explains, "In the end, your commitment to our cause is all that guarantees the Second Amendment survives and thrives for generations to come. Thank you for keeping the flame of freedom burning brightly in American hearts."[43] A decade later, in a 2017 mailing to recruit NRA members, LaPierre stated, "Standing together under the NRA banner is the best guarantee for the long-term survival of our freedom, our heritage and our American way of life." Like Heston had done, LaPierre suggests that the Second Amendment is a direct inheritance from the Founding Fathers, and he too suggests that we must preserve and perpetuate this inheritance to fulfill our obligations to the founders and to America. "Thank you," he says, for your "hard work to keep our Second Amendment rights safe—and our nation free."[44]

Assessing the Appeals to the Founders

When rhetors invoke the Founding Fathers to defend the Second Amendment, the stakes of the debate are heightened: Will we honor and defend a sacred obligation, or will we let it die? The debate is over guns, to be sure, but the debate also becomes a battle over America's past and future, over the character of America and ourselves as Americans. This rhetoric is powerful. But the assumption of immediacy with the Founding Fathers is false.

This rhetoric defending the Second Amendment is just one example of a broader pattern of contemporary rhetoric that invokes the Founding Fathers as the ultimate authority. Historian Jill Lepore describes this unwavering—albeit selective—allegiance to the Founding Fathers as "historical fundamentalism":

> Historical fundamentalism is marked by the belief that a particular and quite narrowly defined past—"the founding"—is ageless and sacred and to be worshipped; that certain historical texts—"the founding documents"—are to be read in the same spirit with which religious fundamentalists read, for instance, the Ten Commandments; that the Founding Fathers were divinely inspired; that the academic study of history (whose standards of evidence and methods of analysis are based on skepticism) is a conspiracy and, furthermore, blasphemy; and that political arguments grounded in appeals to the founding documents, as sacred texts, and the Founding Fathers, as prophets, are therefore incontrovertible.[45]

Lepore points out that even if we wanted to, we "cannot go back to the eighteenth century, and the Founding Fathers are not, in fact, here with us today."[46] To assume such a time collapse is to engage in fiction. Building on Lepore's work, Jeremy Engels highlights that this "time warp" skips over "the messiness of the nineteenth and twentieth centuries" while promising to take us "back to a simpler, purer time."[47] But what gets left out is perhaps most notable about this imagined world. Lepore describes it as "a fantasy of America before race, *without* race." It is a world without women, "aside from Abigail Adams," and without "slavery, poverty, ignorance, insanity, sickness, or misery." In this imagined whitewashed world, all that is left are "the

Founding Fathers with their white wigs, wearing their three-cornered hats, in their Christian nation, revolting against taxes, and defending their right to bear arms."[48]

Historical fundamentalism—or what Andrew Burstein more narrowly calls "founder fundamentalism"—asserts that good Americans must fulfill their "duty to protect the reputation of those unimpeachable sources of authority who carried the eternal word of the founding."[49] Highlighting the complexity of interpretation, Burstein shows how just one founder—Thomas Jefferson—has been cast in different roles throughout U.S. history, including an "FDR liberal, a Reagan republican, and a Tea Party fanatic."[50] Moreover, Jefferson has been invoked as both the enemy and champion of racial equality and as both a defender and a threat to religious liberty. The complexities of interpretation are only amplified when moving from Jefferson to the Founding Fathers in general. To invoke the Founding Fathers is to assume a specific group of men who shared one mind while ignoring questions about who is included and excluded and ignoring the fact that these men did not all agree with one another (or even themselves, since a person's opinion can change over time and circumstance). And to invoke the Founding Fathers as if they offer self-evident truths to us across the breach of more than two centuries ignores how history and our current standpoints and goals shape our reception of the Founding Fathers and their purported lessons.

And then there is the question about obligation. Not only does the NRA assume that the founders reached consensus, that this consensus can be easily discerned, that they would have maintained that consensus despite the social and technological changes over the last two centuries, and that the founders' views reflect those of the NRA. The NRA also assumes that the founders present us with an obligation and that we must accept it. Yet this assumption was debatable even among the Founding Fathers themselves. Thomas Jefferson, for instance, wrote to James Madison on September 6, 1789, asking "whether one generation of men has a right to bind another." Jefferson's conclusion, at least in this letter, was that "'the earth belongs in usufruct to the living'; that the dead have neither powers nor rights over it." Despite Madison's protests, Jefferson imagined that the U.S. Constitution might be updated or even rewritten every nineteen years.[51] At least outside the context of the gun debate, most contemporary Americans recognize that the founders were not infallible and that we are not obliged to carry out everything that they believed, practiced, or enshrined into law (e.g., slavery). Even if we believe that the founders do impose an obligation to uphold a right to bear arms without any restriction (which is contrary to the U.S. Supreme

Court's 2008 *Heller* decision, as I explain later), it is not obvious whether that should be our only obligation or why it should be the most important one.

To be clear, I am not claiming that the NRA gets the Founding Fathers and the Second Amendment right or wrong (although that question is not unimportant). Instead, my claim is more fundamental: the NRA depicts the meaning of the Second Amendment and our obligations to the Founding Fathers as self-evident truths; however, these depictions are actually arguments. But the fact that the NRA and other gun-rights advocates are implicitly arguing when they invoke the founders and the Second Amendment is not a problem; the problem is that they attempt to hide the fact that they are arguing at all.[52] Their concealment allows them to assert rather than argue that their version of the Second Amendment is obviously true. Meanwhile, this assertion of obviousness attempts to hide the fact that there are actually disagreements about the meaning and significance of the Second Amendment. If any disagreement is acknowledged, it is discounted out of hand: arguments opposing a self-evident truth are obviously wrong; to oppose a self-evident truth suggests that the dissenter is not only wrong but also foolish or—given the importance of the Second Amendment—evil and un-American.[53] Invoking the authority of the Founding Fathers further serves as a debate stopper, asking, in effect, Who are *you* to question the founders? Ridicule is used to hide questions about whether the accuser's vision of the founders is accurate and relevant.[54] The Second Amendment, in the NRA's depiction, cannot be argued or debated, just obeyed. As I explore in the next section, this concealment allows the NRA and other gun-rights advocates to hide their own active role in shaping the meaning and significance of the Second Amendment.

The NRA Tips the Scale

Although gun-rights advocates regularly invoke the Second Amendment as if it were a direct, unvarnished inheritance from America's Founding Fathers, such advocates actually play an active role in shaping its meaning and significance. As Michael Waldman explains, "Our view of the Second Amendment is set, at each stage, not by a pristine constitutional text, but by the push-and-pull, the rough-and-tumble of political advocacy and public agitation."[55] Taking a historical perspective on the NRA's rhetoric over the last forty years helps reveal how the NRA actively contributed to this process. Specifically, I trace how the NRA has helped recast the Second Amendment as an absolute right and entangled it with America's culture war. Examining these depictions of the Second Amendment are essential for understanding America's collective inability to talk productively across differences about the Second Amendment and gun policy.

Absolutism

The NRA depicts the Second Amendment as an absolute right. "Absolutes do exist," LaPierre declared on January 22, 2013. "Words have specific meaning in language and in law."[56] On February 13, he explained that the NRA's mission was to "preserve the inalienable, individual human right to keep and bear guns."[57] Notably, he says that this right is "inalienable"—it is unchallengeable, immutable, and absolute—and implies that the NRA's goal is not to establish something new but to "preserve" what has allegedly been inherited. As LaPierre puts it, an absolute Second Amendment comes directly from the Founding Fathers: "We are as 'absolutist' as the Founding Fathers and the framers of the Constitution . . . and we're proud of it."[58]

The NRA's depiction of the Second Amendment as an absolute contradicts how the Supreme Court has interpreted the Second Amendment. Until 2008, the court upheld that the Second Amendment established a collective right to gun ownership so that citizens would be "prepared to carry these arms into battle in defense of the state."[59] The court's 2008 *District of Columbia v. Heller* decision was largely seen as a victory for gun-rights advocates. Overturning Washington DC's handgun ban, the 5–4 majority claimed that the ban violated the Second Amendment. Moreover, the court affirmed that the Second Amendment does in fact protect an individual's right to own and use firearms for self-protection, not just a collective right for militias. Writing for the majority, Justice Antonin Scalia argued that the Second Amendment protects an individual's right to own and use firearms for self-protection. Yet Scalia continued, "Like most rights, the right secured by the Second Amendment is not unlimited." The right was "not a right to keep and carry any weapon whatsoever in any manner whatsoever and for whatever purposes."[60] This legal understanding of the Second Amendment clashes with the NRA's claim that the regulations and the Second Amendment are wholly at odds.

Although the NRA currently maintains that regulations are wholly at odds with an absolute Second Amendment, this has not always been its stance. Karl T. Frederick, who was the NRA's president in the 1930s, testified in congressional hearings over the proposed National Firearms Act, which was passed in 1934. He explained, "I do not believe in the general promiscuous toting of guns. I think it should be sharply restricted and only under licenses."[61] Frederick was not an outlier. Milton A. Reckford, who was then the NRA's executive vice president, told the congressional committee that the NRA was "absolutely favorable to reasonable gun control."[62] Winkler notes that the Second Amendment was "conspicuous in its absence from the NRA's advocacy during this period." For instance, when Frederick was asked during "his testimony on the National Firearms Act whether the proposed law violated any constitutional provision, he responded, 'I have not given it any study from that point of view.'" In other words, "the President of the NRA hadn't even considered whether the most far-reaching federal gun control law to date was affected by the Second Amendment."[63]

For over one hundred years—from its founding in 1871 until its tumultuous change in leadership in 1977—the NRA's mission was primarily focused on gun safety and marksmanship training. Prior to 1977, the NRA had advocated against gun legislation deemed unreasonable, but lobbying was not its primary focus. Things started to change in 1968. Raymond explains, "The Gun Control Act [GCA] of 1968 was considered a watershed in the history of the NRA because it highlighted two changes for the organization. First, the act brought thousands of new members to the organization, increasing its rolls to over 1 million men and women. Second and most important, the debate over the legislation exacerbated a split between the sportsmen and the politicos in the organization."[64] The sportsmen represented the old guard. They wanted the NRA to be devoted to "teaching gun safety, organizing shooting competitions, and running clinics for hunters." They were not as concerned about gun policy. One of these sportsmen was the NRA's executive vice president, General Franklin Orth. He had "testified before Congress in favor of the GCA, saying 'We do not think that any sane American, who calls himself an American, can object to placing into this bill the instrument which killed the President of the United States."[65] The politicos, as represented by Harlon B. Carter, "disagreed vehemently, believing that gun control efforts would eventually restrict all varieties of gun ownership, including that of the sportsmen."[66] They believed that "the NRA needed to spend less time and energy shooting at paper targets and ducks and more blasting away at gun control legislation."[67]

Over the next decade, "these internal divisions brewed."[68] The tensions became unbearable when the sportsmen bought thirty-seven thousand acres of land in New Mexico. The money spent on a new rifle range meant less money for the organization's lobbying efforts. But worse, the sportsmen expressed the desire that this planned National Shooting Center be instead called the National Outdoor Center. The proposed name change signaled that the center's mission would extend beyond shooting to include "camping and wilderness survival training; conservation education; environmental awareness." For the politicos, this "was treason." Carter and the other politicos planned to take control of the organization. When the sportsmen learned of this, they fired "seventy-four NRA employees—most of them members of Carter's hard-line group." In protest of these firings, Carter resigned. "The members of the old guard breathed a sigh of relief," and they moved forward with their plans to make "the NRA into the nation's preeminent outdoors organization." The sportsmen planned to sell their Washington, DC, headquarters and "move all operations to Colorado Springs, not far from the National Outdoor Center."[69]

Six months later, the NRA held its 1977 convention in Cincinnati. NRA leadership hoped that this convention would be an opportunity for reconciling, healing, and moving forward. But that year's convention would become known as the Cincinnati Revolt. Carter and other hardliners "introduced several changes in the group's bylaws that would diminish the power in the hands of the elected officials and give the membership more say in the organization's affairs." But that was just the start. Osha Gray Davidson explains, "The old guard never knew what hit them. The membership overwhelmingly voted for the changes. Plans to move the group's headquarters to Colorado Springs were put on hold, as were those for the hated National Outdoor Center. And then the members overwhelmingly voted against nearly every top NRA official, one by one. When the smoke cleared, leaders of the Federation for the NRA occupied every position of power."[70] Minutes before being elected executive vice president, Carter insisted, "Beginning at this place and at this hour, this period in NRA history is finished."[71] Under Carter's leadership, the NRA "became more than a rifle club. It became the Gun Lobby." As Davidson explains, "Forget about the hunting clinics, forget about target shooting; those activities were now sideshows, mere extras. The new NRA would be devoted single-mindedly—and proud of the fact—to the proposition that Americans and their guns must never, *never* be parted."[72]

With the change in the NRA's mission came an obsessive focus on the Second Amendment. Since 1957, a plaque outside NRA headquarters was inscribed with the motto "Firearm Safety Education, Marksmanship Training, Shooting for Recreation."[73] But after Carter was elected vice president, there was a new motto: "The right of the people to keep and bear arms shall not be infringed."[74] While this motto is taken from the Second Amendment, the amendment's opening—"A well regulated Militia, being necessary to the Security of a free State"—is excised and forgotten. This elision ignores questions about the nature and scope of the Second Amendment, including the text's reference to the "Militia" and what counts as "well regulated." Instead, the Second Amendment is transformed into a simple moral imperative: the right of the people to keep and bear arms shall not be infringed. Although this selective quoting might be savvy marketing, it is a questionable use of history.

The NRA currently insists that the Second Amendment represents an absolute right and that this is obvious. Yet this claim is relatively new. Indeed, the NRA itself did not seem to fully realize it until the late 1970s. The NRA's decision to depict the Second Amendment as an absolute right was a deliberate one. On his path to taking control of the NRA, Carter had written a letter in 1975 to the "entire NRA membership to discuss the fight in Congress over gun control." He explained that "we can win it on a simple concept—*No compromise. No gun legislation.*"[75] Carter's message offered a blueprint for how the NRA has operated since. As just one example, consider Heston's infamous ultimatum to gun-control advocates. After delivering a speech at the 1989 NRA members' meeting, Heston was presented with a "beautiful, handcrafted musket. Lifting the gleaming muzzle-loader high over his head, Heston had intoned in his best Moses-with-the-Tablets voice: 'From my cold, dead hands!'"[76] He repeated that act again on other occasions, including his May 20, 2000, speech before the NRA convention.[77] The implication was clear: Heston saw no room for compromise in the clash between gun-control advocates and gun-rights advocates. The "gun grabbers," Richard Feldman explains, "would have to kill him to trample his Second Amendment rights."[78]

Embracing an absolute Second Amendment has benefited the NRA. Beginning with Carter's leadership, the NRA became "committed to a more rigid approach to gun control" and "became one of the most powerful forces in American politics." As Winkler writes, "Armed with a new philosophy, the organization's membership tripled, its fund-raising multiplied, and its influence soared."[79] "The NRA is a populist organization," William J. Vizzard explains. "They get support when people are mad and stirred up. They want the attention. They're not interested in fixing things. They want to stir things up, and the more they stir things up, the more members they get and the more money they make. What do they gain by compromising? Nothing."[80] Put differently, an NRA that offered a nuanced take on the Second Amendment would not evoke the passionate support evoked by an NRA that says the Second Amendment is absolute and that any restriction must be fought.

Given that the NRA is an advocacy organization, its hardline stance is not altogether surprising. Yet their rhetoric matters because it shapes how all Americans see the Second Amendment, gun policy, and their political opponents. When pollsters ask Americans about their views on gun control, there is generally a partisan divide. The Pew Research Center reports that in early January 2013, for instance, "51% of Americans say it is more important to control gun ownership, while 45% say it is more important to protect gun rights." But those same polls show broad support for specific gun-control measures, such as "background checks for private and gun show sales" (85 percent in favor), "preventing people with mental illness from purchasing guns" (80 percent in favor), a "federal database to track gun sales" (67 percent in favor), and a "ban on semi-automatic weapons" (58 percent in favor).[81] How is it, then, that the same people who oppose "gun control" support specific gun-control measures? One reason is that *gun control* is ambiguous when discussed in the abstract, and the NRA has worked to transform that ambiguity into an all-encompassing threat. In the NRA's telling, gun control means confiscating all guns and stripping all Americans of their right to self-defense. Even though few gun-control advocates propose such radical measures, the NRA insists that gun control equals a total ban and confiscation of all guns for all Americans.

By suggesting that any restriction on guns would constitute a total violation of the Second Amendment, the NRA provides a clear and stable answer in response to calls for gun control. Whenever there is a call for gun restrictions, the answer is always no, regardless of whether it is 1977 or 2017. They will be able to continue to say no in 2047. And the answer is no regardless of the strength of opponents' arguments. If the argumentative standard is an unchanging principle—the right to bear arms shall not be infringed—then no statistics, studies, or cost-benefit analysis will ultimately be persuasive. But even when the argumentative standard shifts to a cost-benefit analysis, the NRA suggests that restrictions of any kind are bad because they lead us down a slippery slope. Expanded background checks might seem like a reasonable restriction, but they are simply a first step toward more and more restrictions—background checks today, a registry tomorrow, confiscation next week.

By depicting the Second Amendment as an absolute, the NRA attempts to erase qualitative judgments so that what might be considered a moderate restriction becomes equivalent to an outright ban. The NRA's rhetoric escalates fear by suggesting that any conversation about the Second Amendment is a zero-sum game: total freedom or an outright ban. Further, it requires us to ignore that gun rights are currently regulated. Citizens cannot simply walk into a store and buy an automatic machine gun, and from 1994 to 2004, there was a ban on semiautomatic assault weapons. Contrary to the NRA's rhetoric, the Second Amendment was not eradicated by these restrictions; restrictions and the Second Amendment have coexisted.

Accepting the NRA's vision of the Second Amendment also requires a relatively narrow understanding of freedom; people have freedom *to* rather than freedom *from*—they have freedom to "walk about with a loaded gun" but not "*freedom from* such things as gun violence."[82] And to accept the NRA's vision of the Second Amendment requires us to ignore that other rights, such as free speech, are regulated rather than absolute.

Depicting the Second Amendment as an absolute shapes not only how Americans see gun policy but also how they see their political opponents. Contrary to Thomas Jefferson's statement that "every difference of opinion is not a difference of principle," the NRA suggests that every difference of opinion is a difference of principle; moreover, a person's opinion about the Second Amendment determines whether that individual is a good person and good American. Take, for instance, LaPierre's statement on February 13, 2013: "We will not surrender. We will not appease. We will buy more guns than ever. We will use them for sport and lawful self-defense more than ever. We will grow the NRA more than ever. And we will be prouder than ever to be freedom-loving NRA patriots. And with your help, we will ensure that the Second Amendment remains America's First Freedom. We will stand and fight."[83] Either we must win or we must "surrender" and "appease." Acceptance of any restriction is rendered as both a political and personal failure. Compromise becomes a sign of weakness and inevitable defeat. In LaPierre's telling, "we" must be vigilant against "them"; they are an unredeemable, dangerous enemy, who cannot be trusted and whose goal is to leave "us" totally defenseless. We should be proud "freedom-loving NRA patriots" who will "stand and fight" for the Second Amendment. While this rhetoric is incredibly powerful, it depends on flawed logic (e.g., there are only these two options) that escalates a difference of opinion into a difference in identity (e.g., you are either a "good" American or not) and that justifies rhetorical, if not physical, confrontation with the enemy (e.g., "We will stand and fight"). Gun-rights supporters are told that being a person of conviction requires writing off all who differ about one issue—the Second Amendment—as wholly bad people and bad Americans. The NRA's rhetoric demands that gun-rights supporters pledge allegiance to the NRA. You are either with them or against them. There is no middle ground, no space for exceptions or doubts. To waiver is to abandon the cause entirely.

Culture War

On February 13, 2013, Wayne LaPierre told NRA supporters, "We can't win the political war if we lose the cultural war."[84] In the NRA's telling, the debate about the Second Amendment is about far more than guns. It is about cultural values and practices. By entangling the Second Amendment with America's culture war, the meaning of the Second Amendment gets transformed, and its significance gets amplified.

The rhetoric of culture war has deep roots in U.S. history, although it fully bloomed in the 1980s and 1990s. In his 1991 book *Culture Wars: The Struggle to Define America*, James Davison Hunter described an America fundamentally divided over social issues such as abortion, gay marriage, and prayer in public schools. Disagreement about prayer in school, for instance, was not simply a disagreement about prayer in school. The rhetoric of culture war suggested that this disagreement revealed fundamentally different systems of morality and visions for America's future. "We" were at battle with "them." To compromise meant far more than to accept an imperfect or even irritating policy; to compromise revealed moral weakness and a threat to one's core beliefs and identity. Hunter suggested that the dividing lines in the culture war between the "orthodox" and the "progressive" were long in the making. Yet savvy politicians and opinion leaders exploited whatever divisions there were. To create a base of passionate supporters, they made the chasms between Americans appear wider and unbridgeable.

Today, the Second Amendment and the culture war are intertwined. But this was by design, not necessity. The NRA's rhetoric during the 1990s helped bring the gun debate and America's culture war together; its rhetoric is both a consequence and a contributor to this larger culture war. Speaking at the NRA's annual convention on May 20, 2000, Heston identified that he had been committed to three goals during the first two terms of his presidency. In addition to bringing the NRA "back to the table of mainstream political debate," he sought "to rebuild our NRA membership" and "to rebuild our NRA war chest."[85] Culture-war rhetoric helped achieve all three of these goals.

Heston delivered perhaps his most notable culture-war speech at the 1997 Conservative Political Action Conference. Although he was not yet

NRA president, he used this very same culture-war rhetoric to advance the NRA's mission. "America," Heston claimed, "yearns to be true to itself again, to return to that warm fireside of common sense and common values."[86] In Heston's telling, then, the fight over the Second Amendment is a fight over America's identity and values. This fight even includes questions about whether truth and morality are situational or absolute. Heston argued that "either we know who we are and what we stand for, or we surrender to situational everything, where there is no absolute truth, no unrelenting conviction, no unshakable policy. This is a definitive moment for America's identity."[87]

Speaking before the Conservative Political Action Conference on January 27, 1998, Heston began with a quote from Lincoln's Gettysburg Address: "We are now engaged in a great civil war, testing whether this nation . . . or any nation so conceived . . . and so dedicated . . . can long endure." He continued, "Lincoln was right. Friends, let me tell you: You are engaged again in a great civil war . . . a cultural war that's about to hijack you right out of your own birthright. And I fear that you no longer trust the pulsing life blood inside you that made this country rise from mud and valor into the miracle that it still is."[88] By likening the culture war of the 1990s to the Civil War of the 1860s, the stakes soar. The Second Amendment becomes a site of battle over America's future. In Heston's telling, our opponents seek to "hijack" our "birthright," so we must go to war against them.

A gun, Heston insisted, "stands for something."[89] Indeed, through the NRA's culture-war rhetoric, guns have come to stand for all sorts of things. Such rhetoric draws wide battle lines. In Heston's telling, the world is clearly divided between the virtuous, conservative, freedom-loving NRA members and their immoral, liberal, freedom-hating NRA opponents who would destroy the Second Amendment. Heston praises "traditional family units, cops who're on your side, clergy who aren't kooky, safe schools, certain punishment, manageable conflict."[90] He argues that good Americans "prefer the America they built—where you could pray without feeling naïve, love without being kinky, sing without profanity, be white without feeling guilty, own a gun without shame, and raise your hand without apology. They are the masses who find themselves under siege and long for you to get some guts, stand on principle and lead them to victory in this cultural war. They are sick and tired of national social policy that originates on Oprah, and they're ready for you to pull the plug."[91] While Heston attempts to unify his supporters against a common enemy, these enemies are notably varied and wide-ranging, including "MTV-bred malcontents" and supporters of "cradle-to-grave socialism."

He routinely rails against President Clinton, the manipulative media, and purveyors of political correctness. According to Heston, what divides the two sides of the battle is an issue of character: "It's a clash between the principled and the unprincipled."[92]

The fact that the NRA participates in and contributes to the culture war is not surprising or new (Scott Melzer's *Gun Crusaders: The NRA's Culture War* does an excellent job of tracing this history.)[93] But what's important here is how the NRA's culture-war rhetoric gets entangled with the Second Amendment. Culture-war rhetoric has been added to debates about the Second Amendment, and this addition is relatively recent. Needless to say, there's no mention of MTV in the Federalist Papers, the Constitution, the Bill of Rights, or the private correspondence of the Founding Fathers. Washington, Franklin, Adams, Jefferson—pick any other founder—did not know about the debates to come concerning political correctness, gay marriage, or Bill Clinton's infidelity.

Adding the culture-war frame to the Second Amendment debate is significant because it shapes how Americans see the Second Amendment and each other. First, the NRA depicts its political opponents as bad people rather than simply mistaken or different. At best, they are unprincipled and uninterested in freedom; at worst, they are "yanking the Bill of Rights from our lives like a weathered handbill stuck under your windshield wiper." Those enemies lack self-control, and their weaknesses are destroying America. "Self-gratification," Heston warned, "has displaced honor, greed has erased good taste, the desires of the moment have undermined basic morality."[94] Second, this allegedly evil opposition is not limited to gun-control advocates; indeed, some opponents might actually have no opinion on gun control. The opposition includes anyone who has joined the other side of the culture war (or who has been placed on that side simply because they are not wholly on "our" side). This logic works enthymematically—listeners can supply their own examples of enemies, whether it is the person who opposes school prayer, the person who watches MTV, or the person they dislike for whatever reason. The fight over the Second Amendment, then, becomes omnipresent. Since there is no escape from the gun debate, we must be ever vigilant.

Finally, this rhetoric attempts to lock in conservatives who are not necessarily gun-rights advocates and transform moderate gun-rights supporters into activists. Beliefs and values come only as a package deal. The NRA's vision of the Second Amendment is placed alongside truth, morality, and decency; if one cares for decency, then they ought to fight for the NRA's vision of the Second Amendment. The debate over guns is just one front of battle, yet it is nonetheless integral to the larger war effort. In the NRA's telling, to fight for one is to fight for all, and to abandon one is to abandon all. There is no middle ground, no space for a gun-rights advocate to waiver. Nor is there any space for a gun-control advocate to still be moral or patriotic.

The Text and Us

Recognizing arguments about the Second Amendment *as arguments*—as claims that could be otherwise, that can be judged persuasive or not, that require adequate evidence and support, and so on—can go a long way to improving public deliberation about the Second Amendment. But we also need to remember that arguments do not simply emerge from the text of the Second Amendment. Because of this, disagreements about the meaning or significance of the Second Amendment are unlikely to be resolved simply by pointing to the text. The text matters for interpretation, but so do the interpreters. My brief rhetorical history has demonstrated that the Second Amendment has gained layers of meaning throughout its use in public discourse, layers that were not present in 1791. Today, any mention of the Second Amendment begins in the middle. The Second Amendment, for better or worse, bears the weight of its rhetorical history, a weight that has accrued in public memory. In turn, public memory shapes how Americans see the Second Amendment, including its significance and meaning.

While I have focused on the NRA's role in shaping the public memory of the Second Amendment, they are not the only contributor. Public memory can include what is remembered from previous deliberations about gun violence and gun policy. And public memory is not limited to the political arena; it can be shaped by representations of guns and gun violence in popular culture, including television and movies. To examine all public memories in their entirety is an impossible task. Yet the concept of public memory draws attention to the deep reservoir of rhetorical resources that we all draw from when interpreting and arguing. In particular, how we remember the Second Amendment is crucially tied to the stories that we are told and that we tell about who we are as individuals and as Americans. In what follows, then, I highlight memory's relationship to narrative and identity to further illustrate how the weight of the past makes public deliberation so difficult.

Memory and Narrative

Gun-control advocates have attempted to rebrand themselves and shift the key terms of the gun debate. Organizations like Everytown for Gun Safety suggest that the issue is about gun reform and gun safety, not gun control. Yet for gun-rights advocates, the issue remains one of control. On January 22, 2013, LaPierre argued that Obama's proposed expansion of background checks would mean "forcing law-abiding people to fork over excessive fees to exercise their rights. Forcing parents to fill out forms to leave a family heirloom to a loved one—standing in line and filling out a bunch of bureaucratic paperwork, just so a grandfather can give a grandson a Christmas gift. [Obama] wants to put every private, personal transaction under the thumb of the federal government, and he wants to keep all those names in a massive federal registry."[95] As I mentioned earlier, LaPierre's allegations were false: the proposal included no federal registry, and the background checks would exclude transfers between family members. He also exaggerates the inconvenience that would be posed by expanded background checks (e.g., "standing in line and filling out a bunch of bureaucratic paperwork") and makes no mention of the potential benefits. But how might we engage with LaPierre's rhetoric? This rhetoric is powerful because it fits into—and perpetuates—a common narrative of a big, untrustworthy government seeking to regulate and thus worsen people's lives.[96] His word choices illustrate this anxiety: the government is the aggressor, and the citizen is the victim; the government is "forcing" us, making us "fork over excessive fees," and putting us "under the thumb of the federal government." And all this is being done to create a "massive federal registry" that will only inconvenience and infringe on the rights of "law-abiding people."

Guns are incidental to this larger narrative, which could encompass any form of perceived overreach by the government, from the regulation of building permits to that of soda size. This narrative of an overreaching government coexists with other narratives that live in memory, both public and individual, including the narrative of our obligation to the founders, the narrative that we are in a dangerous world, the narrative that we are responsible for ourselves and that guns are our best means of self-protection, and so on. Narratives are powerful because they provide an orientation for understanding the world. They run deep yet are easily adaptable to new circumstances. A narrative can provide immunity against more traditional forms of evidence, such as statistics and expert testimony. To challenge someone's narrative, then, requires understanding its narrative logic and perhaps even offering a counternarrative.[97]

Memory and Identity

To argue about values and narratives already implies the importance of identity. Which narratives resonate with individuals and which values and policies they want to triumph in these narratives tell us something about who they are and how they see themselves. Identity matters, of course, yet there is a balance at stake. Taken to their rhetorical extreme, identity claims can supplant any cost-benefit analysis of policy or values. The debate can become transformed into one of warring identities. As Laura J. Collins argues, "The unbridled Second Amendment is more about identity than it is about political action or change."[98] LaPierre's speech on January 22, 2013, provides evidence for this claim: "We are not people to be trivialized, marginalized or demonized as unreasonable. We're not children who need to be parented or misguided 'bitter clingers' to guns and religion. We get up every day, we work hard to pay our taxes, we cherish our families and we care about their safety. We believe in living honorably and living within our means."[99] In LaPierre's rhetoric, "we" are being attacked on all fronts. LaPierre appeals to—and creates—an audience united by a shared sense of victimhood. Illustrating what Engels calls the politics of resentment, LaPierre depicts his audience as victims and blames others as the source for all suffering, imagined or real.[100] The fight over who "we" are as individuals and Americans is simultaneously a fight over who "we" are not, over defining ourselves as unlike or in opposition to "them."[101]

Such identity rhetoric may simply remind some gun-rights advocates of what they already believe. But such rhetoric can also invite audiences to assume a particular identity position and prescribe how they might see the world and interact with others. In LaPierre's rhetoric, the opposition is not reasonable; they are malicious and take joy in humiliating "you": "They portray law-abiding gun owners like you as the members of some lunatic fringe. They attack you in the press and call you a second-class citizen. They say your faith in firearm freedom has no place in today's world. They want to muzzle and marginalize you, and strip you of your political power."[102] Since "they" are so vicious and unreasonable, they must be overpowered, not negotiated with. To overcome their suffering and realize their full potential, NRA members are urged to meet their enemies with "unprecedented defiance, commitment, and determination."[103] The stakes of arguing about the Second Amendment thus become extraordinarily high; more than gun policy, the consequences of this debate get reframed as an all-out battle for identity and dignity, even survival.

Conclusion

Given the NRA's depiction of the fight over the Second Amendment, it is not immediately clear how gun-rights advocates and gun-control advocates might work together. Passion is to be expected in the gun debate because the stakes are perceived as being incredibly high. But that passionate commitment should also have a sense of proportion. The NRA does not own the Second Amendment. Nor do they own the Founding Fathers and patriotism. Gun-rights advocates have a unique obligation to disavow the NRA's more extreme rhetoric.

Although the ritual of demonization and dismissal can help with short-term advocacy, it ultimately undermines the possibility for productive deliberation or peaceful coexistence by splitting Americans further apart. Gun-rights advocates and gun-control advocates alike might resist this ritual by searching for more humane ways of seeing one another. As Collins writes, "Rather than disposing of those arguments that we find irrational or fringe—rejecting the passionate pleas of the 'true believers' or the 'nuts'—we must pay attention to them. To explain them away or to ignore them is to avoid the difficult question of why they exist."[104]

Throughout this chapter, I have drawn attention to the weight of the past in order to highlight that mistrust and misunderstanding have been built up over time, in part through the creation, circulation, and appropriation of public memories. The rhetorical complexity of the fight over the meaning and significance of the Second Amendment suggests that there are no simple and easy solutions for improving public deliberation. But one thing is clear: as long as this rhetorical complexity is ignored, arguments about the Second Amendment will continue to fall on unreceptive ears.

The Second Amendment is inscribed in parchment, but its primary home is in the public memories built by gun-rights advocates. The meaning and significance of the Second Amendment are products of its use and misuse throughout its rhetorical history, particularly over the last forty years. If there is any hope, then, for productive deliberation, we all must reckon with the Second Amendment's accumulated weight.

3

THE FLEETING PAST: MEMORY AND OUR OBLIGATIONS TO THE DEAD

Sooner or later, we are going to get this right. The memories of these children demand it. And so do the American people.

—PRESIDENT BARACK OBAMA, APRIL 17, 2013

Gun-control advocates engage in a back-and-forth with their opponents about the Second Amendment. Yet they also use their own key terms, arguments, and appeals to make their case for gun control. In particular, they regularly make their case by invoking dead victims of gun violence. At the outset, we can observe that invoking the dead to argue for gun control is a choice, not an automatic response. We can also observe that invoking the dead is not the only way to argue for gun control. For instance, Republicans and Democrats in the late 1960s through the early 1990s described gun control as a strategy for cracking down on criminals.[1] Focusing on dead victims of gun violence is different than making a case for gun control by focusing primarily on criminals, guns, or the specific communities in which violence happens. The choice to focus on the dead is different and, as I will illustrate, significant.

In this chapter, I analyze the rhetoric of gun-control advocates by focusing on what I call the warrant of the dead. More than simply mentioning the dead, the warrant of the dead refers to an explicit or implicit claim that the dead place a demand on the living. More than a cost-benefit analysis or a pragmatic argument that suggests a particular action might reduce future deaths, the warrant of the dead is an ethical claim that we must take action because we have an obligation to those who died. The living are called on to act, and the dead are invoked as justification for that action. In gun-control rhetoric, since they died from gun violence, we should support gun-control legislation. In other contexts, since they died, we should do *X*, where *X* can be almost anything (e.g., be kind, cure diseases, pass laws, wage or cease wars, and so on). Seeing this rhetorical move as a warrant is useful because the connection between the dead and the requested action of the living is often assumed rather than argued outright.[2] At times, the living are asked to carry on what the dead were explicitly committed to; at other times, the living are asked to take action in a way that might rectify their deaths in some small way or reduce the chance that what happened to them will happen to others.

The warrant of the dead commonly appears in funeral orations,[3] including national eulogies,[4] but it is not confined to this genre or the immediate aftermath of death. Nor is it distinct to the gun debate or our times. In his famous funeral oration, Pericles praised the Athenians who died in the Peloponnesian War, and he depicted their devotion as a model and obligation for the living.[5] Speaking on the battlefields of Gettysburg in 1863, President Abraham Lincoln argued "that these dead shall not have died in vain" and, in turn, "that this nation shall have a new birth of freedom."[6] Making the case for war nine days after the September 11, 2001, terrorist attacks, President Bush stated, "We have suffered great loss. And in our grief and anger we have found our mission and our moment."[7] Outside the context of war, we can see the warrant of the dead in responses to public tragedies. For example, the NAMES Project AIDS Memorial Quilt was displayed on the Washington Mall to recognize the dead and demand that the federal government address the AIDS epidemic.[8] In short, the dead have long been cast into a central role in our public talk and sight and thus regularly used to justify collective action, including federal policy.

Although the warrant of the dead is not unique to the gun debate, it has nonetheless played a prominent yet largely unexamined role in debates about gun violence and gun policy in the United States. Even gun-rights advocates rely on the warrant of the dead when they claim that the Founding Fathers impose an obligation on us to uphold an absolute Second Amendment. Yet for gun-control advocates, the dead who are most relevant are the recent victims of gun violence. The Gun Control Act of 1968 was proposed after the assassination of President John F. Kennedy in 1963; it gained support after the mass shooting at the University of Texas at Austin in 1966 and was passed after the assassinations of Martin Luther King Jr. and Senator Robert F. Kennedy in 1968. After the 1999 mass shooting at Columbine High School, public leaders disagreed about whether change should come in the form of further gun control or something else, but almost all agreed that we were obligated to the dead to make a change. As Vice President Gore insisted at a memorial service in Colorado, "All of us must change our lives to honor these children." By our doing so, "those who died here this week will not have died in vain."[9]

And in his responses to mass shootings, President Obama consistently relied on the warrant of the dead. In the first term of his presidency, his speeches closely followed the norms of epideictic speech; he claimed that we should honor those who died by recommitting to civic values, such as patriotism, the rule of law, and respect for one another. But his use of the warrant of the dead changed after the shooting at Sandy Hook Elementary School on December 14, 2012: "We honor their memories in part by doing everything we can to prevent this from happening again."[10] Recommitting to civic values was no longer good enough. As he put it after the 2013 mass shooting at the Washington Navy Yard, "Our tears are not enough. Our words and our prayers are not enough." "Wisdom," he explained, "comes through the recognition that tragedies such as this are not inevitable, and that we possess the ability to act and to change."[11] If we really want to honor the dead, Obama repeatedly argued, then we must change our gun laws.

In addition to a verbal expression, the warrant of the dead can also be a visual and embodied argument. The warrant of the dead is visualized in the White House's 2013 plan to reduce gun violence, which features an image of the flag flown at half-staff.[12] And the warrant of the dead is embodied in the presence of victims' families standing behind or beside Obama when he speaks about gun violence, their presence marking the absence of their loved ones. Rhetorically, Obama's or any gun-control advocate's use of the warrant of the dead to support gun control is not entirely surprising. More surprising—indeed, puzzling—is how Obama used it, why, and to what effect. What did he attempt to accomplish rhetorically by relying on the warrant of the dead? And why were these efforts largely ineffective?

As a critical concept, the warrant of the dead illuminates gun-control rhetoric and, more generally, highlights a recurring, significant, yet largely unexamined form of public argument. Specifically, the warrant of the dead sheds light on a central tension between public deliberation and public memory. Unlike deliberation about the Second Amendment, in which the public memory is strong and layered, the public memory of gun violence and its victims is often weak and thin (at least for those who were not directly affected by that violence). As public attention moves from crisis to crisis, the past becomes fleeting and thus forgotten or ignored. And as the past becomes fleeting, so does engagement. In our responses to "terrible, tragic events," Engels explains, "we are moved, and we move on. Moving on, and on, and on *ad infinitum*: this is the cultural ethos of our time, designed for a busy and mobile people constantly on the go."[13] Faced with this challenge, rhetors use the warrant of the dead to strengthen memory and help sustain public attention and engagement. To illustrate these dynamics, this chapter focuses on public deliberation after the shooting at Sandy Hook Elementary School, particularly President Obama's gun-control rhetoric.

My argument develops in four steps. First, I show how the warrant of the dead is specifically rhetorical. Second, if the warrant of the dead could be used differently—or not be used at all—then we can reasonably ask why it is used in a particular situation. In making the case for gun control, what rhetorical problem is Obama using the warrant of the dead to address? Here I describe a problem within the gun debate that Obama himself explicitly identified in his public responses to gun violence: the problem of fleeting engagement. Third, I explore how the warrant of the dead attempts to address this problem. By extending, expanding, and intensifying memories of the victims of gun violence, Obama uses the warrant of the dead to establish sustained concern for those victims and thus sustained commitment to gun control. Finally, I discuss how Obama's effort to transform gun-control supporters into gun-control activists proved largely ineffective. While we cannot expect any argument to immediately transform the gun debate, we can still observe that the warrant of the dead faces rhetorical challenges in helping establish a gun-control movement.

The Warrant of the Dead as Rhetorical

Rhetorical scholars do not need to be persuaded that the warrant of the dead is rhetorical rather than natural, objective, or inevitable. Yet I want to briefly illustrate how the warrant of the dead is rhetorical in order to better account for the warrant of the dead in general and Obama's gun-control rhetoric in particular. First, I show that the needs, goals, and contexts of speakers and listeners determine how or even whether the warrant of the dead is used. Second, I show that the warrant of the dead has been used selectively to draw attention to some dead but not others and, of those who are recognized, not all are recognized equally. Taking these claims together highlights that the warrant of the dead is a strategic response—whether sincere or not—that does important rhetorical work.

Invoking the dead is perhaps most straightforward when a speaker's call for action matches the values of the dead and the cause of their death. Describing the norms of a eulogy, Kathleen Hall Jamieson and Karlyn Kohrs Campbell explain that "the death by cancer of Senator Hubert Humphrey was met with eulogies calling for more research into the causes, prevention, and cure of cancer; Robert F. Kennedy's assassination with a handgun prompted eulogistic demands for gun control." Yet "had Humphrey or Kennedy opposed such legislation, these appeals would have appeared inappropriate and disrespectful."[14]

But what the dead demand of us is often uncertain if not unintelligible. Katherine Verdery points out that for better or worse, "what gives a dead body symbolic effectiveness in politics is precisely its ambiguity, its capacity to evoke a variety of understandings." Without knowing what the victims of gun violence valued, we can reasonably infer that they did not want to die. But it is more of a stretch to infer that they would support gun control. Since the children killed at Sandy Hook Elementary School were so young, we might turn to their parents' opinions about gun control. But the families of the dead disagreed: several parents supported Obama's efforts, and at least one parent supported the NRA's efforts; some family members prioritized mental health reform over guns; and some family members were not politically active at all. Although "the dead" sometimes "present the illusion of having *only one* significance," that is indeed an illusion, given the complexity of one life.[15] The loss of many lives makes questions about significance even more complicated.

Of course, interpreting or ascribing significance in the aftermath of mass shootings often says as much about the interpreter as it does the dead. That is perhaps most clearly on display when observing the same speaker responding to similar types of tragedies in drastically different ways. Before the mass shooting at Sandy Hook Elementary School, Obama responded to several mass shootings by claiming that the dead required the living to recommit to civic values, such as patriotism, the rule of law, and respect for one another. But Obama claimed that the Sandy Hook victims demanded more than a recommitment to civic values; they demanded political action in the form of gun control.

Why the change? Personal, political, and cultural contexts shape how the warrant of the dead is used. We can point to at least five contextual factors that shaped Obama's response to the Sandy Hook shooting. David A. Frank describes the three most important factors. First, the shooting "took place after Obama's reelection, freeing him from the constraints of electoral politics." Second, "the victims were innocent children in an elementary school."[16] Obama later referred to the day of the shooting as "the toughest day of my Presidency," and for many Americans, this shooting felt qualitatively different because most of the victims were young children.[17] Third, "the cultural climate surrounding the Newtown shootings, at least in the immediate aftermath, suggested that his audience was now more open to gun control."[18] Fourth, national tragedies typically require a presidential response. There are genre conventions and expectations that a national eulogy will explain "how the president and the government will ensure that the tragedy will not be repeated."[19] Thus when speaking in the aftermath of a mass shooting, a president needs to hold something or someone responsible for that particular mass shooting (or mass shootings in general). Since the Sandy Hook shooter committed suicide, anger could not be displaced by promises that the criminal justice system would exact justice. Something else needed to be held responsible. Finally, this was not the first or even second time that Obama had responded publicly as president to a mass shooting. Therefore, his recurring claim that the dead should inspire us to recommit to civic values was losing credibility because the violence continued. All five of these factors are important for understanding why Obama turned to gun control after the shooting at Sandy Hook. Yet most important, the fact that there are reasons at all highlights that the warrant of the dead is a strategic response shaped by the needs, goals, and contexts of the living.

But not all dead victims of gun violence are used to argue for policy change (gun control or otherwise); after all, most gun-violence victims are not even nationally recognized in any substantive way. The selective attention to some dead but not others highlights what Judith Butler calls "grievability." Commenting on global violence generally, Butler critiques our "hierarchy of grief."[20] Observing that some deaths are rendered worth grieving, and others are not, she asks, "Who counts as human? Whose lives count as lives? And, finally, *What makes for a grievable life?*"[21] By focusing on gun violence, we might similarly ask, Why do some acts of gun violence—and thus some victims of gun violence—gain national attention while others do not? Which of the dead are invoked to impose an obligation on the living and why?[22]

Mass shootings and their victims have disproportionately claimed national attention, and—at least since the late 1990s—they have been the predominant exigence for national debates about gun policy. Put differently, national debates about gun policy have tended not to happen in response to other forms of gun violence and its victims, such as domestic violence, gang violence, police violence, suicide, or even injuries. From a statistical perspective, that makes little sense because mass shootings account for a relatively small proportion of all gun violence.[23] Yet from a rhetorical perspective, we can see that some numbers matter more than others and that numbers are not all that matters. Magnitude, of course, is not an objective criterion but a consequence of human judgment at particular moments in time.[24] We live in a world with short attention spans and no shortage of problems, so the stakes for what counts as news keep getting higher. Whereas thirty-three people throughout the United States being murdered with a gun each day has become "normal," thirty-three murdered in the same place and at the same time is less normal and can still make the news and garner public attention.

But not all mass shootings gain national attention or produce talk of public policy. That calculus is complicated, but a central factor is the identity of the victims. Age matters: those who are younger are judged more vulnerable and in need of our protection. Location matters too: those who are in spaces presumed safe, such as schools or churches, are more easily presumed innocent than those in a bar. Location also matters in terms of geography: newscasters and leaders often refer to "quiet" or "bucolic" communities as being ripped apart by violence.[25] Saying that "this wasn't supposed to happen here" implies that violence is expected and perhaps even acceptable elsewhere.[26] The mass shootings that have garnered national attention and talk of gun policy tend to be ones that occurred in affluent communities in which nearly all the victims are white. Yet in an analysis of 358 shootings with "four or more casualties," *New York Times* reporters found that most of these mass shootings actually occurred in "economically downtrodden neighborhoods" and that "nearly three-fourths of victims and suspected assailants whose race could be identified were black." "Some experts," they note, suggest that the race and class of the victims help explain why these dead do "not inspire more outrage."[27]

To highlight how the warrant of the dead is rhetorical, I have shown that rhetors and audiences shape the warrant of the dead at particular moments in time. I have also shown that the warrant of the dead represents and reiterates power imbalances. The fact that the warrant of the dead is invoked on some occasions but not others tells us that it is a strategic response that does rhetorical work, regardless of whether the rhetor intends it or an audience recognizes it.

The Problem of Fleeting Engagement

Claiming that the warrant of the dead is a strategic response does not mean that it cannot also be sincere. It can be both. By seeing the warrant of the dead as strategic, however, we can better understand how it is used, why, and to what effect. What rhetorical work does the warrant of the dead attempt to accomplish? Specifically, in making the case for gun control, what problem is Obama using the warrant of the dead to address? I describe here a problem that Obama himself has identified in his public responses to mass gun violence—the problem of fleeting engagement.

On April 17, 2013, the post–Sandy Hook gun-control proposals that Obama initiated failed to reach sixty Senate votes: the proposed expansion of background checks received fifty-four votes, the proposed ban on assault weapons received forty, and the proposed limit on magazine or clip capacity to ten rounds received forty-six votes.[28] The Senate's failure to pass expanded background checks was the most bewildering. The bill had been seen as a bipartisan compromise, cosponsored by a Democrat (Senator Joe Manchin) and a Republican (Senator Pat Toomey). And public opinion, at least for background checks, was not the problem. Polling from January 2013 showed that 85 percent of Americans were in favor of expanding background checks for private and gun-show sales,[29] with public support remaining between 80 percent and 90 percent in April.[30] The problem, as Obama and others argued, was that gun-control supporters were not as committed to the issue as their opponents were or as willing to pressure their representatives. Goss refers to this as the "gun control paradox": "*Why do Americans who want strict gun control not mobilize, in large numbers in a sustained way, to get it?*"[31]

Speaking after the failed Senate vote, a frustrated Obama claimed that the gun lobby used its economic, rhetorical, and political power to circumvent the majority opinion. They had mobilized supporters to help block the vote by making senators fearful that the "vocal minority of gun owners" would "come after them in future elections." He claimed that gun-rights advocates were "better organized. They're better financed. They've been at it longer. And they make sure to stay focused on this one issue during election time."[32] Data from the Pew Research Center support Obama's assessment: they reveal an "activism gap" in which gun-rights advocates are almost twice as likely as gun-control advocates to have contacted "a public official about gun policy (15 percent vs. 8 percent)" and over four times as likely to have contributed money to organizations that support their views (23 percent vs. 5 percent).[33]

The challenge for gun-control supporters, then, is to match their opponents' political power, born from passion, money, and an ability to organize. As Obama explained, "Those who care deeply about preventing more and more gun violence will have to be as passionate, and as organized, and as vocal as those who blocked these common-sense steps to help keep our kids safe."[34] In short, gun-control supporters needed to become gun-control activists.

Although the need for activism was not new for the gun-control movement,[35] it was especially pronounced in 2013. On the day of the Senate vote, Obama noted that everybody had "talked about how we were going to have to change something to make sure this didn't happen again, just like everybody talked about how we needed to do something after Aurora. Everybody talked about we needed to change something after Tucson." Although insisting that "sooner or later, we are going to get this right," Obama sounded exasperated: "I'm assuming our expressions of grief and our commitment to do something different to prevent these things from happening are not empty words."[36] But the problem was not that these expressions were empty words; it was that the words and commitments emptied too quickly—they could not be carried four months from the shooting to the vote. The problem, then, was one of fleeting engagement.

Although not using these specific words, Obama has continued to describe fleeting engagement as a problem for gun-control supporters. After the shooting at the Washington Navy Yard on September 16, 2013, he claimed, "So the question now is not whether, as Americans, we care in moments of tragedy. Clearly, we care. Our hearts are broken—again. And we care so deeply about these families. But the question is, do we care enough?" He directly challenged his audience's emotional, ethical, and rhetorical endurance—to feel an obligation and ensure that that obligation continued long enough and with enough intensity to enact political change: "These families have endured a shattering tragedy. It ought to be a shock to us all as a nation and as a people. It ought to obsess us. It ought to lead to some sort of transformation." But that transformation would not "come from Washington"; it would need to come from "the American people."[37] After the shooting at the Charleston AME Church on June 17, 2015, Obama noted that "for far too long, we've been blind to the unique mayhem that gun violence inflicts upon this nation. Sporadically, our eyes are open." The word *sporadically* is key: attention and engagement are not constant; they come only briefly after the most horrific of tragedies.[38]

Fleeting engagement is perhaps most clearly on display in the aftermath of mass shootings. Concern is intermittent and sporadic because the mass shootings that gain national attention are also intermittent and sporadic. People are most concerned and engaged right after a violent event occurs. As time passes after a high-profile mass shooting, journalists, leaders, and citizens move on to other pressing matters—at least until the cycle begins again with the next high-profile mass shooting.

But fleeting engagement is not wholly unique to mass shootings or the broader debate about gun violence. Our contemporary problem has deep and wide roots. For centuries, rhetoricians have recognized a divide between conviction and persuasion. Conviction is a precondition for persuasion, but conviction alone will not lead to action. Figures such as Francis Bacon in the seventeenth century and George Campbell in the eighteenth century showed that speakers typically need to appeal to emotions and imagination in order to move an audience's will. Yet the divide between conviction and persuasion is even more pronounced now in the twenty-first century. We better understand that this rhetorical problem is also a structural problem. How leaders vote, for instance, is determined not by the best argument alone but rather by how the district they represent is divided, who lives in their district, and who will financially support or oppose them in the next election. Establishing a strong gun-control movement, then, requires more than sustained engagement from individuals; it requires financial support and the ability to organize, among other things. We also face what Andrew Sullivan calls an "epidemic of distraction."[39] Fleeting engagement is not caused simply by a failure of rhetoric or lack of effort. Fleeting engagement is a cultural, economic, and technological problem; it is a problem of limited time, energy, and attention in a world in which our media and our newsfeeds prize speed and the next interesting thing (whether important or not).

Obama has acknowledged some of these structural forces. After the Charleston shooting, for instance, he warned of allowing ourselves "to slip into a comfortable silence again" once "the eulogies have been delivered" and "the TV cameras move on."[40] Yet his repeated decisions to speak in the aftermath of mass shootings affirmed that our collective fate is not solely determined by media companies or cultural scripts. Rhetoric has at least some power for remaking the world. Specifically, rhetoric can help sustain public attention and move people from conviction to action. And a rhetorical resource for countering fleeting engagement, he suggested, is found in the appeals to memory and responsibility—specifically, the warrant of the dead.

The Warrant of the Dead as a Solution to Fleeting Engagement

If we read Obama's use of the warrant of the dead as a strategy for addressing the problem of fleeting engagement, we can see that the warrant is not primarily directed toward gun-rights advocates. The warrant of the dead might appeal to gun-rights advocates, but they are not Obama's primary audience: gun-rights advocates often reject the notion that there is any obligation to the dead by claiming that now is the time for mourning, not action; that if there is an obligation to the dead, it is not as important as the obligation to support the Second Amendment; or that if an obligation to the dead is in fact most important, that obligation is for greater access to guns to make sure that citizens can protect themselves—that a "good guy" is not defenseless against a "bad guy."[41] Instead, Obama directed the warrant of the dead at gun-control supporters. More precisely, Obama used the warrant of the dead to transform those who support or are open to gun control into activists who are as committed as their opponents are to the rhetorical and political struggle over gun policy. His goal is what social-movement scholars describe as mobilization: "Raise the consciousness level of the people so significant numbers will pressure institutions" to enact change.[42]

To mobilize his audience, Obama attempted to make the dead present—not literally, of course, but symbolically and imaginatively. Rhetoricians have used a variety of labels to describe this language function, including Aristotle's "bringing-before-the-eyes"[43] and Chaïm Perelman and Lucie Olbrechts-Tyteca's "presence."[44] This function of rhetoric reflects the etymology of epideictic—showing forth. But showing forth is not simply a speaker's display of ingenuity or artistry; instead, as Ned O'Gorman argues, it is a speaker's drawing of an audience's attention to what has been absent.[45] In this vein, several contemporary rhetoricians have revived the classical term *phantasia*, describing it as the "capacity through which images of stimuli past, passing, or to come are generated and made present."[46] Michele Kennerly describes *civic phantasia*—"a mode of distance collapse whereby rhetors move subjects or objects so as to enable or impede particular judgments."[47] Such "visualization" and "distance collapse" help explain how Obama attempted to make the dead symbolically and imaginatively present. As I will illustrate, the resource Obama uses to undertake such rhetorical work is memory.

As public-memory scholars have long noted, memory is not "a simple act of recall"; it is a selective interpretation that is "usable" to "defend different aims and agendas."[48] By extending, expanding, and intensifying the memory of the victims of gun violence, Obama has used the warrant of the dead to establish sustained concern for those victims and thus sustained commitment to gun control. First, Obama's rhetoric extends memory by placing a particular mass shooting within a larger history of mass shootings and thus highlights our failed obligation to the dead. Second, his rhetoric expands memory by recognizing the broader context of gun violence and its victims. And third, his rhetoric intensifies memory by claiming that we should view the dead as if they were our own family members.

Extending Memory: Remembering Past Mass Shootings

Placing a particular mass shooting within the larger history of mass shootings is significant. It is possible, for instance, to depict a mass shooting as an aberration, an act that exists in its own moment, disconnected from other violent events and immune to understanding. President George W. Bush, for instance, suggested that the 2007 shooting at Virginia Tech was an aberration: "It's impossible to make sense of such violence and suffering."[49] Responding to mass shootings during the first term of his presidency, Obama also sidestepped the question of cause and avoided referencing previous mass shootings. But his rhetoric changed after the mass shooting at Sandy Hook Elementary School on December 14, 2012. While acknowledging that the "causes of such violence are complex" and that "no set of laws can eliminate evil from the world," he insisted that these limitations "can't be an excuse for inaction."[50]

Speaking on the day of the Sandy Hook shooting, Obama explained, "As a country, we have been through this too many times." Since one mass shooting could rightly be called "too many," he is making a claim that this shooting is a turning point, that this is the one that is one too many: "Whether it's an elementary school in Newtown, or a shopping mall in Oregon, or a temple in Wisconsin, or a movie theater in Aurora, or a street corner in Chicago—these neighborhoods are our neighborhoods, and these children are our children."[51] His repeated conjunctions—or, or, or, or—emphasize that history has accumulated abundant examples, thereby offering an inductive line of reasoning that builds to a generalization: mass shootings are a public problem that requires our attention and action. In his December 16, 2012, speech in Connecticut, he went even further back in time by mentioning the 1999 shooting at Columbine High School and the 2007 shooting at Virginia Tech. Since these shootings were not confined to any one geographic region, he suggested that the problem of gun violence is a national problem. With the exception of Chicago (which I will discuss in the next section), this is a sequence of mass shootings. Syntactically, then, he moved back in time to suggest that what happened in Newtown was part of a larger history of such mass shootings. And if there is a larger history, then that suggests that we might search for causes of—or at least patterns in—mass shootings and thus seek potential solutions.

Obama's response to the Sandy Hook shooting was not an anomaly but rather a turning point in his rhetoric. After the Washington Navy Yard shooting in September 2013, he again argued for gun control. And he again asked us to remember previous mass shootings and the victims of those shootings. He explained that at least for the families, "there is nothing routine about this tragedy. There is nothing routine about your loss." Yet for the nation, tragedy had become routine: "And so, once again, we remember our fellow Americans who were just going about their day doing their jobs." He then repeated the phrase several more times: "Once more our hearts are broken. Once more we ask why. Once more we seek strength and wisdom through God's grace." Although this repetition suggests frustration, it also works to make the past present, thus giving the past presence.[52] Obama explained, "As President, I have now grieved with five American communities ripped apart by mass violence. Fort Hood. Tucson. Aurora. Sandy Hook. And now, the Washington Navy Yard."[53] Since gun violence was going to be discussed in the aftermath of only the most horrific instances and since that discussion would be brief, Obama connected the particular moment to the larger history of mass shootings in order to make multiple moments of gun violence and multiple victims symbolically present at once. And he has continued to do so in response to subsequent mass shootings: he stated in 2014, after the second mass shooting at Fort Hood, "Once more, soldiers who survived foreign warzones were struck down here at home, where they're supposed to be safe";[54] in 2015, after the mass shooting at Umpqua Community College, "There's been another mass shooting in America";[55] and in 2016, after the mass shooting of police in Dallas, "Another community torn apart."[56]

By extending back to previous mass shootings, Obama was making a numerical argument, but it was also an argument rooted in obligation. By mentioning previous mass shootings, he was asking us to remember the victims of those shootings, even if abstractly. "Remembering," Susan Sontag explains, "*is* an ethical act"—an act that "has ethical value in and of itself."[57] Yet sometimes remembering is not enough. By asking us to remember the victims of gun violence, Obama was not merely paying respects. He was making a case for intervening in the present to secure a better future.

Remembering served as a counterforce to forgetting and a justification for change. "We're not forgetting," he insisted on April 8, 2013. He praised the "citizens determined to right something gone wrong," those who were using their "grief to make a difference."[58] While people might resolve to change after a particular mass shooting, his pointing to several previous shootings throughout recent history—shootings in which people might similarly have resolved to change—reveals that we have failed to meet our obligations to the dead. And without human intervention, we will continue failing to meet our obligation. Our debt, in short, has been compounding.

Expanding Memory: Recognizing Victims Beyond Mass Shootings

While Obama extended memory by referencing previous mass shootings, he expanded memory by referencing other forms of gun violence and thus additional victims of gun violence. Since his response to the mass shooting at Sandy Hook, Obama has acknowledged the much broader context of violence beyond mass shootings. Let us return again to his speech on December 14, 2012: "We've been through this too many times," he explained, "whether it's an elementary school in Newtown, or a shopping mall in Oregon, or a temple in Wisconsin, or a movie theater in Aurora, or a street corner in Chicago."[59] Whereas Newtown, Oregon, and Wisconsin refer to specific mass shootings, Chicago refers to recurring but not primarily mass shootings. The generality is notable: it is "a" street corner, not "that" street corner. While Chicago refers to homicides in a specific city, it also represents the broader problem of firearm homicides across the United States.

Obama's expansion from talking about mass shootings to talking about gun violence more generally was subtle, but the stakes were not. In his telling, the crisis pertained not only to the mass shooting at Sandy Hook Elementary School but to the recent history of mass shootings; moreover, the crisis was not just mass shootings but gun violence generally—gun violence that happens daily yet fails to capture national attention. He suggested that the problem of mass shootings and the problem of gun deaths in general were one and the same—that, in short, they all represented a gun problem. Given Obama's framing, inadequate gun laws not only contributed to twenty-six deaths at an elementary school in Connecticut; they contributed to the more than thirty thousand lives lost each year due to gun homicides and suicides.[60]

It is significant that Obama chose Chicago and "a street corner" to represent the larger context of gun violence. Gun violence in Chicago has been extreme. In 2012 alone, there were 506 murders in Chicago,[61] and approximately 87 percent involved guns.[62] The violence was so bad that some referred to Chicago as "the nation's murder capital" (although the city is safer than many other U.S. cities when crime is "viewed on a per-capita basis").[63] And gun homicides in Chicago, like gun homicides nationwide, have disproportionately affected black Americans. A *New York Times* headline from January 3, 2013, described "A Chicago Divided by Killings." The authors concluded from their analysis of homicide and census data that "residents living near homicides in the last 12 years were much more likely to be black, earn less money and lack a college degree."[64] Obama did not discuss this racial disparity at length, but he invokes the race and class dimensions of gun violence with the phrase "a street corner in Chicago."

The move from mass shootings to other forms of gun violence attempts to expand memory, yet this expansion is risky. Whereas victims of mass shootings are presumed wholly innocent, questions about the guilt or innocence of victims of other forms of gun violence can be complicated (and, in turn, so can questions about the responsibility of guns). There is a risk that racist and classist stereotypes will lead some audiences to avoid identifying with those who die on "a street corner in Chicago." And there is a risk that some audiences will see these deaths as a rationale for taking up arms for self-protection.

Given these potential risks, Obama's choosing Hadiya Pendleton to represent those who died from nonmass gun violence is notable. As part of his post–Sandy Hook push for gun control, Obama focused on Pendleton in his February 12, 2013, State of the Union Address and his February 15, 2013, speech in Chicago. Pendleton was from Chicago and was black. Obama made it clear that she, like so many others who have died from gun violence, was innocent and good: the fifteen-year-old honors students was "so good to her friends that they all thought they were her best friend. Just three weeks ago, she was here, in Washington, with her classmates, performing for her country at my inauguration. And a week later, she was shot and killed in a Chicago park after school, just a mile away from my house."[65] Thus in telling the story of Pendleton's death, Obama used the warrant of the dead to expand listeners' memories to more fully recognize and identify with all victims of gun violence.

By invoking this wider context of gun violence, Obama was again making a numerical argument (i.e., the problem is much larger than a specific incident). And again, he was making an argument rooted in a sense of obligation. That so many have died increases our obligation. We should feel obliged not just to the victims of the most horrific of mass shootings but also to those whose deaths do not capture national attention. Obama was trying to make us grieve those deaths that typically go ungrieved or unnoticed and, in turn, to mobilize that grief in the service of gun control. He pointed out that rather than be outraged every few months or years by a horrific mass shooting, we should notice the gun violence that happens daily in America, to remember those victims and thus feel an unwavering obligation to support gun control. The fact that these shootings happen every day should offer a daily reminder of our obligation to those who have died.

Intensifying Memory: Viewing the Dead as Our Own

Obama's rhetoric extends memory by having us remember previous mass shootings and expands memory by having us remember the broader context of gun violence and its victims. But recognizing these victims is not enough. He also intensifies memory so that we recognize these dead as our own. Obama wanted gun-control supporters—and especially those who have not been directly affected by gun violence—to feel an obligation to all whose lives have been ended by gun violence. Using what George Lakoff calls the "nation-as-family metaphor," Obama asked us to see these dead as part of the American family.[66] Moreover, Obama asked us to see these dead as if they were members of our own family—as if they were our own children, parents, brothers, or sisters. By representing the dead in this way, Obama sought to intensify our obligation to the dead and thus establish an enduring commitment to gun control.

Although Obama sought to intensify memory, he also did not want to exhaust his audience or appear indecorous. Kennerly's commentary on rhetoric's capacity to "bring before the eyes" is instructive here. She warns that a speaker should avoid two extremes. Too little visualization can keep an audience from seeing the "essential aspects of a subject" necessary to "jolt judgment into nimble action." But "overstimulation of the emotions throws judgment off-kilter." Thus visualization "must be directed with tact and care."[67] Obama attempted to find this balance.

After the shooting at Sandy Hook Elementary School, Obama did not describe the dead victims' personalities or hobbies, as he had in eulogies for previous and subsequent mass shooting victims. I suspect this choice was largely pragmatic: describing twenty-six lives would take a long time, and emotions were already especially raw. Yet he still humanized the dead by depicting them as "our children." On December 16, 2012, he explained, "We come to realize that we bear a responsibility for every child because we're counting on everybody else to help look after ours; that we're all parents; that they're all our children."[68]

On January 16, 2013, Obama and Vice President Biden spoke from the White House to introduce their gun-control proposals. Rather than beginning his speech by appealing to policy experts or law enforcement, Obama quoted three letters he received from children throughout the United States who were concerned about the Sandy Hook shooting. Those children were at the White House for Obama's speech. Before quoting each of their words, he encouraged them to "go ahead and wave" so that their presence would be noticed. Obama concluded that "we should be thinking about our responsibility to care for them, and shield them from harm, and give them the tools they need to grow up and do everything they're capable of doing." Further, our obligation to protect the living is compounded by our failure to protect those who were killed. As Obama claimed, "While reducing gun violence is a complicated challenge, protecting our children from harm shouldn't be a divisive one."[69] If Obama had said "should have protected," he would have been rendering blame to the past, and if he had said "will protect," he would have been rendering responsibility to the future, but by saying "protecting," he suggested that our obligation to protect is ongoing—it applies to the past, present, and future.

Obama could have referred to the dead as citizens or simply people; after all, six of the twenty-six killed at the school were adults. And in describing the dead as "children," he could have referred to the dead as "the" children, "their" children, or even "U.S." children; instead, he said that they are "our" children. Obama thus attempted to establish a specific relationship with the dead that, in turn, would lead to a distinct understanding of gun control. Gun control, in this telling, is not about the government exerting its control and disarming citizens. Government is not "them"—those who impose their will on us. Government is "us," and all of us must work together to secure a better future: "It's a government of and by and for the people."[70] If gun control is paternalistic, Obama suggested, it is paternalistic in a good way: the parent-child relationship is not one between equals; it is a disproportionate one in which those with power are obliged to protect those without it.[71] Obama thus attempted to transcend political divisions. As I have argued elsewhere, Obama wrongly suggested that the gun debate was "not between those who support gun control and those who oppose it but between those who recognize and accept their obligation" as citizen-parents to care for "our children" and those who do not.[72]

Obama continued making his case for gun control between January and April of 2013, and he continued framing gun control as a parental responsibility. Notably, the parent-child relationship entails an enduring obligation. It is more acceptable for citizens to fail to recognize and care for fellow citizens than it is for parents to fail to recognize and care for their children. Parents do not forget or easily move on. As Obama insisted on March 28, 2013, "Grace's dad is not forgetting. Hadiya's mom hasn't forgotten. The notion that two or three months after something as horrific as what happened in Newtown happens and we've moved on to other things, that's not who we are. That's not who we are."[73] Obama used these parents of the dead to make the case that all Americans—with or without children—have an enduring obligation to act as metaphoric parents. They have an obligation to empathize by acting as if their own child might become a victim of gun violence or as if the dead were their own children.

In Obama's responses to shootings subsequent to Sandy Hook, he continued using familial language to argue for gun control. In his response to the 2013 shooting at the Washington Navy Yard, Obama briefly provided details about each of the twelve who were murdered. He then concluded, "These are not statistics. They are the lives that have been taken from us. This is how far a single act of violence can ripple. A husband has lost his wife. Wives have lost their husbands. Sons and daughters have lost their moms and their dads. Little children have lost their grandparents. Hundreds in our communities have lost a neighbor, and thousands have lost a friend."[74] Obama attempted to humanize the dead, not just for those directly affected, but also for those who have not been directly affected by gun violence.

Many leaders of the gun-control movement have personally lost someone to gun violence, but a national movement is severely limited if it is confined just to those who have experienced loss firsthand. Obama thus tried to expand who is part of the gun-control movement by asking us to view the dead differently. We must do more than just see the dead as statistics or as part of an abstract, mediated spectacle; we must recognize that the dead were real people with real families and friends and neighbors who have been left behind. The dead would no longer be able to celebrate "birthdays and anniversaries and graduations."[75] Moreover, he asked us to imagine the dead as if they were part of our families and, more subtly, to recognize that our own loved ones—whether we imagine our partner, child, parent, grandparent, friend, neighbor, or someone else—could become victims of gun violence. Finally, he urged us to identify with all of the dead, even those forgotten or ignored. Race and class should not matter. Proximity should not matter. And questions about guilt and innocence are not the only ones that matter.

Of course, empathy and imagination have their limits; they cannot bridge some gaps, nor should they be confused with having firsthand experience. Yet Obama described empathy as a counterforce to inaction. If we can see the dead as our own—with that kind of intensity—he suggested, then we will feel an enduring obligation toward them and establish an enduring commitment to gun control.

Two Rhetorical Challenges for the Warrant of the Dead

By extending, expanding, and intensifying memories of gun-violence victims, Obama used the warrant of the dead to counter fleeting engagement and thus transform gun-control supporters into activists. But his efforts have not resulted in new federal gun-control legislation. And at the state level, nearly "two-thirds of the new laws" passed in the year after the Sandy Hook shooting have actually loosened gun restrictions, making it easier for people to carry weapons legally in public spaces.[76] Yet we should not write off Obama's gun-control rhetoric as a complete failure. First, it would be unfair to expect the warrant of the dead or any other argument to transform our deeply complex and ingrained gun debate, especially immediately: the gun debate depends on the give and take of many arguments; moreover, turning arguments into votes depends on grassroots organization, financial support, and political clout. Second, there are other ways to evaluate the effectiveness of an argument besides looking at votes; for instance, we might examine "more subtle, indirect, and long-term effects," such as "framing an issue in specific ways, or influencing the national understanding of an issue over time."[77]

Nonetheless, Obama's gun-control rhetoric did not lead to federal legislation and does not appear successful at establishing a gun-control movement. I have discussed the broad challenge of fleeting engagement, including its structural and rhetorical dimensions. But now I focus on two rhetorical challenges that the warrant of the dead in particular faces. The first challenge comes from opponents who charge that the warrant of the dead violates decorum and manipulates emotion. The second challenge comes from trying to organize and sustain a movement by appealing to responsibility and obligation.

Does the Warrant of the Dead Violate Decorum and Manipulate Emotions?

When the warrant of the dead is explicitly acknowledged in the gun debate, it elicits controversy. Opponents of gun control charge that those who argue for gun control in the aftermath of gun violence are violating decorum and manipulating emotions. But the problem is not with how the dead are depicted: indeed, Obama sanitized his depiction; he does not describe the site of tragedy or provide any imagery of bodies riddled with bullets. Instead, opponents decry any talk of policy in the aftermath of tragedy. NRA Executive Vice President LaPierre explained that the NRA was reluctant to speak after the Sandy Hook shooting "out of respect for those grieving families." He further explained, "While some have tried to exploit tragedy for political gain, we have remained respectfully silent."[78] LaPierre's message echoed the NRA's message after the Columbine shooting thirteen years earlier. Then-president Heston claimed that "the dirty secret of this day and age is that political gain and media ratings all too often bloom upon fresh graves." Heston harkened back to "a better day," when "no one dared politicize or profiteer on trauma" and when "simply being silent is so often the right thing to do."[79] By appealing to decorum—a sense of what is appropriate in particular moments—Heston and LaPierre insisted that the aftermath of tragedy is the time for mourning and that proper mourning should include no talk of policy.

Obama has defended the warrant of the dead (although not in that precise language) since his post–Sandy Hook gun-control proposals were voted down in the Senate. On April 17, 2013, he directly addressed the charge that it was improper to invoke the dead, including using the families of victims to make a case for gun control: "I've heard folks say that having the families of victims lobby for this legislation was somehow misplaced. 'A prop,' somebody called them. 'Emotional blackmail,' some outlet said. Are they serious? Do we really think that thousands of families whose lives have been shattered by gun violence don't have a right to weigh in on this issue? Do we think their emotions, their loss is not relevant to this debate?"[80] According to Obama, mentioning the dead and the emotional turmoil left in their wake is not only legitimate but central to the gun debate. While opponents of gun control have regularly charged that Obama has "politicized" mass shootings, he claimed after the 2015 Umpqua Community College shooting that "this is something we should politicize. It is relevant to our common life together, to the body politic."[81] And he went even further in his response to the 2016 shooting at a gay nightclub in Orlando by claiming that "to actively do nothing is a decision as well."[82]

There are, of course, legitimate reasons for disagreeing on this issue. Obama expressed the view that grief is not necessarily passive and private but can be active and public. Political action can legitimately coexist with grieving and can even be a form of grieving. Emotions relevant to the issue at hand have an important place in policy making. Yet the worry—present since rhetoric's beginning—is that emotion will trump logic; the moral authority and pathos granted to the dead can blind us and, in turn, bind us to ill-conceived and reactionary policies that in the long term might do more harm than good. I think that a balance can be struck between these two views and that this is a debate worth having.

In wrestling with disagreements about decorum, though, we should not ignore the strategic dimension of appeals to decorum, particularly in the aftermath of mass shootings. Both gun-rights and gun-control advocates appeal to decorum in order to diminish their opponents' character. LaPierre charged that gun-control advocates lack judgment and decency for speaking about gun control in the aftermath of tragedy, whereas Obama charged that his opponents lack judgment and decency for not doing so. Moreover, whether one accepts a particular form of the warrant of the dead may very well depend on whether one already agrees with LaPierre's defense of gun rights or Obama's defense of gun control. In other words, arguments about decorum can be used to rationalize what we already believe and to dismiss what we do not.

Rhetorical criticism can help reveal the strategic dimension of appeals to decorum. For instance, by appealing to decorum, the NRA attempts to dismiss any gun-control arguments based on their timing rather than quality.[83] Precluding talk by gun-control advocates works to the NRA's advantage since its primary legislative goal is to resist gun-control legislation. "Not now" effectively means "not ever." Although LaPierre disparaged talk of policy at the outset of his December 21, 2012, speech, what he actually opposed was talk of gun-control policies.[84] Indeed, by the end of his speech, LaPierre used the warrant of the dead to justify his own policy as the best response to the shooting. He argued that placing armed guards in schools fulfills our obligation to ensure that others are not harmed: "They're *our* kids. They're our *responsibility*. And it's not just our *duty* to protect them—it's our *right* to protect them."[85] In addition to revealing the strategic dimension of appeals to decorum, then, rhetorical criticism can help us assess these appeals by tracking whether they are used consistently. And if they are not used consistently, then we ought to ask why.

Can Responsibility and Obligation Sustain a Movement?

Rights has long been the key term of the gun debate. Obama has used the language of rights by arguing that gun control is consistent with the Second Amendment. He has also tried to expand the scope of rights by arguing that an unwavering defense of the Second Amendment infringes on other rights enshrined in the Bill of Rights. On January 16, 2013, Obama made the following claim:

> The right to worship freely and safely, that right was denied to Sikhs in Oak Creek, Wisconsin. The right to assemble peaceably, that right was denied shoppers in Clackamas, Oregon, and moviegoers in Aurora, Colorado. That most fundamental set of rights to life and liberty and the pursuit of happiness—fundamental rights that were denied to college students at Virginia Tech, and high school students at Columbine, and elementary school students in Newtown, and kids on street corners in Chicago on too frequent a basis to tolerate, and all the families who've never imagined that they'd lose a loved one to a bullet—those rights are at stake.[86]

Although Obama used the language of rights, he also tried to displace rights as the only key term in the gun debate. In his rhetoric of gun control, responsibility and obligation—as exemplified in the warrant of the dead—are at least as important as rights. As he put it, "As Americans, we are endowed by our Creators with certain inalienable rights that no man or government can take away from us. But we've also long recognized, as our Founders recognized, that with rights come responsibilities. Along with our freedom to live our lives as we will comes an obligation to allow others to do the same. We don't live in isolation. We live in a society, a government of, and by, and for the people. We are responsible for each other."[87] After the shooting at Sandy Hook, he explained that "our first task" is "caring for our children. It's our first job. If we don't get that right, we don't get anything right. That's how, as a society, we will be judged. And by that measure, can we truly say, as a nation, that we are meeting our obligations?"[88]

But establishing and sustaining a gun-control movement predicated on responsibility and obligation presents its own challenges. First, there is a gap between accepting responsibility for others and embracing gun control. Gun-control advocates must argue not only that we are responsible for protecting others but that this responsibility for others entails gun control; it is possible to accept the first step but not the second. Indeed, gun-rights advocates have used the language of obligation and responsibility to justify greater access to guns and greater visibility of guns in public spaces (e.g., open carry). These gun-rights advocates see themselves as "citizen-protectors," Jennifer Carlson's label for gun carriers who "use firearms to actively assert their authority and relevance by embracing the duty to protect themselves and others."[89] Supporters and opponents of gun control, then, can agree on our obligation to protect others yet still disagree about whether gun control is a good way to do so. But for gun-rights advocates, there is no such gap; their appeal to rights is assumed to necessitate the rejection of gun control.

Second, gun-control supporters who believe that they are responsible for others and that this responsibility entails gun control face the challenge of motivating people. On the one hand, the rhetoric of responsibility entails a sense of urgency. Obama asserted that all Americans should see the dead victims of gun violence as members of the American family and as if they were or might be members of our individual families. He claimed that reducing gun violence ought to "obsess us."[90] But on the other hand, the solution he espoused—expanded background checks and a ban on assault weapons and high-capacity magazines—can only promise a relatively modest reduction in gun violence. Obama rightly acknowledged that "there is no law or set of laws that can prevent every senseless act of violence completely." Yet he insisted that incremental progress is worthwhile: "If there is even one thing we can do to reduce this violence, if there is even one life that can be saved, then we've got an obligation to try."[91] Such incremental progress, even if realistic, is typically not inspiring. Because of the mismatch between the passion that gun-control supporters are supposed to feel and the incremental benefit that might come from their action, Obama has tried to create activists who are paradoxically moderate.

In contrast, gun-rights advocates have a motivational advantage built into the gun debate: they do not need to craft or argue about the best plan; their policy, in short, is to oppose any policies restricting guns.[92] Moreover, many gun-rights advocates see the gun debate as a stark, all-or-nothing battle that will determine their own autonomy and safety, the future of the Second Amendment (and all that entails), and the future of America. The NRA sends that message consistently to its members through its magazines, mailings, and online platforms, amplifying that message at key moments in order to mobilize gun-rights advocates to oppose any and all gun legislation. Gun-control advocacy groups have been unable to match the organizational power of the NRA. Yet this organizational mismatch is also coupled with a rhetorical mismatch. Whereas gun-rights advocates' rhetoric of rights and self-defense portrays the gun debate as having personal, immediate consequences, gun-control advocates' rhetoric of responsibility does not convey that sense of immediacy, particularly for those who have not been directly affected by gun violence. The warrant of the dead tries to get audiences to feel a sense of responsibility for and obligation toward unknown victims, but such challenges as I have indicated make it ethically complicated and rhetorically difficult to sustain a gun-control movement.

Conclusion

Further examination of the warrant of the dead could provide additional insight about gun-control rhetoric, including the rhetoric of advocacy groups such as Moms Demand Action and the Brady Campaign to Prevent Gun Violence. We might further question how the warrant of the dead functions, for whom, and to what effect—whether in the gun debate or beyond. Some questions pertain to the rhetoric and politics of representation. Who, after all, presumes to speak on behalf of the dead, and who is accepted as speaking on behalf of the dead? Which dead are spoken for and which are not, and how come? Other questions pertain to decorum and ethics. When and why is it deemed appropriate or inappropriate to speak on behalf of the dead? How might we distinguish between alleged obligations that honor the dead versus those that misuse or exploit them? Would we still feel obliged to honor the dead if we disagreed with the cause being advocated in their name? And if we are obliged to the dead, what is the extent of this obligation, and what is its relationship to our other obligations and needs (including the need to not be paralyzed by grief)? Still other questions pertain to its deliberative dimensions. Does the warrant of the dead allow for open debate, or does it presume privileged and thus unquestionable knowledge? On what values or evidence does the warrant of the dead depend, and on what basis can or should it be challenged?

Above all, we should pause to question the movement from the dead to obligations ascribed to them. Why are the living called upon to take *this* action—whether it is legislation, war, or something else—rather than other actions? Beyond our obligation to the dead, what other arguments are there, if any, for the proposed action? Would we still find the case persuasive without appeals to the pathos and ethos of the dead? In asking these questions, among others, we can bring the warrant of the dead out into the open and better understand how it operates. Rather than treating this warrant as a given—something assumed or taken for granted—we can see it as a significant rhetorical move that is worth our explicit attention as both users and scholars of rhetoric.

Future research might also focus on the situation that the warrant of the dead is responding to—fleeting engagement. Thought of in terms of the relationship between public memory and deliberation, gun-rights and gun-control advocates are in different positions. Whereas the Second Amendment has accumulated meanings and accrued weight, the victims of gun violence have not. Given this imbalance, the speed of news media and contemporary life are alone insufficient explanations. Gun-rights advocates have been able to build memories of the Second Amendment. The weight of the past—as demonstrated by the Second Amendment—highlights that memory can be strengthened if a message is simple, urgent, and repeated again and again.

To better understand the implications of the fleeting past and fleeting engagement for the gun debate and for America's deliberative culture more generally, rhetorical scholars might foreground "attention." Describing rhetoric as "the economics of attention," Richard A. Lanham encourages us to think of rhetorical theory and practice as telling us "how to allocate our central scarce resource."[93] To what extent is fleeting engagement a structural problem, and to what extent is it a rhetorical problem? Beyond the warrant of the dead, what strategies have been used or might be used to counter fleeting engagement in the gun debate and in other public debates? Asking these questions can help us better understand the challenges and potential barriers involved not only in gaining attention but in ethically sustaining it long enough to move audiences from conviction to action.

4

THE IMPLICIT PAST: MEMORY AND RACISM

In Charleston, South Carolina, a small group gathered in a church basement on June 17, 2015. They were there for a Bible study. A visitor had joined the group and sat with them for nearly an hour.[1] When they stood to pray, the visitor began shooting.[2] Nine people were murdered.

Again, the nation looked on in horror and wondered, Why? Politicians, reporters, and opinion leaders redeployed their talking points about mental illness and guns. But the conversation also addressed a topic rarely discussed after mass shootings: racism. The turn toward the topic of racism made sense because all nine victims were black. Although violence against people of color is often ignored by politicians and opinion leaders in the United States, the combination of circumstances in this case was distinct: it was a mass shooting, it happened in a church, and one of the victims—Clementa Pinckney—was a state senator. Moreover, the shooter—by this point, I have grown tired of repeating and recirculating the names of mass shooters—was white and explicitly racist. His "manifesto" described his belief in the superiority of whites and the inferiority of blacks, Jews, and Hispanics.[3] He deliberately chose to target a black church—the Emanuel African Methodist Episcopal Church—hoping to ignite a larger "race war."[4]

Since the shooter was unambiguously racist, the debate that followed centered on whether cultural forces had sustained the shooter's racism and, if so, whether these forces might be changed. The debate focused on the Confederate flag, which was soon removed from the South Carolina capitol building.[5] Other commentators suggested that the violence represented problems much larger than the flag. Noting that this was "not the first time that black churches have been attacked," President Obama reminded listeners that the Charleston shooting occurred just over fifty years after "four little girls were killed in a bombing in a black church in Birmingham, Alabama."[6] This history of targeting black churches was part of a much broader history of racist violence and terror. The shooter's "act of race hate," according to Michael Eric Dyson, "is a tragic monument in the landscape of white racial terror."[7] That landscape extends back to America's haunting legacy of lynching and slavery.

The Charleston shooting is rightly understood within this larger landscape of white racial terror. Yet the conjunction of racism and gun violence in the Charleston shooting also helps illuminate the much larger role that racism has played—both implicitly and explicitly—in debates about gun violence and policy throughout U.S. history. In chapter 3, I began to describe how racism shapes which victims of gun violence are recognized and which ones are not. This chapter extends that point and explores the much larger and pervasive role of racism. Specifically, I examine how the ideology of white supremacy has regularly been at work in debates about gun violence, policy, and possession.

The ideology of white supremacy runs deep in America. Its fundamental assumption is that whites are superior to nonwhites, and its fundamental goal is to maintain that power imbalance. To upset that imbalance—if whites begin to lose psychological, cultural, political, or economic power or if people of color begin to gain power—can lead to white fear and backlash. As an ideology, white supremacy is a dominant belief system that often operates unnoticed by seeming "normal." Moreover, it renders material and symbolic privileges to white people and material and symbolic burdens to people of color. In its most extreme and explicit form, the ideology of white supremacy is a rallying point for explicitly racist groups such as the Ku Klux Klan. But the ideology of white supremacy remains influential in less overt, implicit ways, even in the twenty-first century. We do not need to go deep into America's past or far from the mainstream of politics to see white supremacy at work. Indeed, consider the speech that Donald Trump delivered on June 16, 2015—the day before the Charleston shooting. The man who would eventually receive over sixty-two million votes and become president of the United States announced his candidacy by insisting, "When Mexico sends its people, they're not sending their best. They're not sending you. They're not sending you. They're sending people that have lots of problems, and they're bringing those problems with us. They're bringing drugs. They're bringing crime. They're rapists." He then backtracked by adding, "And some [immigrants], I assume, are good people."[8]

Unfortunately, white supremacy is not limited to a few people or a few outrageous statements. The breadth of white supremacy is wide, and it includes those who explicitly or implicitly embrace the ideology of white supremacy as well as those who reject it. Its influence extends to those who have hate in their hearts and those who do not, to racists and antiracists and to those in between. It is not confined to any political party. All people of all colors can use this ideology and be used by it. As a form of racism, white supremacy is not simply "an individual aberration" but is "something systemic, institutional, and pervasive."[9] It is illustrated by disproportionate incarceration rates and job opportunities, segregated schooling and housing, unequal wealth and health, and so on.

My basic claim here is that the ideology of white supremacy filters how Americans understand and deliberate about gun violence, policy, and possession. This ideology represents an implicit past: America's history of white supremacy functions as a lens or filter that sorts and distorts interpretation and deliberation as well as perception (including what is seen and heard and what is not).[10]

First, I trace how white supremacy has been used both to support and to oppose gun-control legislation. This historical legacy highlights how white supremacy continues to shape the contemporary gun debate, including which violent events, perpetrators, and victims gain national attention and which do not. Second, I demonstrate that white supremacy shapes how publics understand the sources of and potential solutions to gun violence; in turn, these understandings help direct conversations about public policy while also unfairly distributing privileges and burdens. Overall, I suggest that if Americans are going to address the problem of gun violence, we need to talk about explicit and implicit racism. To understand—let alone change—debates about gun violence, policy, and possession, we need to acknowledge and then challenge the ideology of white supremacy. In fundamental ways, the problems of racism and gun violence are inseparable.

White Supremacy in the Case for and Against Gun Control: A Brief Rhetorical History

The Charleston shooter claimed that "the event that truly awakened [him] was the Trayvon Martin case."[11] Martin was a seventeen-year-old African American who, while walking home from a convenience store, was confronted and killed by George Zimmerman, a neighborhood watch volunteer. After the February 26, 2012, shooting, public debate centered on whether Zimmerman was actually threatened—and thus responded in self-defense—or whether he engaged in racial profiling by viewing Martin as dangerous and then overreacting to that perception.[12] For the eventual Charleston shooter, though, the media narrative about racial profiling was completely backward. After finding a defunct website describing "black on White crime," he stated, "I realized that something was very wrong. How could the news be blowing up in the Trayvon Martin case while hundreds of these black on White murders got ignored?"[13] From his perspective, the immediate problem was media bias. But the larger problem was something that media bias was overlooking. In his telling, we are in a world where dangerous and inferior blacks are targeting virtuous and superior whites.

The Charleston shooter's racism is startling because it is so explicit and because it motivated mass murder. In that respect, he is an anomaly. But to render him wholly "other" would be a mistake. He was raised in the United States, a place where gun violence and debates about gun policy have been infused with racist fear from the very beginning. Understanding this context helps us see the Charleston shooter not only as an advocate of white supremacy but also as a product of it.

From America's Founding to 1994

The ideology of white supremacy has been central to debates for and against gun control throughout U.S. history. "In colonial times and in the early republic," Brett Lunceford explains, "laws in many states prohibited Native Americans, African Americans (both slave and free), and those of mixed race from owning guns."[14] Adam Winkler writes that "America's founders strictly prohibited slaves and even free blacks from owning guns, lest they use them for the same purpose the colonists did in 1776: to revolt against tyranny."[15] Guns were necessary for sustaining white domination, and they also became an essential resource for challenging white supremacy. "Throughout the 1850s," writes Michael Waldman, "many foes of slavery had abandoned pacifist ideals, gravitating toward radical action."[16] Rev. Henry Ward Beecher, for instance, "rallied supporters to send crates of guns and Bibles to Kansas" after he "declared 'more moral power in [a Sharps rifle,] so far as the slaveholders of Kansas were concerned, than in a hundred Bibles.'"[17] Abolitionists relied on these rifles, known as "Beecher's Bibles."[18] "In 1859, John Brown—carrying arms sent by the abolitionists for use in Kansas—raided the U.S. Arsenal at Harpers Ferry, West Virginia" with hopes to ignite a slave rebellion.[19] The rebellion failed, but "fear of armed abolitionists intensified through the South."[20]

After the Civil War, this fear of armed rebellion became a rationale for disarming African Americans. Winkler emphasizes that the newly formed Ku

Klux Klan "made their first objective the confiscation of all guns from newly freed blacks, who gained access to guns in service to the Union army."[21] But black disarmament was also enshrined in law. As Waldman notes, "State governments passed Black Codes seeking to restore slavery in all but name. These laws disarmed African Americans but let whites retain their guns."[22] Further, as Philip J. Cook and Kristin A. Goss point out, "African Americans seeking protection in the Second Amendment found none, for in 1875 the Supreme Court ruled in *U.S. v. Cruikshank* that the amendment applied only to acts of Congress, not vigilante groups [such as the KKK] or other usurpers of gun rights."[23]

During the civil rights movement nearly a century later, gun laws continued to be used to maintain white supremacy. For some civil rights activists, guns offered a means of self-defense. Some activists committed to the cause of nonviolence kept guns in briefcases or in their homes in case their lives were threatened by white supremacists.[24] When nonviolent activism gave way to more militant modes during the 1960s, activists increasingly wielded their guns in public. Black Panthers cofounder Huey Newton described their strategy of "policing the police." With "weapons in our hands, we were no longer their subjects but their equals."[25] While conservative leaders today celebrate open-carry protests as an expression of the right to bear arms and the right to free speech, such was not the case in the 1960s. Norms have changed, of course, but it also mattered that the Black Panthers were black, whereas the open-carry protestors today are predominantly white.[26] In response to the armed protests by Black Panthers, the state of California passed the Mulford Act. Under this law, Winkler explains, "anyone caught carrying a loaded gun on a public street in California would face five years in prison."[27] In 1967, Republican governor Ronald Reagan signed the Mulford Act into law, claiming that guns were "a ridiculous way to solve problems that have to be solved among people of good will."[28]

Democrats also relied on the white fear of black Americans to pass gun-control legislation. One of the most significant pieces of federal gun legislation passed in the twentieth century was the Gun Control Act of 1968. The act regulated the interstate sale of guns, including the transfer of rifles through the mail, and restricted certain types of criminals and mentally ill individuals from owning firearms.[29] In my introductory chapter, I followed the narrative offered by many histories of the gun debate by pointing out that this legislation was initiated after the 1963 assassination of President John F.

Kennedy, who was slain with a rifle ordered through the mail. Then the mass shooting at the University of Texas at Austin in 1966 and the assassinations of Martin Luther King Jr. and Robert F. Kennedy in 1968 helped push this proposal into law. Yet it was not only this violence that created a desire for gun control. President Lyndon B. Johnson signed the Omnibus Crime Control and Safe Streets Act in June 1968 after "250 separate incidents of urban civil disorder—what policymakers, journalists, and most of the public at large called 'riots.'"[30] The riots represented disorder and a threat to white power; in turn, the Safe Streets Act represented an effort to restore order. Johnson made his case for the Gun Control Act of 1968 by framing it within this broader context: this was not a narrow piece of legislation meant solely as a reaction to the assassination of public figures or the mass shooting in Austin; instead, it was part of his War on Crime. Johnson argued that the act would allow the government to "protect its citizens against the random and the reckless violence of crime at gun point."[31]

Reducing crime is an important goal, but we need to be careful because "crime" and "criminal" are not neutral categories. "In the USA," Carol A. Stabile writes, "various institutions and agents have waged long, bitter struggles over the power to define crime—to criminalize various acts to the exclusion of others."[32] As Richard Delgado and Jean Stefancic point out, "The disproportionate criminalization of African Americans is a product, in large part, of the ways we define crime."[33] They continue,

> Many lethal acts, such as marketing defective automobiles, alcohol, or pharmaceuticals or waging undeclared wars, are not considered crimes at all. By the same token, many things that young black and Latino men are prone to do, such as congregating on street corners, cruising in low-rider cars, or scrawling graffiti in public places, are energetically policed, sometimes under new ordinances that penalize belonging to a gang or associating with a known gang member. Crack cocaine offenses receive harsher penalties than those that apply to powder cocaine. Figures show that white-collar crime, including embezzlement, consumer fraud, bribery, insider trading, and price fixing, causes more deaths and property loss, even on a per capita basis, than does all street crime combined.

What counts as a crime, who gets the benefit of the doubt and who does not, what sort of punishment seems fair, and even whether punishment is less urgent than reform and prevention—these are all questions that are formed across time in the crucible of culture, politics, and law.

Beyond legal definitions, who is seen as a criminal or potential criminal is informed by a history of conflating blackness and criminality that dates back to colonial America.[34] That long history was brought to bear on debates about crime in the 1960s. Elizabeth Hinton charges that "Republican policymakers employed the racially coded politics of crime control to appeal to disenchanted white voters."[35] Yet Democrats were also guilty. Hinton traces how both the War on Poverty and the War on Crime disproportionately targeted and affected black Americans: "From the ashes of the Watts 'riot' in August 1965, a growing consensus of policymakers, federal administrators, law enforcement officials, and journalists came to understand crime as specific to black urban youth. They concluded that only intensified enforcement of the law in black urban neighborhoods, where contempt for authority seemed widespread, would quell the anarchy and chaos of the nation's streets."[36] Johnson's Safe Streets Act of 1968 "invested $400 million worth of 'seed money' in the War on Crime." "The result," Hinton explains, "was a significant expansion of America's carceral state"—a trend that has continued for forty years.[37] As of 2014, "Black Americans and Latinos together constitute 59 percent of the nation's prisoners, even though they make up roughly a quarter of the entire U.S. population."[38]

The "crime" frame was again central to passing gun-control legislation in the 1990s, particularly the 1994 Federal Assault Weapons Ban, formally known as the Public Safety and Recreational Firearms Use Protection Act. As I noted in my introductory chapter, the bill had its origins in recent mass shootings, yet it was framed much more broadly. President Bill Clinton helped pass the bill by selling it as "anticrime rather than antigun." He framed it within America's War on Crime, which dated back to the 1960s. At "every opportunity," Clinton "surrounded himself with police officers." Moreover, the assault-weapons ban survived because it was part of a much larger "criminal justice bill"—a "$30 billion package" that included "financing for one hundred thousand new police officers, an expansion of the federal death penalty, and funds for crime prevention programs."[39] Gabrielle Giffords and Mark Kelly praise Clinton's successful packaging of the assault-weapon ban as anticrime, yet this framing depended on the racially coded fear appeals of America's larger War on Crime and War on Drugs. In addition to tapping into racist fear, the crime bill disproportionately targeted and incarcerated Americans of color.[40]

From 2012 to 2013

Rather than trying to prevent criminals from getting guns, gun-rights advocates argue that Americans have a duty to arm and defend themselves against criminals and others who are dangerous. Polls show that among all gun owners, protection has become the primary reason for owning guns: "In 1999, far more gun owners cited hunting, rather than self-protection, as the main reason they owned guns. By 2013, those attitudes had shifted: 48% said protection was the main reason to own a gun, while 32% pointed to hunting."[41] Notably, the Second Amendment is fourth on that list: only 4 percent of gun owners in 1999 and only 2 percent of gun owners in 2013 listed the Second Amendment as the reason they owned guns.[42] These data suggest that Americans do not own guns simply because they believe in the Second Amendment; instead, they invoke specific readings of the Second Amendment to justify their desire for guns. And they want guns because they want protection. But it is worth asking, From what or whom do they want protection? There are many possible answers, but in the NRA's rhetoric, the perceived threat is largely imagined as nonwhite.[43] This critique should not be misinterpreted as suggesting that all or even most who oppose gun control are racist, nor is it to suggest that the gun-rights cause is always predicated on racism—they are not, and it is not. Yet the NRA's rhetoric relies on fear in general and racist fear in particular.

Let us turn again to the NRA's rhetoric after the 2012 shooting at Sandy Hook Elementary School. Wayne LaPierre briefly recognized the victims of the recent mass shooting. Yet his speech focused on the perpetrators of violence. He asked his listeners to imagine themselves as potential victims who are "utterly defenseless" against such "genuine monsters." LaPierre depicted the world as a dangerous place. Rather than claiming that mass shooters were rare, he asked, "How many more copycats are waiting in the wings for their moment of fame?" He continued, "A dozen more killers? A hundred? More?" LaPierre tapped into his audience's fear of mass shooters—whether white shooters or shooters of color—to encourage Americans to arm and defend themselves. This focus on the *perpetrators* of mass shootings is itself remarkable. Yet LaPierre's rationale for gun access and self-defense extends beyond the threat of mass shooters to criminals more generally: "the much larger and more lethal *criminal* class: Killers, robbers, rapists and drug gang members who have spread like cancer in every community in this country."[44]

Self-defense, from LaPierre's perspective, is not an abstract concern. The threat is immediate, and the need for self-defense is urgent. He asked the audience to imagine themselves as potential victims of gun violence: "When you hear the glass breaking in your living room at 3 a.m. and call 911, you won't be able to pray hard enough for a gun in the hands of a good guy to get there fast enough to protect you." His fear appeals make the case both against gun restrictions and for gun possession. Gun restrictions, in his telling, will not stop criminals; restrictions will only disarm citizens and leave them defenseless. Police, or even armed guards, are an insufficient defense. In LaPierre's narrative, the problem was not that there was a lack of gun restrictions but that there were too many restrictions that kept people from defending themselves. The Second Amendment obliges us to bear arms to defend ourselves and others. Otherwise, "our children" will be left "utterly defenseless," while the "monsters and predators of this world know it and exploit it."[45]

LaPierre suggested that danger comes primarily from outsiders. Yet FBI statistics show that in 2011—the year before the shooting at Sandy Hook—more than half of the people who were killed in the United States were "killed by someone they knew (acquaintance, neighbor, friend, boyfriend, etc.)," and nearly half of those "murder victims were slain by family members."[46] By excluding these details, LaPierre painted a rather distorted picture of crime and murder. Violence, in his telling, comes from "them," not from "us." Violence comes from outsiders, in terms of geography (e.g., people from outside of America), politics (e.g., people who do not support the NRA), identity (e.g., people who are unlike "us"), and race (e.g., people who are not white).

In his February 2013 statement titled "Stand and Fight," LaPierre argued against President Obama's post–Sandy Hook gun-control proposals, indicating from the start that "good Americans" are "prudently getting ready to protect themselves." What were they getting ready to protect themselves against? Protection was needed from "violent criminals who prey on decent people." Protection was needed from "Latin American drug gangs" that have "invaded every city of significant size in the United States." Protection was needed from "criminals" crossing the Mexican border, "whose jobs are murder, rape, robbery and kidnapping."[47] And protection was needed from "agents of al Qaeda and other terrorist organizations." LaPierre's rhetoric suggests that "we" need guns to protect ourselves from outsiders who might invade the borders of "our" homes, communities, and country. This general fear of being "invaded" by outsiders was, in actuality, a specific fear of nonwhites.

Vigilance against crime and terrorism are typically good things—but not when such vigilance relies on racist stereotypes and exacerbates racist fears. LaPierre wrote, "After Hurricane Sandy, we saw the hellish world that the gun prohibitionists [such as New York City Mayor Bloomberg] see as their utopia. Looters ran wild in south Brooklyn. There was no food, water or electricity. And if you wanted to walk several miles to get supplies, you better get back before dark, or you might not get home at all."[48] LaPierre did not need to specify the race of these "looters" who would "run wild." His audience understood. His division between us and them—of good Americans versus bad Americans or non-Americans—is especially troubling since the majority of gun owners in the United States are white men. According to the Pew Research Center, "Roughly three-quarters (74 percent) of gun owners are men, and 82 percent are white. Taken together, 61 percent of adults who own guns are white men. Nationwide, white men make up only 32 percent of the adult U.S. population."[49] More troubling still, the world of immense danger that LaPierre depicted was a fantasy. As Waldman points out, "LaPierre's version of the hurricane mystified those who lived through it. Coney Island was unusually peaceful: There were no murders, no rapes, and no shootings that week, according to the New York City Police Department."[50]

My brief rhetorical history has highlighted how both gun-control and gun-rights advocates have relied on and perpetuated the ideology of white supremacy. I do not mean to imply that they are equal offenders; they are not. Yet I am impatient with arguments about who is more racist. Although targeting one's political opponents can be justified, the better target to focus on is white supremacy, wherever it lives. All Americans need to consciously work to critique and challenge white supremacy, including its use and consequences—even when these are unintentional.

The Consequences of White Supremacy: Selective Attention and Action

White supremacy shapes which events, perpetrators, and victims gain national attention and which do not. It also shapes how publics understand the sources and potential solutions to gun violence. In turn, these understandings help direct conversations about public policy while also unfairly distributing psychological and material privileges and burdens. To help illustrate these complex dynamics, I first focus on white supremacy's relationship to the victims of gun violence and then white supremacy's relationship to the perpetrators of gun violence.

Selectively Recognizing the Victims of Gun Violence

For too long, we've been blind to the unique mayhem that gun violence inflicts upon this nation. Sporadically, our eyes are open: When [9] of our brothers and sisters are cut down in a church basement, 12 in a movie theater, 26 in an elementary school. But I hope we also see the 30 precious lives cut short by gun violence in this country every single day.

—PRESIDENT OBAMA, JUNE 26, 2015

Selective attention to some violent events and victims—but not others—is in some sense inevitable given the plethora of violence that happens each day and given that our time, attention, and empathy are not unlimited. But who gets recognized and how they get recognized are not natural or inevitable. They are products of human choices, even if those choices are far removed and not reducible to one person. For example, America's news industry profits from breaking news not because of one individual but because of the accumulated choices of media executives, stockholders, advertisers, reporters, and viewers. Our "norms of recognition" are not easy to change, even at the individual level.[51] But they are also not set in stone. They can be changed and should be changed in order to reduce racism and its consequences.

Whether intended or not, America's selective focus on high-profile mass shootings—and notably, we only pay attention to *some* mass shootings—perpetuates inequity by displacing attention from forms of gun violence that disproportionately affect people of color, particularly black men. According to the Department of Justice, "From 2002 to 2011, the average homicide rate for males was 3.6 times higher than the rate for females." But race matters even more than gender: "The average homicide rate for blacks was 6.3 times higher than the rate for whites."[52] Thus black men in the United States are in an incredibly precarious position: data from 2016 show that "black men are 14 times more likely than white men to die by firearm homicide."[53]

Chapter 3 described how the ideology of white supremacy shapes which violent events and victims of gun violence are recognized nationally. But here I want to highlight that even if victims of color are recognized and even if that recognition leads to discussion of potential solutions (which are two big ifs), white supremacy still exerts its force by shaping the conversation about potential solutions. To illustrate this point, I focus on President Obama's rhetoric that attempts to recognize the broader contexts of gun violence and its victims.

As America's first black president, Obama has been uniquely positioned to talk about racism, but according to Dyson, he has been reluctant to do so. The institution of the presidency establishes certain constraints: Obama is not a prophet who is free to say anything, Dyson notes, but is a politician tasked with building coalitions and thus constrained in what he can and cannot say.[54] Given Obama's general reluctance to talk about racism, it is not surprising that Obama has had a conflicted history when responding to gun violence against people of color. When a jury acquitted George Zimmerman of murder charges against Trayvon Martin, Obama spoke publicly. On July 19, 2013, Obama acknowledged that racist stereotypes render some bodies, but not others, threatening. Whereas white victims and even white perpetrators of violence are presumed innocent until proven guilty, black perpetrators and even victims are presumed guilty until proven innocent. In this racist logic, Martin's black skin and hoodie rendered him as a threat that justified lethal force against him. By saying that Martin could have been his son and that Martin "could have been me 35 years ago," Obama attempted to contextualize why Americans of color were so upset by the verdict. He noted that "African American young men are disproportionately involved in the criminal justice system; that they're disproportionately both victims and perpetrators of violence." But as he further explained, "Black folks do interpret the reasons for that in a historical context. They understand that some of the violence that takes place in poor black neighborhoods around the country is born out of a very violent past in this country, and that the poverty and dysfunction that we see in those communities can be traced to a very difficult history."[55] Although Obama referenced racism in the United States, he only passingly referred to Florida's Stand Your Ground law, which enabled Zimmerman to kill Martin without punishment. Rather than a time for policy talk, Obama suggested that now was a time for "soul-searching."[56] However, others saw this as a moment for reflection *and* action. Three organizers—Alicia Garza, Patrisse Cullors, and Opal Tometi—initiated the Black Lives Matter movement.[57]

I have noted that Obama's post–Sandy Hook push for gun control focused on the problem of mass shootings yet regularly invoked other forms of gun violence, captured by his recurring reference to gun violence in Chicago. Let us return to Chicago. On February 15, 2013, Obama spoke at the Hyde Park Academy High School on the South Side of Chicago. Reflecting on the Sandy Hook shooting, he noted, "There was something profound and uniquely heartbreaking and tragic, obviously, about a group of 6-year-olds being killed." "But," he continued, "there were 443 murders with a firearm on the streets of this city, and 65 of those victims were 18 and under. So that's the equivalent of a Newtown every four months."[58] His focus on children attempted to bridge Chicago and Newtown and thus bridge the divide between homicides and high-profile mass shootings, between predominantly black victims and predominantly white victims. His focus on children also attempted to challenge some people's presumption that black victims were always already guilty and, in some sense, responsible for their deaths.

Notably, Obama spoke in Chicago to gain support for his post–Sandy Hook gun-control proposals, but the violence in Chicago was not the impetus for his gun-control proposals. Although he might have been more explicit in describing how violence in Chicago was rooted in a history of racist oppression, and although he might have addressed the violence in Chicago sooner and on its own, he nonetheless deserves credit for drawing attention to gun violence in Chicago and throughout the United States. But Obama's speech in Chicago highlights that even when black victims of violence are recognized, white supremacy shapes how blame is distributed and what kinds of solutions are offered for potentially reducing future violence.

Critics charged that Obama offered his predominantly black audience different solutions to gun violence—solutions that emphasized personal responsibility—from those he offered to his predominantly white audience in direct response to the Sandy Hook shooting. This is "not just a gun issue," Obama explained to his Chicago audience; it is also "an issue of the kinds of communities that we're building." He mentioned the need for educational and job opportunities. Yet he also argued that there was "nothing that would be more important for us reducing violence than strong, stable families—which means we should do more to promote marriage and encourage fatherhood." Stable families, he suggested, might "teach integrity and responsibility, and discipline and delayed gratification."[59]

In contrast, Obama's speeches in direct response to the Sandy Hook shooting included no talk of "strong, stable families" even though the white shooter's parents were divorced. Nor did his speeches in direct response to the Sandy Hook shooting include any talk of families and communities needing to "teach integrity and responsibility, and discipline and delayed gratification."[60] He depicted gun violence at Sandy Hook as America's national problem but gun violence in Chicago as Chicago's personal problem, giving white families a pass while blaming black families. This racial disparity was especially pronounced because Obama's blame of predominantly black families was overly simplistic. As Melissa Harris-Perry argued in her systematic critique of Obama's speech, "The recipe to stopping gun violence is much more complicated than 'Just add Dad.'"[61] Building on her critique, Dyson argued that Obama "lost his moral balance by stressing personal responsibility while slighting the forces that harm black families," including "huge unemployment" and "over-incarceration of black people."[62]

The problems represented in Obama's speech, however, are much larger than Obama. Indeed, his attempt to acknowledge the violence in Chicago—but not too much—highlights that the violence in Chicago evoked different reactions for different audiences. For some audiences, the more that Obama mentions street violence in Chicago, the more he feeds racist fear (including LaPierre's dystopian vision of "our" communities being invaded by purported outsiders). For those audiences, the violence in Chicago becomes a warrant not for gun control but for taking up arms in self-defense.

Obama's speech in Chicago represents another challenge that extends beyond the gun debate to our deliberative culture more generally. Obama begins to indicate the complexity of gun violence by implying that the problem of gun violence actually consists of several different problems. He suggests that the sources of and potential solutions for mass shootings might overlap with but are not identical to the sources of and potential solutions for other forms of gun violence—whether gang violence, domestic violence, suicide, or something else. But he does not fully make this point. Given that our deliberative culture is predicated on speed and simplicity (and the need to attract the interest of a busy people), given that Obama is a politician trying to change public policy, and given that gun violence is only one among many problems that a president must confront, it makes sense that he avoids complexity by suggesting that all gun violence is primarily a gun problem. Yet if we only talk about gun violence within the context of mass shootings, then we risk muddying the problems of gun violence and, in turn, offering blunt solutions for complex problems. Moreover, we risk reaffirming white supremacy, including its unequal distribution of benefits and burdens.

(Mis)interpreting the Perpetrators of Gun Violence: Blinded by Whiteness[63]

Maybe we now realize the way racial bias can infect us even when we don't realize it, so that we're guarding against not just racial slurs, but we're also guarding against the subtle impulse to call Johnny back for a job interview but not Jamal. So that we search our hearts when we consider laws to make it harder for some of our fellow citizens to vote.

—PRESIDENT OBAMA, JUNE 26, 2015

Whiteness functions powerfully in discourse about gun violence even though—or perhaps because—whiteness is rarely discussed explicitly. Understanding how whiteness "wields power" is challenging, Thomas K. Nakayama and Robert L. Krizek argue, because whiteness "endures as a largely unarticulated position."[64] As Raka Shome puts it, "The power of whiteness is the power to remain unmarked and thus occupy a position of universality and normalcy."[65] Scholars, commentators, and everyday citizens can benefit from acknowledging and critiquing how whiteness shapes understandings of the sources and solutions to gun violence, including its perpetrators. To be clear, I am not suggesting that the whiteness of a mass shooter is all that matters or even that it is the most important factor—or that the actions of one white person should be used to indict all white people. As Linda Martín Alcoff cautions, it is not that "whiteness overdetermines every encounter, or overpowers every other aspect of one's identity, nor would I hold that whiteness is relevant in every interaction." "But," she continues, "it is a danger to believe that whiteness can be left behind."[66]

To begin to illustrate how whiteness shapes our understanding of gun violence and its perpetrators, consider the shooting at Columbine High School on April 20, 1999. In the aftermath of that shooting, some commentators suggested that racism might have been a contributing factor, given the two white perpetrators' interest in Nazi Germany, their choice to attack their school on Adolf Hitler's birthday, and their use of racist epithets before murdering a black student, Isaiah Shoels. Other interpreters downplayed the role of racism by highlighting that the other twelve who were murdered were white. Moreover, the fact that the perpetrators planted bombs in the cafeteria (which failed to detonate) suggests that their killing was indiscriminate.[67] But less acknowledged is how whiteness functioned implicitly yet powerfully before and after the shooting. Whiteness kept the two perpetrators from being found out before they acted and oriented public responses in the aftermath of the shooting.

Commentary after mass shootings often points to warning signs that might have prevented the tragedy. Hindsight offers unusual clarity, of course, since no one person possesses all the pieces of the puzzle beforehand. Moreover, violence radically changes the meaning of each puzzle piece: in the aftermath of violence, *of course* a student's stories with violent themes indicated impending violence; in the absence of violence, such stories might simply be stories. Yet before violence occurs, ideas about race mediate the perceived significance and implications of so-called warning signs. Tim Wise asks us to reimagine Columbine—to imagine "a handful of black students who say they feel like outcasts" and who "begin talking openly about how they hate everyone":

> They start dressing alike: perhaps wearing the same jackets, or black berets; and they show off their gun collection in a video they produce for a class project. In this video, they act out the murders of dozens of students and teachers. In addition, the students are known to operate a website which praises a mass murderer, and on which they have been known to post hit lists, letting everyone know who they hate most, and intend to kill first. One of the targets of their hatred discovers the list, tells his father, and the two of them inform police of the thinly veiled threat.[68]

These details were true of the white perpetrators at Columbine (just replace the berets with trench coats), but no one stopped them. In part, no one stopped them because these details did not have the same associations in 1999 as they do now that mass shootings have become more familiar. But even in 1999, racist stereotypes shaped how these details were perceived. Wise argues that the perpetrators' whiteness allowed them to be presumed innocent and allowed their peers and parents, as well as the police, to not take their threats seriously. By contrast, if they had been black, their actions and their threats would have been interpreted much differently. If they had been black, Wise asks, "How long would it take, given this information, for school officials, teachers, and parents to make sure these kids were expelled? How long would it take for their families to be run out of town? Does anyone believe this scenario would have been met with apathy, indifference, or even amusement?"[69] Whiteness, in short, provided the perpetrators a presumption of innocence rarely granted to people of color.

In the aftermath of the Columbine shooting, the turn to collective and cultural examination was no doubt due to the relative newness of mass shootings. But this search for understanding was also predicated on the whiteness of the perpetrators. In the days and even years following the shooting, commentators puzzled through the fact that these shooters defied conventional stereotypes: they came from middle-class families, were well educated, and lived in a suburb of Denver. Given these advantages, how could they do this? What these commentators likely wondered but did not ask outright was, How could two *white* boys do this? Analyzing news coverage of the Columbine shooting, Cynthia Willis-Chun found that depictions of the shooting implied that violence was "imaginable and even expected in urban areas" but "nearly inconceivable in the suburbs and from suburban kids." "Urban" functioned as "a code for racialized and financially unstable," whereas "suburban" invoked "whiteness and middle class-ness."[70]

Speaking at a memorial service a month after the tragedy, President Bill Clinton proclaimed, "These dark forces that take over people and make them murder are the extreme manifestation of fear and rage with which every human being has to do combat."[71] To Clinton, "dark forces"—not the shooters—had agency and thus bore responsibility for the murders. Having commentators and national leaders identify so closely with the perpetrators, remove their responsibility, and search for explanations to understand their violence are privileges typically afforded only to white perpetrators of violence. As Bernadette Marie Calafell put it, "Narratives that embrace" the shooter as a "victim, misunderstood, or simply mentally ill, is white privilege."[72]

Consider how different the public responses to mass shootings are when the perpetrator is identified as nonwhite. After the April 16, 2007, shooting at Virginia Tech, for instance, public responses did not suggest that we should identify with the perpetrator or depict him as one of "us" who went astray. Although some commentators critiqued America's approach to mental health care and how students' information was shared among campus units,[73] on the whole, there was not the same kind of search for understanding as there was with Columbine. In part, times had simply changed: it was now a post-9/11 world, and mass shootings had become more common. But the ideology of white supremacy also shaped understandings of the perpetrator as well as the sources of and potential solutions to gun violence. Initial commentary implied that the shooter might have been a terrorist. He was at first described as an "Asian male," which led to "a flurry of speculation," as Douglas Kellner notes.[74] One commentator alleged that this man "might be a 'Paki' Muslim and part of a 'coordinated terrorist attack.'"[75] Some speculated that he was "a Chinese national here on a student visa," thereby concluding that the United States needed "tougher immigration laws."[76] When it was revealed that the shooter emigrated from South Korea, "racist comments emerged about the violent authoritarianism of Koreans." "Frightened Korean students," in turn, "began leaving the Virginia Tech campus."[77] Several South Koreans living in the United States apologized on behalf of the gunman, "citing a sense of collective guilt and shame simply by virtue of a shared ethnicity."[78] Meanwhile, "South Korea's Ambassador to the U.S., Lee Tae Shik, pledged to fast for 32 days to show his sorrow"[79] and to demonstrate that South Koreans were a "worthwhile ethnic minority in America."[80] For some audiences, South Korea and South Koreans were perceived as being at fault even though the shooter had immigrated to the United States with his family when he was eight.

The fact that the Virginia Tech shooter was from South Korea and thus read as nonwhite unlocked a series of questions not typically asked of white perpetrators. Questions asked of a Seung-Hui are not typically asked of white men named Jared or Adam. Very few people asked of the white perpetrator after the 2011 shooting at a political rally in Tucson, the 2012 shooting at a movie theater in Aurora, or the 2012 shooting at an elementary school in Newtown, Why are white men so violent? What was life like in the United States as a white male, and what was it about those life experiences that might have motivated his act of terror? And no white people fled their communities and cities for fear that they would be persecuted because another white man committed mass murder.

To help us understand why some mass shootings happen in the first place, Michael Kimmell suggests that we should explicitly talk about whiteness, particularly white masculinity. Tracing the rise of "angry white men," Kimmell explains that white men in the United States have historically been in a position of power and expected to remain in that position of power. Losing power—whether through bullying, getting laid off, failing to meet expectations, or for whatever reason—can be devastating for anyone, but it can be especially devastating for those white men who have felt entitled to power: "Raised to expect unparalleled social and economic privilege, white men are suffering today from what Kimmel calls 'aggrieved entitlement': a sense that those benefits that white men believed were their due have been snatched away from them."[81] The pressures can be especially powerful in cultures where men are taught to ignore certain emotions and "toughen up" when confronting signs of depression and mental illness. After all, the suicide rate in the United States is highest among white men.[82] The point of examining white masculinity is certainly not to excuse the behavior of angry white men—mass shooters or otherwise—but rather to better understand, for instance, how norms of white masculinity work beneficially and detrimentally for white men and others and how white masculinity—especially heterosexual white masculinity—might be productively reimagined and dissociated from the need for dominance, the stigma of failure, and the imperative for violence.

Focusing on the privileges that white supremacy affords to white perpetrators of gun violence also reveals how people of color have been denied those benefits and rendered with distinct burdens. Whiteness has worked to protect white perpetrators, granting them a presumption of innocence even when the evidence suggests otherwise. Perpetrators of color are denied that presumption of innocence. Indeed, black men—even when nonviolent—regularly "face a world that sees them as violent."[83]

After the Charleston shooting, some commentators urged Americans to push beyond a debate in which the only two options were racist or not racist. Instead, they urged us to see how the ideology of white supremacy structures our shared language and directs our collective attention regardless of whether a specific individual is racist. Anthea Butler highlights that shooters of color are called "terrorists" or "thugs," whereas white shooters are often referred to as mentally ill.[84] Similarly, Britt Bennett highlights the selective and racialized use of the word *terrorist*. "In America's contemporary imagination," Bennett explains, "terrorism is foreign and brown." She continues, "Those terrorists do not have complex motivations. We do not urge one another to reserve judgment until we search through their Facebook histories or interview their friends. We do not trot out psychologists to analyze their mental states. We know immediately why they kill. But a white terrorist is an enigma. A white terrorist has no history, no context, no origin. He is forever unknowable. His very existence is unspeakable. We see him, but we pretend we cannot."[85] Calling shooters terrorists or thugs forecloses the possibility for humanizing them, empathizing with the challenges that they faced, or encouraging systemic reform, whereas calling shooters mentally ill at least allows for these possibilities (even though, as I explored in chapter 1, *mental illness* can also become a stand-in for *evil*, thus shutting down conversation and stigmatizing mental illness and the mentally ill). All three labels—terrorist, mentally ill, or evil—are problematic, but the unequal use of labels should make us pause. The labeling and naming practices regarding perpetrators of gun violence matter because they reveal and perpetuate racist bias. Moreover, they shape public understandings of perpetrators and their violent acts and, in turn, determine which potential solutions, if any, are proposed to help reduce gun violence.

Perceiving a (Nonviolent) Person with a Gun

Wayne LaPierre of the NRA famously claimed, "The *only* thing that stops a *bad* guy with a gun is a *good* guy with a gun."[86] For many gun-rights advocates, this message of personal responsibility is incredibly empowering. Yet as Carlson notes, this message "shifts responsibility from the state to citizens" and redefines "social functions as personal responsibilities."[87] This reasoning suggests that people who become victims of gun violence are to blame because they were not armed to defend themselves. Moreover, responsibility for reducing gun violence shifts from police or lawmakers (or even those who perpetrate violence) to "good" individuals who need to buy guns and use them to take care of themselves. Yet data suggest that the problem is not a shortage of guns. Even though Americans make up "less than 5% of the world's population," they "own nearly half (48%) of the estimated 650 [million] civilian-owned guns worldwide."[88]

But we should also note that determining who is a "bad guy" or a "good guy" is not always simple. A "law-abiding citizen" who draws a weapon publicly in self-defense could be mistaken for a perpetrator of violence. Although carrying a weapon might provide individuals with a sense of security, the prospect that others could be armed might amplify citizens' fear and distrust. It also makes the job of police officers incredibly more difficult since they then have to discern whether armed civilians are simply exercising their Second Amendment right or are planning to do harm. Moreover, risk assessment and judgment about who is a "good guy" or a "bad guy" are never neutral even when well intentioned. Such judgments are shaped by the ideology of white supremacy.

On July 6, 2016, Philando Castile; his girlfriend, Diamond Reynolds; and her four-year-old daughter were pulled over in Falcon Heights, Minnesota, a suburb of St. Paul. They were on their way home from the grocery store. Castile had a permit to carry a gun, and he informed the officer that there was a gun in the car. The situation escalated quickly. Reynolds later testified that Castile was reaching for his ID, but the officer worried that he was reaching for his gun. The officer shot at Castile seven times. The dashcam video shows that before dying, "Castile moaned and said, 'I wasn't reaching for it.'"[89] Charges against the officer were eventually dropped. Nonetheless, it seems unlikely that Castile would have been killed that day had he not been black and thus perceived as exceptionally threatening. Indeed, Castile might not have been pulled over in the first place. The officer had stopped the car because he thought Castile and Reynolds might have been involved in a recent robbery. The officer had called in his plan to pull over the couple: "The driver looks more like one of our suspects, just because of the wide-set nose."[90]

White supremacy shapes who can and cannot exercise their Second Amendment right, who can and cannot exercise their First Amendment right, and indeed, who can and cannot exercise their right to life. As Lunceford explains, "The white male subject has been a prominent figure in open carry actions—for good reason. They are the ones who are able to exercise this right most freely."[91] Carlson points out that "what a gun 'says' is, in part, determined by who is carrying it." And these judgments are informed by a broad "constellation of racial and gendered meanings."[92] While white supremacy allows for white men to be armed in public, it frequently renders armed black men as deadly threats. Lunceford cites an Internet commentator who succinctly highlights this racist double standard: "An angry white man with a gun is a patriot. An angry Muslim man with a gun is a terrorist. An angry black man with a gun is a corpse. Nothing exemplifies the stark racial divide in America like putting a gun in the hands of men of different races."[93] Indeed, white supremacy renders people of color as dangerous even without being armed (e.g., Trayvon Martin). As Dyson puts it, "Living when you might otherwise be dead if you were black or brown is the ultimate form of white privilege."[94]

Who gets perceived as violent—or who becomes violent—is not inevitable. How and why does the ideology of white supremacy work to render people of color as a threat? More broadly, how has the ideology of white supremacy perpetuated racist inequality? And how can we initiate systemic reform designed to reduce gun violence—by and against people of color—and generally improve quality of life without further perpetuating racist inequality? Hinton reminds us that we had a chance to do so in the 1960s, but the war on poverty was soon transformed into a war on crime, which in turn represented a shift in priorities from strengthening the social safety net to letting people languish and then punishing them when they committed crimes in an effort to survive.[95] Policing and prisons—and a general "tough on crime" solution—cannot fully address this problem; indeed, this approach often perpetuates the problem by tearing families apart and creating economic insecurity. People of color have disproportionately suffered as a result of these choices. Addressing the problems of gun violence and racism, then, requires that all Americans see these problems not as "theirs"—whether a specific race or community—but as "ours." The history of racism and gun violence is America's. To change that requires us to focus on the ideology of white supremacy, including how it has unequally distributed psychological and material benefits and burdens.

Conclusion

As the Charleston shooting recedes further into the past, we do not know what the lasting legacy of the shooting will be, if it is remembered at all. It could be reduced to the shooting that led to controversy about the Confederate flag. It could be remembered for the memorial service in which President Obama led the church in singing "Amazing Grace." The passage of time tends to simplify memory, and that is especially true in our increasingly busy times. But public memory is never predetermined or fixed—even when it is etched in stone. So here is a more productive way to remember this tragedy: in 2015, the explicitly racist white male perpetrator purposefully targeted and killed nine black people whom he did not know—Cynthia Marie Graham Hurd, Susie Jackson, Ethel Lee Lance, Depayne Middleton-Doctor, Clementa C. Pinckney, Tywanza Sanders, Daniel Simmons, Sharonda Coleman-Singleton, and Myra Thompson. The point of foregrounding racism in remembering is not to suggest that all gun violence is predominantly about racism or that white and black Americans are fundamentally at odds; it is not, and they are not. Instead, the point is that remembering in this way helps us do what Obama challenged us to do—to "see where we've been blind."[96]

The discussion of racism that followed the Charleston shooting highlights how racism has subtly and not so subtly shaped responses to other tragedies and debates throughout U.S. history. In particular, we can see how the ideology of white supremacy shapes Americans' understanding of and deliberation about gun violence, policy, and possession. This ideology—built up over time from a variety of sources—bears on the gun debate even in moments when race and racism are not explicitly discussed. Operating as an implicit past, the ideology of white supremacy functions as a lens or filter that sorts and distorts interpretation and deliberation as well as perception (including what is seen and heard and what is not).

Further research might examine other implicit pasts, including gender relations. If the question is "Who commits mass shootings?" then gender is a better predictor than race. One estimate from 2015 indicates that white people commit a proportionate number of mass shootings: they make up 63 percent of the U.S. population and commit approximately 64 percent of the mass shootings. What is striking, however, is that mass shooters of all races are almost exclusively men.[97] How come? Why are masculinity and gun violence so tightly linked? By focusing on gender as an implicit past, we can see how norms of masculinity (as well as femininity and nonbinary genders) have worked throughout history, shaping and misshaping how we imagine and discuss gun violence, policy, and possession.[98] For instance, we might ask, How has patriarchy—an ideology of male supremacy, which comes with psychological, emotional, and material consequences—worked to enable and at times even excuse public and domestic violence? We should also ask about the intersection of social categories (such as class, gender, race, and sexual orientation) and the relationship between systems of discrimination (i.e., How do patriarchy and white supremacy work together?).[99]

And we should ask about still other implicit pasts. Thought of in terms of the relationship between public memory and deliberation, the implicit past affirms that any given debate is about far more than what is on the surface. Our initial questions should be these: What is brought to debates about guns—or any other issue? What do we bring as individuals—whether consciously or unconsciously—and what is brought by other rhetors, the news media, indeed our very language? Once we make this implicit past explicit, we will be prepared to examine how such preconceptions shape and misshape how we understand, let alone argue about, gun violence or any other public problem.

5

CONCLUSIONS FOR MOVING BEYOND GRIDLOCK

America does not ask us to be perfect. Precisely because of our individual imperfections, our founders gave us the institutions to guard against tyranny and ensure no one is above the law; a democracy that gives us the space to work through our differences and debate them peacefully, to make things better, even if it doesn't always happen as fast as we'd like. America gives us the capacity to change.

—PRESIDENT OBAMA, JULY 12, 2016

In the year after the Charleston shooting, several mass shootings captured national attention—at least momentarily. On October 1, 2015, nine people were killed at Umpqua Community College in Roseburg, Oregon. On December 2, 2015, fourteen people were killed at a workplace Christmas party in San Bernardino, California. On June 12, 2016, forty-nine people were killed at Pulse, a gay nightclub in Orlando, Florida.[1] On July 7, 2016, five police officers were killed during a protest in Dallas, Texas. This high-profile violence happens against a backdrop of violence that typically does not gain national attention or initiate talk of solutions. Throughout the United States, gun homicides continue at an average of thirty-three per day, and gun suicides continue at an average of fifty-nine per day.[2] And each day, there is an average of 215 nonfatal firearm injuries.[3] We should not forget that behind all these numbers are people, their families, and their communities.

How do we move beyond this routine of violence and inaction? How do we break the gridlock? It depends. On some matters, the majority of Americans agree with one another. Polls have regularly shown that 80–90 percent of Americans support doing background checks of individuals purchasing guns through private sales and at gun shows. Moreover, there is strong support among both Democrats and Republicans. A 2017 poll from the Pew

Research Center showed that 90 percent of Democrat and Democrat-leaning respondents and 77 percent of Republican and Republican-leaning respondents support background checks.[4] Even 77 percent of gun owners support background checks for private sales and at gun shows.[5] Since consensus has been reached on background checks, there is no need for further deliberation or persuasion—just action. Legislators ought to hear the majority of Americans rather than be intimidated by the most vocal gun-rights advocates or special interest groups. For that to happen, the majority of Americans need to make their views known; if their views are continually ignored, then they need to vote accordingly.

Yet other matters are more complicated. Americans disagree about the causes of gun violence. After the 2012 shooting at Sandy Hook Elementary School, for instance, 47 percent of Americans thought that such shootings reflected broader problems in society, whereas 44 percent of Americans thought that they were just isolated acts of troubled individuals.[6] Americans also disagree about the potential solutions to gun violence, including various gun policies. The Pew Research Center's polling offers a snapshot of these divides. A 2017 poll, for instance, showed that 68 percent of Americans support banning assault-style weapons, and 65 percent of Americans support banning high-capacity magazines.[7] Yet there is a partisan divide. Among those who identify as Democrat and Democrat leaning, 80 percent support banning assault-style weapons, and 79 percent support banning high-capacity magazines, whereas among those identifying as Republican or Republican leaning, 54 percent support banning assault-style weapons, and 47 percent support banning high-capacity magazines.[8] On the gun-rights side of things, 46 percent of Americans support allowing concealed carry in more places, and 45 percent of Americans support allowing teachers and officials to carry guns in K–12 schools.[9] But again, there is a partisan divide: allowing concealed carry in more places has 72 percent support from those identifying as Republican and Republican leaning and only 26 percent support from those identifying as Democrat and Democrat leaning.[10]

Given that compromise is so regularly eschewed in America's current political culture, it is hard to imagine Democrats and Republicans working together to address the problem of gun violence. More likely, change will happen at the national level when one of the parties controls the presidency and has a comfortable majority in both the House of Representatives and the Senate. That's often how policy change happens.

But even if such policy change is to come, what will life be like the morning after? Sometimes public support leads and legislation follows, and sometimes legislation leads and public support follows. But at other times, a president signs a bill into law or the Supreme Court renders a ruling, and public opinion remains divided. Despite the civil rights legislation of the 1960s, racism persists. Despite the Supreme Court's 1973 ruling on abortion in *Roe v. Wade*, public opinion about abortion remains divided, with 59 percent of Americans saying abortion should be legal and 37 percent saying it should be illegal.[11] And in the case of the gun debate, neither gun-control advocates nor gun-rights advocates are likely to concede defeat and simply move on if their opponents score a legislative or judicial victory. With actions come reactions—or in some cases, with actions come festering resentment. "In democracies," David Zarefsky reminds us, "there are no final victories."[12] Short-term wins matter. Policy change matters. Such change can have significant consequences, for good or bad. But we also need to think about the long term. We need to find a way to live peacefully with one another. We need to be able to argue and disagree without wishing to destroy one another.

At a memorial service in Dallas, Texas, on July 12, 2016, President Obama spoke about the possibility of change in an age of political gridlock. He puzzled through whether the divides in America could "ever be bridged." He claimed that the inability to communicate across differences has kept Americans from addressing shared problems, including racism and gun violence: "If we cannot talk honestly and openly not just in the comfort of our own circles, but with those who look different than us or bring a different perspective, then we will never break this dangerous cycle." He suggested that for us to have more productive deliberation—and thus better address public problems—we need a "new heart," an "open heart."[13]

By way of concluding, I want to further examine Obama's speech in Dallas. First, I consider the context and content of this speech. Then I use the mixed reception of his speech to reflect on the broader challenges that Americans face in moving beyond gridlock. Drawing together my chapters, I suggest that the concept of public memory—though not sufficient—is necessary to understand and move beyond our age of gridlock.

Obama in Dallas

By the summer of 2016, police across the United States had come under increased scrutiny for using excessive and sometimes deadly force against Americans of color. Two recent events had gained national attention: on

July 5, 2016, Alton Sterling was killed by a police officer in Baton Rouge, Louisiana, and on July 6, 2016, Philando Castile was killed by a police officer in Falcon Heights, a suburb of St. Paul, Minnesota. For some—though not all—Americans, the shootings added further proof of racial injustice and contributed to long-standing mistrust between African American communities and those who police them.

As news of the recent violence spread, people in several cities across the United States went to the streets in solidarity and protest. One such protest was held on July 7 in Dallas, Texas. The protest started out peacefully: "In fact, the police had been part of the protest's planning. Dallas PD even posted photos on their Twitter feeds of their own officers standing among the protestors. Two officers, black and white, smiled next to a man with a sign that read, 'No Justice, No Peace.'" But then, "around nine o'clock, the gunfire came."[14] A gunman shot and killed five police officers. Before police killed the shooter, he told negotiators that he was "upset about recent police shootings" and wanted to "kill white people."[15] The shooter's actions and motives were met with nearly universal condemnation. President Obama responded on July 8 by describing the violence as a "vicious, calculated and despicable attack on law enforcement." Although investigators would search to understand the shooter's motives, Obama insisted, "There is no possible justification for these kinds of attacks or any violence against law enforcement."[16]

On July 12, Obama traveled to Dallas and spoke at a memorial service for the five officers who had been killed. In a sign of unity, he appeared on the stage with First Lady Michelle Obama, former President George W. Bush and First Lady Laura Bush, Vice President Joe Biden and Second Lady Jill Biden, and Dallas Mayor Mike Rawlings and Police Chief David Brown. When it was Obama's turn to speak, he began by eulogizing the five officers: Lorne Ahrens, Michael Krol, Michael Smith, Patrick Zamarripa, and Brent Thompson. But then, in the last quarter of his speech, he also mourned the loss of Alton Sterling and Philando Castile. And rather than limit his comments to the recent violence by police in Baton Rouge and Falcon Heights and against police in Dallas, Obama claimed that this recent violence illustrated broader and persisting problems in the United States. He eulogized the dead and attempted to comfort the families and communities torn apart by this violence, but he also spoke about gun violence, racism, police and policing, and protestors and protesting. He used the occasion to speak about who we are—and who we might become—as Americans. The speech, in short, is a complex balancing act that attempts to address multiple audiences and purposes. As I will explore in the next section, some audiences claimed that

Obama lost his balance. But for now, I want to examine Obama's description of America's problem and his proposed solution.

"Faced with this violence," Obama explained,

> we wonder if the divides of race in America can ever be bridged. We wonder if an African-American community that feels unfairly targeted by police, and police departments that feel unfairly maligned for doing their jobs, can ever understand each other's experience. We turn on the TV or surf the Internet, and we can watch positions harden and lines drawn, and people retreat to their respective corners, and politicians calculate how to grab attention or avoid the fallout. We see all this, and it's hard not to think sometimes that the center won't hold and that things might get worse.

"I understand," he continued. "I understand how Americans are feeling. But Dallas, I'm here to say we must reject such despair. I'm here to insist that we are not as divided as we seem. And I know that because I know America." America, properly understood, "gives us the capacity for change." Our democracy "gives us the space to work through our differences and debate them peacefully, to make things better, even if it doesn't always happen as fast as we'd like."[17]

How, asked Obama, are we to "work through our differences and debate them peacefully?" His claim that "we are not as divided as we seem" suggests that at least some of our divisions are exaggerated, perhaps even illusory. Part of the solution, then, requires us to move beyond binary, either-or thinking. Americans might feel like they need to choose between supporting protestors or police, but that is not necessarily an either-or choice. Obama described Shetamia Taylor, who participated in the Dallas protests and was "shot trying to shield her four sons." Obama revealed that although Taylor participated in the protests, she also admired the police. She thanked the Dallas PD for "being heroes." Meanwhile, "her 12-year old son wants to be a cop when he grows up." Obama also described how "Mayor Rawlings and Chief Brown, a white man and a black man with different backgrounds" had worked together "to unify a city with strength and grace and wisdom."[18] These descriptions challenge either-or thinking by highlighting that it is possible to be black and support the police, to be white and support the protestors, and to be any color and support both the police and the protestors. By rejecting such either-or choices, then, we might better understand the complexity and nuance of the controversies and each other.

Yet the violence in Dallas, Falcon Heights, and Baton Rouge demonstrates that our divisions—whether illusory, real, or a bit of both—can have devastating consequences. Obama claimed that to address these divisions, Americans needed to have a new and an open heart: "I am reminded of what the Lord tells Ezekiel: I will give you a new heart, the Lord says, and put a new spirit in you. I will remove from you your heart of stone and give you a heart of flesh." This new heart requires us to be "open to the fears and hopes and challenges of our fellow citizens." It can help us "abandon the overheated rhetoric and the oversimplification that reduces whole categories of our fellow Americans not just to opponents, but to enemies."[19] At its best, an open heart can help us build empathy, understanding, and common ground.

Reflecting on the many eulogies he delivered over the course of his presidency, Obama acknowledged, "I've seen how inadequate words can be in bringing about lasting change. I've seen how inadequate my own words have been." The pressing question was whether the American people would be willing to open their hearts to one another and to keep them open: "Can we find the character, as Americans, to open our hearts to each other? Can we see in each other a common humanity and a shared dignity, and recognize how our different experiences have shaped us?"[20] An open heart requires that we attempt to understand others' perspectives, including how their different experiences and values have shaped their worldviews. Obama admits that this is difficult work and, in some situations, impossible. But he insists that we must try.

He describes the "open heart" as a mode of engaging with others: "Because with an open heart, we can learn to stand in each other's shoes and look at the world through each other's eyes, so that maybe the police officer sees his own son in that teenager with a hoodie who's kind of goofing off but not dangerous—and the teenager—maybe the teenager will see in the police officer the same words and values and authority of his parents." After explaining this mode of engagement, Obama attempts to enact it by voicing and contextualizing the experiences of African Americans and police. He describes the "centuries of racial discrimination" and the fact that "bias remains":

> When African Americans from all walks of life, from different communities across the country, voice a growing despair over what they perceive to be unequal treatment; when study after study shows that whites and people of color experience the criminal justice system differently, so that if you're black you're more likely to be pulled over or searched or arrested, more likely to get longer sentences, more

> likely to get the death penalty for the same crime; when mothers and fathers raise their kids right and have "the talk" about how to respond if stopped by a police officer—"yes, sir," "no, sir"—but still fear that something terrible may happen when their child walks out the door, still fear that kids being stupid and not quite doing things right might end in tragedy—when all this takes place 50 years after the passage of the Civil Rights Act, we cannot simply turn away and dismiss those in peaceful protest as troublemakers or paranoid. We can't simply dismiss it as a symptom of political correctness or reverse racism. To have your experience denied like that, dismissed by those in authority, dismissed perhaps even by your white friends and coworkers and fellow church members again and again and again—it hurts.

Then, contextualizing the experiences of police, Obama suggests that "so much of the tensions between police departments and minority communities that they serve is because we ask the police to do too much and we ask too little of ourselves." Police are told, "You're a social worker, you're the parent, you're the teacher, you're the drug counselor." We tell them to "keep those neighborhoods in check at all costs, and do so without causing any political blowback or inconvenience. Don't make a mistake that might disturb our own peace of mind. And then we feign surprise when, periodically, the tensions boil over."[21]

By voicing and contextualizing the experiences of African Americans and police, Obama attempts to build empathy and understanding between these two groups, as well as between audience members who align with each group. In my judgment, his goal is not to take sides and declare a winner. Instead, the goal is to explain why people disagree with and distrust one another. He is suggesting that an open heart is crucial for countering gridlock and addressing the problems that confront us all. And while this mode of engagement requires us to be open and generous—at least momentarily—it does not require that we feign neutrality or embrace relativism. Obama makes judgments, and these judgments acknowledge the limits of understanding and respect. For example, he critiques the excesses of some protestors, noting that when anyone characterizes "all police as biased or bigoted, we undermine those officers we depend on for our safety." He also critiques those who fail to acknowledge that racial bias and discrimination remain: "Although most of us do our best to guard against it and teach our children better, none of us is entirely innocent. No institution is entirely immune. That includes our police departments."[22]

One risk of Obama's call for an open heart is that it can localize blame by suggesting that change must come from individual action rather than collective action and structural reform.[23] Although he suggests that individual acts are necessary for reworking social norms, he also acknowledges that violence and racism are multifaceted and systemic problems that require multifaceted and systemic solutions. For instance, he laments that many communities are being flooded with guns, though he also acknowledges that guns alone are not responsible for gun violence. He acknowledges the need for "decent schools," "drug treatment and mental health programs," and "gainful employment."[24] Ultimately, he suggests that an open heart can thus complement and perhaps even function as a prerequisite for such systemic change.

Another risk of Obama's call for an open heart is that it assumes shared responsibility. But the responsibility to practice an open heart has historically fallen to marginalized people. Those with power have been able to safely ignore those without power. Obama acknowledges that "some suffer far more under racism's burden, some feel to a far greater extent discrimination's sting."[25] Yet he does not explore the implications of this inequity for practicing an open heart. In some situations, asking those who have suffered to empathize with their oppressors might be unfair, even cruel. To be clear, all of us might benefit from an open heart, whether we are deliberating racism, gun violence, or any other public problem. Yet being "open to the fears and hopes and challenges of our fellow citizens" is an obligation that is especially urgent for those who have historically evaded it.

The Challenges for Moving Beyond Gridlock

Many opinion writers and television commentators praised Obama for his speech in Dallas, calling him "a consoler-in-chief" and suggesting that he worked to help Americans bridge their divides. Mike Barnacle wrote an article titled "In Dallas, Our President Meets the Moment."[26] On MSNBC's *Morning Joe*, panelist Mike Lupica called it "the speech of President Obama's life," noting that—at least briefly—"this was not the country that really does seem to be as divided as it has ever been." Host Joe Scarborough likened Obama to President Kennedy and suggested that Obama's speech in Dallas was in the same league as President Reagan's 1986 *Challenger* address. Panelist Joshua DuBois said that Obama was essentially advocating an "empathy revolution," redrawing "the lines of civic discourse" and inviting Americans to join him in the "process of American renewal."[27]

But not everyone reacted so favorably to Obama's speech in Dallas. Responding to a video of Obama's speech on YouTube, some commenters objected that Obama violated a sense of decorum: "Great speech until he used it for things other than honoring these fallen officers." Another commenter argued, "This was a memorial of 5 murdered police officers." It was "no place for a speech calling out bad cops. Do that somewhere else." Commenters further suggested that, irrespective of timing, police were wrongly being blamed and that Sterling, Castile, and protestors were wrongly being praised. One commenter referred to Castile and Sterling as "two thugs." Another asked, "Why is he making a memorial for criminals?" Another suggested that rather than blaming cops, "Obama should be preaching for perpetrators to stop resisting arrest." "The man is a divider," another commenter claimed. "He definitely called out the cops but made excuses for the BLM [Black Lives Matter] movement over and over." Commenters also repeatedly claimed that Obama was racist, implying that the very act of talking about racism is racist. Obama was a "divisive race baiter." Another commenter alleged that Obama "throws gas on the race tensions." Others alleged that Obama was exploiting tragedy as an excuse to take away guns: "Is this a memorial or a ploy for gun control!?" Another claimed that Obama "never loses a chance to push gun control." And another asserted that "this p.o.s. wants to take our guns so bad he can't stand it."[28]

Hosts and commentators on Fox News also voiced several objections to Obama's speech. Some claimed that Obama was wrongly "political." For instance, George W. Bush's former White House press secretary, Dana Perino, praised Bush's speech in Dallas by claiming that it just focuses on the violence against police—unlike Obama's speech.[29] Across several Fox News programs, commentators regularly claimed that racial tensions were worse under President Obama (a claim that seems to assume that talking about racism causes racial tensions and, moreover, that Obama is the cause of such racial tensions). On Sean Hannity's program, Milwaukee County Sheriff David Clarke proclaimed that "this has been, in my 38 years in law enforcement, the most anti-police president I have ever seen."[30] Hannity attempted to build a case that Obama is antipolice by repeating comments that Obama has made about police, including Obama's 2009 statement that police "acted stupidly" when they arrested Henry Louis Gates Jr.—a black Harvard University professor—for trying to break into his own home. Moreover, Hannity alleged that Obama had been courting BLM members by inviting them to the White House. Offering a straw-person argument, Hannity showed video footage of some BLM members calling for dead cops, implying that these members were representative of the movement and Obama's views. Hannity implied that the choice is either-or: by siding with such radical protestors, Obama—and those who side with him—clearly hate police.

Almost no one would claim that the comments section of YouTube or that cable news represents the highest quality of public discourse that America offers. But such reactions, even in their exaggerated form, illustrate several challenges for moving beyond gridlock. Although these reactions reinforce Obama's call for an open heart—since many did not seem to listen with the kind of openness he recommended—these reactions also highlight that listening with an open heart can be far more difficult than Obama suggests. The negative reactions suggest that some people benefit from *not* listening. Yet even for those who are well intentioned, there are several factors that make communicating with an open heart difficult.

To be clear, there are legitimate reasons for disagreeing with Obama's speech; just because he says that we need to listen to one another does not mean that his analysis about race relations, for instance, is correct or that people lose their right to disagree. What's peculiar about the negative reactions, however, is that Obama's arguments in the speech almost seem irrelevant. And while this problem seems exaggerated in the case of Obama, it is not distinct to him. These negative reactions invite us to reflect further on what might be called *partisan reception*—how an "us versus them" mentality shapes the ways that audiences encounter, interpret, and understand an argument, event, issue, text, and so on. Put simply, not all audiences heard Obama's speech in the same way. Trying to understand partisan reception can provide insight about the broader challenges for listening to—let alone deliberating with—one another.

Since at least the time of Michael McGee's work in the 1980s, rhetorical scholars have recognized that speeches circulate and are often received as fragments rather than as whole objects.[31] For instance, we might see a clip on YouTube or the news, overhear a line on the radio or television as we move about our day, or see a quote pulled out and shared on Facebook or Twitter. Commentators preface, explain, and repurpose these fragments to achieve their own goals. Moreover, whether the received text is an entire speech or just a fragment, audiences also play a role in the process of meaning making. Reception scholars—including scholars who are trained in hermeneutics, literary criticism, media studies, rhetoric, and so on—have pointed out that audiences do not always encounter, let alone interpret, a text in the way that its creator might have intended or imagined. Individually and collectively, audiences bring their own moods, understandings, and goals to their act of interpretation. Even Aristotle observed that "our judgments when we are pleased and friendly are not the same as when we are pained and hostile."[32]

Many factors influence how individuals encounter, interpret, and understand a text, such as their own sense of identity, including their party affiliation. Identity, of course, is not destiny. But in general, an audience of Democrats is more likely to agree with and defend a speech by a Democrat than one by a Republican, whereas an audience of Republicans is more likely to agree with and defend a speech by a Republican than one by a Democrat. This is not only because the content of the speech is more likely to reflect one's beliefs. Even if we disagree with the content of a speech, we are more likely to excuse a speaker who is on our own side because we perceive the speaker as like or unlike ourselves—he or she is one of "us." And we are more likely to focus on the faults of the speaker who is not on our side because we do not perceive the speaker as being like ourselves—he or she is one of "them." At times, the best policy becomes the one that reaffirms our identity and gives "us" power—or that denies "them" power. Even agreement about policy can become less important than making sure "we" win and "they" lose.[33] Whether we refer to this mentality as the rhetorics of identification and division,[34] in-group and out-group identities,[35] tribalism,[36] or something else, the same challenge remains: if identity is at least as important as reasoned arguments—or if identity skews what we understand to be good arguments—then how do we deliberate with those who are unlike ourselves? How do we talk—and listen—across our divides? And how do we honor our differences without letting these divisions become destructive?

Partisanship is nothing new in American life. Yet the Pew Research Center reported that as of October 2017, the "gap between the political values of Democrats and Republicans is now larger than at any point in Pew Research Center surveys dating back to 1994, a continuation of a steep increase in the ideological divisions between the two parties over more than a decade." This problem extends beyond the gun debate. For example, Republicans and Democrats responded to the following prompts:

- "Blacks who can't get ahead in this country are mostly responsible for their own condition." In 1994, 66 percent of Republicans and

53 percent of Democrats agreed with this statement (a gap of 13 percent). But in 2017, 75 percent of Republicans and 28 percent of Democrats agreed with the statement (a gap of 47 percent).

- "The best way to ensure peace is through military strength." In 1994, 44 percent of Republicans and 28 percent of Democrats agreed with this statement (a gap of 16 percent). But in 2017, 53 percent of Republicans and 13 percent of Democrats agreed with this statement (a gap of 40 percent).
- And to take just one more example, "Stricter environmental laws and regulations cost too many jobs and hurt the economy." In 1994, 39 percent of Republicans and 29 percent of Democrats agreed with this statement (a gap of 10 percent). But in 2017, 58 percent of Republicans and 20 percent of Democrats agreed with this statement (a gap of 38 percent).[37]

The report concludes, "Across 10 political values Pew Research Center has tracked since 1994, there is now an average 36-percentage-point gap between Republicans and Republican-leaning independents and Democrats and Democratic leaners. In 1994, it was only 15 points."[38]

Partisanship, like disagreement more generally, is not inherently bad. At times, political polarization can signal that one side is right and the other side is wrong. In such cases, rather than decry the lack of common ground, we should decry the failure of one side (and celebrate their opponents). At other times, partisanship can be a sign that democracy is healthy—that people are engaged in public life and committed to addressing problems. Citizens and leaders might disagree not simply because they are being cantankerous or because one side is right and the other is wrong but because they are seeking to address urgent and difficult problems.

Yet extreme and broad partisanship should give us pause. We know, for instance, that cooperation and persuasion require at least some common ground. Without shared beliefs, facts, narratives, and values, we have little basis to trust our political opponents, let alone work with them to address public problems. Indeed, as the partisan divide widens, we are less capable of even agreeing on what is a shared problem.

Scholars and opinion leaders point to a variety of factors to help explain America's growing partisan divide. They help us see that listening is not simply a matter of individual will; there are structural forces that enable and constrain our ability to listen to some facts, people, and narratives but not others. Some commentators point to America's political system, which rewards politicians for amplifying disagreements by disparaging compromise and demonizing their opponents.[39] Partisan gerrymandering, for instance, undermines democracy by dividing up districts so that a candidate needs to speak only to Republicans or Democrats, not both. Meanwhile, campaign finance laws allow billionaires and special interest groups to skew elections by spending millions of dollars to sustain candidates who share their vision and to sink those who do not. Others point to the decline of civic institutions and activities that bring diverse groups of people together,[40] as well as to the clustering of Americans so that regions, cities, and workplaces are populated by the like-minded.[41] Still others note that our news media and social media profit from conflict and drama. And while conflict and drama can make good entertainment, it can also tear us apart. The labels "echo chamber,"[42] "filter bubble,"[43] and "social media bubble"[44] highlight that technological advances provide a steady stream of information and stories that reinforce our worldviews but ignore or disparage information and stories that do not. Paradoxically, our technological advances have enabled us to connect with people throughout the world but have also made it possible to feel like those who disagree with us live on an entirely different planet.

The challenges for moving beyond gridlock are much bigger than what any single book or individual could hope to resolve. The scope and complexity of the problem can feel overwhelming. We should not deny those feelings or pretend that the solutions are simple or easy. At the same time, however, we should not let the problem's scope and complexity paralyze us. We must persist in the best ways that our knowledge and abilities allow.

Memory and Gridlocked Deliberation

Throughout the preceding chapters, I have drawn attention to the concept of public memory, arguing that it plays a central, though often unrecognized, role in public deliberation. Even though memory alone cannot fix our gridlocked debates, it is nonetheless a necessary component. By recognizing memory as both a resource and a constraint, we can better appreciate the rhetorical complexity of our deliberations and our interlocutors. Focusing on the interplay between memory and deliberation can help us become better listeners and understand why listening is so difficult, practice empathy and build trust, identify opportunities for rhetorical invention and intervention,[45] and, above all, break the cycle of dysfunctional deliberation and identify ways to honestly address public problems such as gun violence.

As scholars, as educators, and as rhetors, we might work to become more attuned to the relationships between memory and deliberation, including the three relationships that I have theorized in the previous chapters. First, examining the weight of the past (chapter 2) shows us how arguments and values accrue meaning and significance over time. This can be especially problematic when such meaning and significance are not shared in common, as is the case with the Second Amendment. By identifying the weight of the past, we can recognize that meaning and significance are not natural but are human creations; thus, we can begin to examine how a particular argument or value is imbued with meaning and significance. Second, examining the fleeting past (chapter 3) shows us how inattention and forgetting (whether willful or not) shape public deliberation. By recognizing the fleeting past, we can begin to assess the structural and rhetorical forces that sustain inattention and forgetting, as well as the changes that might help circumvent them. And third, examining the implicit past (chapter 4) shows us that deliberation can be difficult because unchecked assumptions shape what we do and do not see, say, and hear when interpreting and deliberating gun violence. By recognizing the implicit past, we can begin to make implicit assumptions explicit and thus deliberate more openly and purposefully.

Scholars might further analyze, theorize, and refine these three common relationships—the weight of the past, the fleeting past, and the implicit past—and identify additional relationships between public memory and public deliberation. The thematic histories I have discussed here focused on the Second Amendment, our obligations to the dead, and racism because these three topics seem most pertinent for understanding deliberation about gun violence and gun policy. But these three topics are by no means exhaustive. Scholars might examine other topics central to the gun debate (e.g., masculinity)—as well as topics central to other public debates—in order to further account for the relationship between public memory and public deliberation.

At times, however, it makes sense to proceed more informally. To help scholars, educators, and rhetors become more attuned to the relationships between memory and deliberation, I recommend four basic practices: practice openness with others, isolate the point of disagreement, search for the unstated, and adopt a historical perspective. These practices, in turn, can help us articulate and understand our disagreements, thus serving as a necessary first step for moving beyond gridlock.[46]

Practice Openness with Others

Openness entails "the willingness to engage in communication, the willingness to listen to opposing views, and, if they are persuasive, the willingness to be changed by them."[47] Openness, of course, is not automatically good (nor is closure automatically bad). Choosing not to listen to others might be strategically and even ethically justified in specific situations. Especially in face-to-face encounters, openness can "demand a kind of vulnerability that is not always possible or advisable for all people in all situations."[48] Moreover, we cannot listen indefinitely; at some point, we need to decide and act. We should not be expected to have infinite patience, especially with those who are arguing in bad faith or those whom we have listened to but judged as malicious. Nonetheless, openness offers several potential benefits. Chiefly, it can help us rehumanize others and build trust. We should not hide disagreements. Nor should our goal necessarily be to resolve them. Instead, we need to find ways to live together peacefully, even with our differences. *E pluribus unum*—out of many, one. Or as Danielle Allen puts it, out of many, a whole. We are together, with our differences.[49]

Whether conversing face-to-face with strangers or friends, communicating online, or analyzing public texts, we can practice openness. Peter Elbow's description of the "doubting game" and "believing game" illustrates what openness looks like in practice. Elbow claims that we are relatively skilled in the doubting game—at finding faults in an argument or an arguer. By contrast, we are less skilled in the believing game—giving an argument and arguer a fair hearing by trying to "get inside the head of someone who saw things this way."[50] When we are confronted with ideas or practices that seem unfamiliar or indefensible, the believing game urges us to ask (at least momentarily), Why might someone believe this? What experiences or concerns might lead someone to accept this belief as reasonable? We can find answers through research and reflection—or by actually engaging with others who think differently than we do. Elbow insists that we need both modes of engagement: If we only practice the believing game, then we are likely to be duped by anyone into believing anything. Yet if we only practice the doubting game, then we will never learn or change our minds. While both modes of engagement are valuable, we need more practice and skill in the believing game.

While openness with others might lead to persuasion, it also might simply teach us why persuasion is often gradual and difficult. As I have traced throughout these chapters, debates about gun violence and gun policy are regularly intertwined with our own senses of identity—about who "I" and "we" are and how "I" and "we" are different from "you" or "they."[51] Given the importance of identity, it is no wonder that what "we" consider as strong evidence and sound reasoning might fall on unreceptive ears and vice versa. To see oneself as a supporter of gun control or gun rights can be a deep commitment linked to narratives, values, practices, and affiliations (e.g., to a political party, family, friends, or coworkers). To ask individuals to change their minds, then, can mean asking them to change their senses of self. It is a great deal to ask, especially when the stakes are perceived to be so high. It requires generosity and humility (and as I will explore later, critical reflection on how such links have been exaggerated).

Ultimately, we might conclude that others are wrong, perhaps even dangerous. But practicing openness requires that we give others a chance—even if their experiences and beliefs are not the same as our own. Doing so can help us understand others' worldview (and help them understand our worldview), including how different lived experiences, values, and narratives inform and justify that worldview.

Isolate the Point of Disagreement

A spirit of openness encourages us to try to isolate the point of disagreement. For instance, the term *gun control* is slippery: some gun-rights advocates interpret gun control to mean a ban and confiscation of all guns, whereas most gun-control advocates interpret it to mean instituting relatively modest measures such as universal background checks. Purported gun-control advocates and gun-rights advocates might argue past one another—even though they share the belief that a total ban goes too far and that modest restrictions make sense. In other words, when people claim to disagree about gun control, it might help to ask which policies they actually disagree about.

And when arguing about gun policy and gun violence, it might help to identify the type of claims being made. Stasis theory teaches us that trying to persuade others about proposals to prevent gun violence (i.e., "What should we do about this?") is especially difficult when interlocutors do not agree about presupposed questions, such as the stasis of cause (i.e., "How did this come to happen?"), definition (i.e., "What should we call it?"), or in some cases, fact (i.e., "Does a shared reality exist?").[52] When engaging with others who have different views—whether to persuade them or to learn from them—we might benefit from starting with basic questions to establish common ground (e.g., Can we at least agree that gun violence happens frequently and that it's a problem worth our attention and action?). From there, we can collaboratively work toward more advanced questions to discover the point at which we start to disagree; if we disagree at the stasis of cause, for instance, we should pause there. Why do we disagree? Can we resolve our disagreement—or at least better understand it? If so, how? If not, can we still find proposals that address our divergent understanding of the cause? The stasis questions can help us get out of our argumentative ruts.

But the spirit of openness does not oblige us to waste our time with those who argue in bad faith. To argue in "good faith" means "debating and discussing controversial issues in a spirit of mutual respect, with a commitment to telling the truth, backing up arguments with sound reasoning and evidence, and remaining open to changing one's mind."[53] When others are not interested in deliberating in good faith, then we are justified in not bothering to engage with them; similarly, if we are not interested in deliberating in good faith, then others are justified in not bothering to engage with us.

We should be cautious of those who seem to present reasonable arguments or who appeal to values like openness yet do so for the sake of either closing down or needlessly extending a debate. In discussing "manufactured" scientific controversy, Leah Ceccarelli highlights how unscrupulous rhetors can shift the conversation to previous stases to muddle the debate, using this manufactured complexity to justify inaction on an issue. For example, climate-change deniers suggest that there is disagreement about whether climate change is happening (the stasis of fact)—even though there is scientific consensus—in order to derail conversations about how to address that issue (the stasis of proposal/policy).[54]

Applying Ceccarelli's insight, we can similarly critique those who attempt to derail conversations about potential solutions to gun violence by shifting from the stasis of policy to the stasis of cause (e.g., using the causal complexity of gun violence to justify continued inaction)—or in one of the most egregious examples, conspiracy theorists who allege that the Sandy Hook Elementary School shooting was a hoax attempt to shift the debate from questions of policy to more basic questions of fact. Engaging on their terms can be a rhetorical trap. Ceccarelli urges us to guard against those who would exploit our open-mindedness, using our willingness to hear the "other side" as a weapon against us. Sometimes there is not an "other side" worthy of debate or attention.[55]

Search for the Unstated

Since at least when Aristotle described the enthymeme, those who study rhetoric have recognized that human communication depends on the unstated. In the vocabulary of argumentation scholars, the unstated often functions as a warrant to bolster or justify particular conclusions. Those conclusions might seem obvious to those who share a warrant but irrational or incomprehensible to those who do not. However, by making these assumptions explicit—by stating the unstated—we make them available for shared understanding and scrutiny. Doing so can improve communication and serve as a check on our own reasoning.[56]

Rhetorical education—particularly courses in rhetorical theory and rhetorical criticism—offers formalized training in analyzing and assessing rhetoric, including what is stated and unstated. Less formally, however, we might get into the habit of periodically pausing when interpreting and deliberating to reflect on what is absent, unstated, or implied. What assumptions are our interlocutors making? What assumptions are we making? Are these assumptions justified? What experiences, evidence, stories, beliefs, fears, and so on might lead someone to accept or reject these assumptions?

By recognizing that the arguments we make and hear rely on memory, we can better identify the experiences, values, and narratives that are brought to particular debates—and in turn, identify whether these are shared in common. Moreover, we can see more clearly how the debate over gun policy, for instance, has become about far more than guns. We can untangle each other's reasoning to see the connections that have been made and taken for granted. And in some cases, we may wish to decouple positions from values or narratives by showing, for instance, that the link between an individual's view on guns and sense of patriotism is human-made, not inevitable.

Furthermore, Krista Ratcliffe's account of rhetorical listening points out that we must do more than just analyze claims, whether stated or not; we must also examine cultural logics. As she explains, "If a claim is an assertion of a person's thinking, then a cultural logic is a belief system or shared way of reasoning within which a claim may function."[57] In chapter 4, for instance, I examined the cultural logic of white supremacy and its influence on how we interpret and deliberate about gun violence and gun policy. But we might consider how other cultural logics—say, that of individual responsibility—function as shared ways of reasoning, which make specific claims seem natural or obvious to some groups but not others.

Adopt a Historical Perspective

Adopting a historical perspective requires us to pause and consider the larger context of a particular event or argument. As I have suggested throughout, the accelerating speed of our news cycle means that Americans regularly bounce from one breaking news story to the next. We are placed in a perpetual now, with little time or space for reflecting or placing events in their broader context. Since our ways of seeing and communicating typically have a history, a historical perspective can remind us of what has come prior. Moreover, a historical perspective can help us see how others—and we ourselves—use and are used by the language and habits that we have inherited.

Writing and studying history are two modes of adopting a historical perspective and thus of making and remaking public memory. In the spirit of Obama's claim that history can offer a "roadway toward a better world,"[58] this book has begun to answer the call that Hogan and I made for rhetorical scholars to craft a rhetorical history of the gun debate. There are, of course, more rhetorical histories to be written of the gun debate and other public debates. Such rhetorical histories can further illuminate how arguments develop or fail to develop across time. Scholars in rhetoric and other disciplines can benefit from studying "key players, important policy texts, and transformative moments in debates over guns and gun control policies,"[59] but it is also instructive to examine the failures, absences, and exclusions.

But adopting a historical perspective does not have to be a formalized process. There is value in simply pausing to ask, What is the broader context of this event or argument? What historical forces led to this current predicament? What memories do various actions and arguments depend on? What has been forgotten, and who benefits from such forgetting? What changes need to be made to create a better future?

Of course, the appeal to history is never neutral. Nor does it always provide easy answers. We can choose different moments in time: a gun-rights advocate might point to Nazi Germany to claim that gun control leads to confiscation and eventual tyranny; a gun-control advocate can point to gun-control measures in England and Australia in the mid-1990s that radically reduced the level of gun violence without leading to tyranny. Moreover, we can draw different lessons from the same moment in history (e.g., the conflicting lessons drawn from the shooting at Columbine). Nonetheless, a historical perspective at least gives us the potential to see beyond our current moment. And by placing events and arguments in their broader context, we can better understand the interplay of public deliberation and public memory.

These four practices—practicing openness with others, isolating the point of disagreement, searching for the unstated, and adopting a historical perspective—can be of value to scholars who teach and study deliberation about public problems, as well as to those who are directly engaged in public deliberation.

Beyond Gridlock

The cycle of violence and inaction at the national level has been imprinted on our consciousness. It has been made to seem unsurprising. Since little has changed, we assume that nothing will. We assume that the past predicts the future—or worse, that the cycle of violence and inaction is inescapable. Recall again Obama's September 22, 2013, speech at a memorial service for the victims of the Navy Yard shooting: "Sometimes I fear there's a creeping resignation that these tragedies are just somehow the way it is, that this is somehow the new normal."[60] This narrative of violence and inaction has been built across time. It resides in public memory, available for us to reuse whenever we hear of gun violence. Many Americans feel the truth of this narrative in their bones.

We need to challenge the gridlock narrative and offer an alternative in its place. I am not suggesting that gridlock is imaginary, without any basis in reality. Nor am I denying that there are structural forces that sustain gridlock. There are. My point, quite simply, is that gridlock is not inevitable. We are not bound to this cycle of violence and inaction; we need not be forever cursed with the problem of gun violence and our futility to address it. "Wisdom," Obama explained, "comes through the recognition that tragedies such as this are not inevitable, and that we possess the ability to act and to change."[61] To address this problem of gun violence—or other urgent public problems that we face—requires enormous work for all Americans. But perhaps our first and most urgent task is to affirm that, yes, change is possible.

The concept of public memory can help us move beyond gridlock. By looking and listening for memory, we can better understand how shared and unshared histories are brought to bear on any particular debate. And by acknowledging that our debates are often about far more than what is on the surface, we can more fully appreciate the rhetorical complexity of these debates and our interlocutors. Given the stakes of the gun debate, there are moments to be angry and insistent, yet there are also moments to be humble, curious, and generous. Acknowledging that we are always after gun violence requires us to recognize that we inherit language and habits; these influence what we see, hear, say, and feel—as well as what we do not. The world is not entirely of our own making, but that does not mean that we are powerless. The language and habits that we inherit are not the ones that we must perpetuate. Rather than reacting to gun violence with the same old scripts, we might identify and enact different ways of perceiving, feeling, interpreting, thinking, talking, and acting. Rather than recycle clichés for or against particular policies, we might identify and enact different ways of perceiving, feeling, interpreting, thinking, talking, and acting. Things can be otherwise.

EPILOGUE

Throughout the process of writing this book, I have had to accept that a project like this will in some sense always be out of date. The prevalence of gun violence and the relative slowness of scholarly publishing necessitate this unfortunate fact. Since the 2016 Dallas shooting, gun violence has of course continued, and several more mass shootings have captured national attention. On October 1, 2017, a gunman killed 58 people and injured 546 who were attending a music festival on the Las Vegas strip. On November 5, 2017, a gunman killed 26 people (including an unborn child) during a Sunday morning church service in Sutherland Springs, Texas. On February 14, 2018, a gunman killed 17 people at Marjory Stoneman Douglass High School in Parkland, Florida. And by the time you read these words, the list will probably need to be updated. I hope I am wrong.

When it comes to the routine of violence and inaction, I hope that this book feels ancient to you. I hope that it seems like a relic of a bygone era that America has moved beyond. By the time you read this, I hope that gun violence has decreased and is no longer a significant problem. And I hope that gun-control advocates and gun-rights advocates have found common ground and can talk with rather than just past one another. For that to happen, however, we must change how we talk and act in response to gun violence.

Catastrophe, according to its Greek origins, means "overturning."[1] When life has been overturned by gun violence, it is common to assert order, virtue, and hope by saying, in effect, This awful thing happened, but people demonstrated heroism in response to it. Some public officials and reporters even imply that the communities directly affected by this recent violence in Nevada, Texas, and Florida will become stronger as a result. Maybe that's true. But maybe not. In any case, innocent people were injured and killed. We should not forget that or move past it so quickly. The rush to optimism seems especially callous when mass shootings happen again and again. The pivot to goodness, while understandable, feels awfully quick. At some point, if we're being honest, those of us who have not been directly impacted by gun violence need to acknowledge the brutality of what happened and dwell with the horror (yet at the same time, not become paralyzed by grief or fear).

If there is any hope of interrupting the cycle of violence and inaction, we need to find the courage, strength, and resolve to not move on so quickly.

We also regularly affirm order by separating ourselves entirely from the shooter: he is wholly evil, and we are wholly good; he is wholly guilty, and we are wholly innocent. To an extent, this separation makes sense. Clearly, the shooter is to blame: he undertook such violence; none of us did. Given the magnitude, meanness, and sheer stupidity of his violence, blame and anger toward him seem wholly warranted. But this clear separation also risks oversimplifying matters and distorting how we understand the problem of gun violence. The shooter came from "us"—indeed, before he undertook his violence, he was one of "us." And he is not the first mass shooter. The fact that such violence happens again and again suggests that all might not be well with "us." Recall again that the frequency of mass shootings[2] and gun homicides[3] is a uniquely American problem. What distinguishes the United States from other high-income countries? Researchers point out that the United States has "more guns and weaker gun laws."[4] Even those who dispute that answer ought to at least dwell with the question. Put differently, what is it about American life that enables—and perhaps even encourages—such violence by this shooter and others? And why have we repeatedly decided as a country—and perhaps individually too—that it is acceptable to do little or nothing in the face of such violence? As a country, we need to find ways to recognize that the responsibility for gun violence is not limited only to "him" (although he is still to blame). Nor does America's failure to address gun violence rest solely with "them" (although they may be partially to blame). The cycle of gun violence and inaction is not just someone else's problem. It is America's problem. The problem is ours. And it waits for us to claim it as our own.

I am writing this epilogue six weeks after the Parkland shooting. The shooting is still in the news, which is unusual. It will take much longer to see and assess the long-term impacts of this shooting and the responses to it, but there have already been some notable shifts in public talk and action. Florida leaders have made modest—and imperfect—changes to their state gun laws.[5] Several companies previously offering benefits to NRA members felt pressure to cut ties with the NRA.[6] And several retail chains—including Dick's Sporting Goods, Kroger, and Walmart—have elected to raise the age for purchasing firearms in their stores from eighteen to twenty-one. These shifts in state politics and the private sector have come in part from the work of grassroots activists in Parkland and throughout the United States. More broadly, the activism movement that has developed—especially among students—reveals a fundamental frustration with the cycle of violence and inaction coupled with the insistence that change is both possible and necessary.

Just three days after the shooting, Emma González, a senior who survived the school shooting in Parkland, delivered an impassioned speech that went viral. González argued, in short, that America needed to reform its gun laws. In making her case for change, she illustrated how memory serves as both a rhetorical constraint and a resource. Looking to the past, she stated, "Since the time of the Founding Fathers and since they added the Second Amendment to the Constitution, our guns have developed at a rate that leaves me dizzy. The guns have changed and the laws have not." Looking to the present, she stated, "Every single person up here today, all these people should be home grieving. But instead we are up here standing together because if all our government and President can do is send thoughts and prayers, then it's time for victims to be the change that we need to see." And looking to the future, she stated, "We are going to be the kids that you read about in textbooks. Not because we're going to be another statistic about mass shootings in America, but because, just as David said, we are going to be the last mass shooting."[7]

She concluded her speech with irreverence, for which she was later criticized. But it was an irreverence earned through the shock and grief of having endured a mass shooting and through the accumulated frustration of having grown up in a world where mass shootings and inaction are accepted as normal. Born in 2000, González has forever lived in a post-Columbine world. Her irreverence attempted to unsettle habituated ways of thinking, arguing, and acting: "Politicians who sit in their gilded House and Senate seats funded by the NRA telling us nothing could have ever been done to prevent this, we call BS. They say that tougher guns laws do not decrease gun violence. We call BS. They say a good guy with a gun stops a bad guy with a gun. We call BS. They say guns are just tools like knives and are as dangerous as cars. We call BS. They say no laws could have prevented the hundreds of senseless tragedies that have occurred. We call BS." She then concluded her speech with a call to action: "If you agree, register to vote. Contact your local congresspeople. Give them a piece of your mind."[8]

Although González has become a leading voice in what appears to be a growing movement, other students from her school have been active as well. Several students have appeared on television, including a CNN Town Hall Forum, where students questioned Florida Senator Marco Rubio and NRA spokesperson Dana Loesch. More broadly, students from Parkland

and throughout the United States have organized online with the Twitter hashtag #NeverAgain. They organized a national school walkout for March 14, 2018, to protest gun violence. And they organized the March for Our Lives in Washington, DC, and in cities throughout the United States and the world. In anticipation of the march, the website stated, "On March 24, the kids and families of March For Our Lives will take to the streets of Washington DC to demand that their lives and safety become a priority and that we end gun violence and mass shootings in our schools today."[9]

Their efforts have been met with resistance. In response to the planned national school walkout, a countermovement emerged online, organized by the hashtag #WalkUpNotOut. A viral Facebook post from a "Maryland youth minister and mom" helped spark this movement:

> Instead of walking out of school on March 14, encourage students to walk up—walk up to the kid who sits a lone [*sic*] at lunch and invite him to sit with your group; walk up to the kid who sits quietly in the corner of the room and sit next to her, smile, and say Hi; walk up to the kid who causes disturbances in class and ask what he is doing; walk up to your teachers and thank them; walk up to someone who has different views than you and get to know them—you may be surprised at how much you have in common.

On its face, there is nothing wrong with calling for kindness, and Parkland student David Hogg, among others, highlighted that it is possible to "#walkoutandwalkup."[10] Critics pointed out that the message of #WalkUpNotOut seems to engage in victim blaming by implying that the Parkland shooter would not have done what he did if students had just been nice to him. This message also seemed to place responsibility for addressing gun violence "on the shoulders of young people who are in school to learn, while demanding nothing of the policymakers who are actually in positions to make change." Similar to chapter 4, where I highlighted ways that white privilege benefited the Columbine killers before and after their attack, critics have highlighted the racial politics of #WalkUpNotOut. Kylie Cheung claims that the message "exhibits a gaping racial blindspot,"[11] while Rebecca Wald points out that "this argument only applies to crimes overwhelming committed by white boys. Their crimes are tragic betrayals of an underlying innocence that is never attributed to black boys selling drugs on the corner."[12]

The March for Our Lives also met resistance from some gun-rights advocates. In the week after the Parkland shooting, the number of people contributing to the NRA "increased almost 500% from the week before."[13] This upsurge in donations coincided with a rise in gun sales, which often happens in response to high-profile mass shootings, as people rush to buy guns out of fear for their safety and fear that gun-control legislation might follow. After planning began for the March for Our Lives, the NRA responded by calling for an online March for Freedom, a membership push to gain twenty-five thousand new NRA members to help defeat the "gun-ban extremists who want to BAN and CONFISCATE our guns." According to the NRA, the March for Our Lives protestors were not actually planning to march for life or safety, nor were they planning to march against gun violence. Instead, they were "anti-gun protestors."[14] In a similar vein, commentators on Fox News depicted the student-activists as dangerous and rebranded the march as the "March Against Guns."[15]

Despite this resistance, the school walkout happened on March 14, 2018. And ten days later, approximately eight hundred thousand people attended the March for Our Lives in Washington, DC, while even more people attended smaller protests in cities throughout the United States and the world.[16] The number and diversity of attendees challenged the NRA's assertion that "gun-hating billionaires" and "Hollywood elites" orchestrated the March for Our Lives.[17] Moreover, the number and diversity of attendees demonstrated that becoming a protestor or an advocate does not demand a radical transformation. It does not require training, status, or great wealth. Everyday people become advocates when they take time out of their regular routines to say, in effect, "We must do better than this." An advocate can simply be anyone who speaks up or shows up.

The amount of rhetorical activity related to the March for Our Lives—in terms of signs, T-shirts, music, conversations, speeches, tweets, and so on—is hard to imagine, let alone analyze. I leave most of that work to others. In closing, I simply want to draw attention to three speeches. The first speech urges us to recognize the human toll of gun violence; the second speech urges us to consider which victims of gun violence are recognized and remembered and why; the third speech urges us to view gun violence as partially a structural problem with structural solutions. These speeches extend my claims that gun-control rhetoric regularly relies on the warrant of the dead (chapter 3) and that debates about gun violence and gun policy have been shaped by explicit and implicit racism (chapter 4). Moreover, these speeches urge us to embrace different ways of thinking, talking, and acting to better address the problem of gun violence. I quote them at length without much comment because I think that their eloquence speaks for itself.

Parkland student Emma González began her March for Our Lives speech by saying, "Six minutes and about twenty seconds. In a little over six minutes, 17 of our friends were taken from us, 15 were injured, and everyone—absolutely everyone—in the Douglas community was forever altered." She then proceeded to name her classmates and the teacher who died:

> Six minutes and twenty seconds with an AR-15 and my friend Carmen would never complain to me about piano practice. Aaron Feis would never call Kira, "Miss Sunshine." Alex Schachter would never walk into school with his brother Ryan. Scott Beigel would never joke around with Cameron at camp. Helena Ramsey would never hang out after school with Max. Gina Montalto would never wave to her friend Liam at lunch. Joaquin Oliver would never play basketball with Sam or Dylan. Alaina Petty would never. Cara Loughran would never. Chris Hixon would never. Luke Hoyer would never. Martin Duque Anguiano would never. Peter Wang would never. Alyssa Alhadeff would never. Jamie Guttenberg would never. Meadow Pollack would never.[18]

She stopped abruptly. At first, it seemed like she needed time to collect herself. But then it became clear that her silence was purposeful.[19] She stood staring forward, resilient. She did not speak for over four minutes. The crowd was unsure how to react. Some people yelled out words of encouragement. At one point, the crowd joined together in chanting, "Never again!" Tears streamed down González's face, but she remained silent until her alarm beeped. Then she concluded with these words: "Since the time that I came out here, it has been six minutes and twenty seconds. The shooter has ceased shooting, and will soon abandon his rifle, blend in with the students as they escape, and walk free for an hour before arrest. Fight for your lives before its someone else's job."

Naomi Wadler, an eleven-year-old coleader of a walkout at her school in Virginia, spoke at the March for Our Lives about America's tendency to pay attention to some acts of gun violence but not others and to care about some victims but not others. Drawing attention to the racial and gendered dynamics of gun violence, she mourned the loss of the seventeen students in Parkland but also asked us to remember Courtlin Arrington, "an African American girl who was the victim of gun violence in her school in Alabama after the Parkland shooting." Wadler continued, "I am here today to represent Courtlin Arrington. I am here today to represent Hadiya Pendleton. I am here today to represent Tiana Thompson, who at just 16 was shot dead in her home here in Washington, D.C. I am here today to acknowledge and represent the African American girls whose stories don't make the front page of every national newspaper, whose stories don't lead on the evening news." The eleven-year-old concluded her speech as follows: "I urge everyone here and everyone who hears my voice to join me in telling the stories that aren't told, to honor the girls, the women of color, who are murdered at disproportionate rates in this nation. I urge each of you to help me write that narrative for this world and understand so that these girls and women are never forgotten."[20]

Trevon Bosley, a nineteen-year-old from Chicago, spoke in honor of his brother who was shot and killed while leaving church in 2006. Bosley talked about the everyday gun violence that happens in Chicago and cities throughout the nation. In doing so, he drew attention to the systemic sources and solutions of gun violence, and he challenged local and national leaders to reflect on their priorities. "Chicago's violence epidemic," he explained, "didn't start overnight. It was caused by many problems that we are still not dealing with to this day." He noted, for instance, that when "you have a city that feels it's more important to help pay for a college's sports complex rather than fund schools and impoverished communities, you have gun violence. When you have a city that feels we need more Divvy bikes in downtown Chicago for tourists rather than more funding for workforce programs that get guys off the streets real jobs, you have gun violence." He continued, "It's time for the nation to realize gun violence is more than just a Chicago problem or a Parkland problem, but it's an American problem. It's time to care about all communities equally."[21]

At six weeks out from the Parkland shooting, I am amazed by the bravery and wisdom of America's youth. These children and young adults have filled a void and assumed responsibility for leading the nation on this difficult problem while many of our elected leaders play political games.[22] Whether or not one supports the recent calls for gun-control legislation,[23] all Americans might take inspiration from these young people's insistence that the cycle of gun violence and inaction is neither normal nor acceptable. They have begun to imagine a future after gun violence. But the test will be whether there are enough people—young, old, and in between—who have the endurance to sustain this call for change.

NOTES

INTRODUCTION

1. Lysiak, *Newtown*, 1.
2. Ibid., 2.
3. Ibid., 4.
4. Stephen King further describes this ritualized response to mass shootings in his audio essay, *Guns*.
5. Obama, "Shooting in Newtown, CT."
6. Rood, "Racial Politics of Gun Violence."
7. Obama, "Press Conference."
8. Ibid.
9. White House, "Now Is the Time."
10. Obama, "Navy Yard Shooting."
11. Obama, "Shootings at Umpqua Community College."
12. Brad Serber deserves special thanks for helping me think through this issue.
13. Krouse and Richardson, "Mass Murder with Firearms."
14. Nichols, "How Is a 'Mass Shooting' Defined?"
15. See http://www.shootingtracker.com/.
16. Fox, "How US Gun Culture Compares." See also Lankford, "Mass Shooters Unique?," 178.
17. Birkland, "Focusing Events."
18. Murphy, Xu, Kochanek, Curtin, and Arias, "Deaths," 34.
19. Kochanek, Murphy, Xu, and Tejada-Vera, "Deaths," 44.
20. Murphy, Xu, Kochanek, Curtin, and Arias, "Deaths," 33.
21. Fowler, Dahlberg, Haileyesus, and Annest, "Firearm Injuries," 5.
22. Grinshteyn and Hemenway, "Violent Death Rates," 266.
23. Lopez, "America's Unique Gun Violence."
24. Spitzer, *Politics of Gun Control*, 14.
25. This point has been made by rhetoricians, historians, and journalists. See, for instance, Ceccarelli, "Manufactured Scientific Controversy"; Lipstadt, *Denying the Holocaust*; and Greenhouse, *Just a Journalist*.
26. For example, in communication, see Hollihan and Smith, "Special Issue on Civility"; in criminology, Kleck, *Point Blank*; in history, Strain, *Reload*; in law, Winkler, *Gunfight*; in media studies, Kellner, *Guys and Guns Amok*; in philosophy, DeBrabander, *Do Guns Make Us Free?*; in political science, Goss, *Disarmed*; in public health, Hemenway, *Private Guns, Public Health*; in psychology, Langman, *Why Kids Kill*; and in sociology, Newman, *Rampage*.
27. For example, see Lavergne, *Sniper in the Tower*; Cullen, *Columbine*; Lysiak, *Newtown*.
28. Langman, *Why Kids Kill*.
29. Kellner, *Guys and Guns Amok*.
30. For example, see Winkler, *Gunfight*; Waldman, *Second Amendment*.

31. Haag, *Gunning of America.*

32. Hemenway, *Private Guns, Public Health*; Webster and Vernick, *Reducing Gun Violence.*

33. Goss, *Disarmed*; Melzer, *Gun Crusaders*; Carlson, *Citizen-Protectors.*

34. Ratcliffe, "Current State of Composition."

35. Zarefsky, "Democratic Rhetoric," 119.

36. Zhang, "Why Can't the U.S. Treat Gun Violence?"

37. Kahan, "Gun Control Debate," 10.

38. Rood, "'Our Tears Are Not Enough,'" 48.

39. Hogan and Rood, "Rhetorical Studies," 364.

40. Kurtz, "Civility, American Style"; Amsden, "Dimensions of Temporality"; Hollihan and Smith, "Special Issue on Civility"; Engels, *Politics of Resentment*; Meyers, "Barack Obama"; and Landau and Keeley-Jonker, "Conductor of Public Feelings."

41. Lunceford, "Second Amendment Remedies"; Collins, "Second Amendment as Demanding Subject"; Lunceford, "Armed Victims"; Gunn, "Tears of Refusal"; Hogan and Rood, "Rhetorical Studies"; Collins, "Rights Talk."

42. Two exceptions are Hayden, "Family Metaphors," and Frank, "Facing Moloch."

43. Hogan and Rood, "Rhetorical Studies," 364.

44. Rood, "Racial Politics of Gun Violence."

45. For more on rhetorical history, see Turner, *Doing Rhetorical History*. Scholars have written rhetorical histories of several public debates, including abortion debates (e.g., Condit, *Decoding Abortion Rhetoric*), education reform (e.g., Hlavacik, *Assigning Blame*), nuclear policy (e.g., Hogan, *Nuclear Freeze Campaign*), and poverty (e.g., Zarefsky, *President Johnson's War*; Asen, *Invoking the Invisible Hand*).

46. Zarefsky, "Making the Case," 12.

47. Lavergne, *Sniper in the Tower*, 98–123.

48. Selby, "Steve Adler Wrong."

49. Clark, *Open Square.* Rosa Eberly deserves credit for first drawing my attention to Clark's novel and its potential influence on Whitman. This potential connection is also mentioned in Akers, Akers, and Friedman, *Tower Sniper*, 216.

50. Lavergne, *Sniper in the Tower*, back cover.

51. Holloway, "40 Years Later."

52. "KTBC News UT Tower Shooting."

53. Lavergne, *Sniper in the Tower*, 258–62.

54. Shown in the Netflix animated documentary *Tower.*

55. Victor, "Mass Shooters Are All Different."

56. Kellner, *Guys and Guns Amok*, 139.

57. Rood, "Racial Politics of Gun Violence."

58. Johnson, "Firearms Control Legislation."

59. Cook and Goss, *Gun Debate*, 56.

60. Johnson, "Remarks upon Signing."

61. Raymond, *From My Cold Dead Hands*, 250.

62. Ibid., 251.

63. Davidson, *Under Fire*, 40.

64. Reagan, "Annual Members Banquet."

65. Reagan, "Why I'm for the Brady Bill."

66. Cook and Goss, *Gun Debate*, 102–3.

67. Ibid., 13–14.

68. Wilson, *Guns, Gun Control, and Elections*, 96.

69. Mohr, "U.S. Bans Imports of Assault Rifles."

70. Giffords and Kelly, *Enough*, 127.

71. Ibid.
72. Quoted in Eaton, "Ford, Carter, Reagan."
73. Quoted in Feldman, *Ricochet*, 233.
74. Ibid., 236.
75. Ibid., 238.
76. Erickson, *Columbine Review Commission*.
77. "Why? Portraits of the Killers."
78. "Gun Spree at Columbine High."
79. Brooke, "'Suicide Mission,'" A1.
80. Clinton, "Columbine HS Shooting (1999)."
81. Goodman, "With Abundance of Confusion," A16.
82. Cullen, *Columbine*, 193.
83. Quoted in Brown and Merritt, *No Easy Answers*, 180.
84. Brown and Merritt, *No Easy Answers*, 252.
85. Cullen, *Columbine*, 107.
86. Clinton, "Reporter Q&A."
87. Brown and Abel, *Outgunned*, 100.
88. "Gunned Down."
89. Baum, *Gun Guys*, 270.
90. Cook and Goss, *Gun Debate*, 102.
91. Winkler, *Gunfight*, 74.
92. Newman, *Rampage*, 271.
93. Hogan, Andrews, Andrews, and Williams, *Public Speaking*, 17.
94. See, for instance, Gastil, *Political Communication*.
95. See, for instance, Mutz, *Hearing the Other Side*.
96. See, for instance, Gutmann and Thompson, *Why Deliberative Democracy?*
97. See, for instance, Asen, *Democracy, Deliberation, and Education*.
98. Booth, *Rhetoric of Rhetoric*, 171.
99. Longo, Manosevitch, and Shaffer, "Introduction," xxiv.
100. Fraser, "Rethinking the Public Sphere"; Young, "Activist Challenges."
101. Longo, Manosevitch, and Shaffer, "Introduction," xxiv.
102. Ivie, "Rhetorical Deliberation," 278.
103. Asen, *Democracy, Deliberation, and Education*, 9.

CHAPTER 1

1. Obama, "Fallen Dallas Police Officers."
2. Johnson, "Firearms Control Legislation."
3. Haidt, *Righteous Mind*.
4. In history, see, for example, Bodnar, *Remaking America*; Blight, *Race and Reunion*. In philosophy, see Casey, *Remembering*; Ricoeur, *Memory, History, Forgetting*. In rhetoric, see Browne, "Texture of Public Memory"; Phillips, *Framing Public Memory*; Vivian, *Public Forgetting*; Blair, Dickinson, and Ott, "Introduction." In sociology, see Halbwachs, *On Collective Memory*; Schwartz, *Abraham Lincoln in the Post-Heroic Era*.
5. Browne, "Texture of Public Memory," 248.
6. Blair, Dickinson, and Ott, "Introduction," 6.
7. Casey, "Public Memory," 25.
8. Browne, "Texture of Public Memory," 248.
9. Carruthers, "How to Make a Composition," 15.
10. Quoted in Ede, Glenn, and Lunsford, "Border Crossings," 410.

11. Ede, Glenn, and Lunsford, "Border Crossings," 410.
12. Williams and Enos, "Vico's Triangular Invention," 201.
13. Carruthers, "How to Make a Composition," 16.
14. Aristotle, *On Rhetoric*, 41–42.
15. Zarefsky, "Four Senses," 28.
16. Casey, *Remembering*, xix.
17. Hawhee, "Kairotic Encounters," 24.
18. Cullen, *Columbine*.
19. Matthews, "Virginia Tech Shooter."
20. Indeed, a review panel commissioned by Virginia Governor Timothy Kaine found little evidence that Cho played video games. Their report indicated that, according to a roommate, "the only activities Cho engaged in were studying, sleeping, and downloading music." The roommate also reported that he "never saw him play a video game." Ironically, the roommate interpreted Cho's failure to play video games as "strange," rather than a badge of honor, since "he and other students play them." Virginia Tech Review Panel, *Report*, 64.
21. Blair, Dickinson, and Ott, "Introduction," 6.
22. Larkin, *Comprehending Columbine*, 176.
23. See Cullen, *Columbine*.
24. Porter quoted in Larkin, *Comprehending Columbine*, 49.
25. Doss, *Memorial Mania*, 105.
26. Nimmo and Scott, *Rachel's Tears*, 167.
27. Ibid., 162.
28. Ibid., 158.
29. "'Columbine' Author on Newtown Massacre."
30. Gore, "Columbine Memorial Address."
31. Clinton, "Columbine High School Community."
32. Clinton, "Reporter Q&A."
33. Clinton, *It Takes a Village*.
34. Gore, "Protect Children."
35. Cloud, *Control and Consolation*, 3.
36. In "Deranged Loners and Demented Outsiders," Kristen E. Hoerl, Dana L. Cloud, and Sharon E. Jarvis pursue a similar line of questioning by analyzing newspaper coverage of presidential assassination attempts between 1973 and 2001. Although the attackers were "only sometimes mentally ill" (101), major news media nonetheless presented them as lonely and demented outsiders. The authors argue that some coverage "acknowledged economic and professional hardships," but reporters failed to connect "the personal hardships of the attackers to the broader social context of economic recession and generalized economic anxiety" (96–97).
37. Foucault, *History of Madness*.
38. Burke, *Rhetoric of Motives*.
39. Office of the Press Secretary, "Press Briefing by Dana Perino," April 16, 2007.
40. Ibid. The reporter's comment about the "Amish school shooting" was in reference to a shooting on October 2, 2006, in Nickel Mines, Pennsylvania, where five "girls were killed and six others wounded" (CNN Library, "Mass Killings at U.S. Schools").
41. Ibid.
42. Bush, "President Bush Offers Condolences."
43. Office of the Press Secretary, "Press Briefing by Dana Perino," April 18, 2007 (emphasis added).
44. Virginia Tech Review Panel, *Report*, 26.
45. "Killer's Manifesto."

46. Office of the Press Secretary, "Press Briefing by Dana Perino," April 19, 2007.
47. Bush, "President's Radio Address."
48. Eberly, "Deliver Ourselves from 'Evil,'" 552.
49. Engels, *Politics of Resentment*, 2.
50. Quoted in ibid.
51. Quoted in ibid., 107–8.
52. Quoted in ibid., 111.
53. Smith and Hollihan, "'Out of Chaos Breathes Creation,'" 598.
54. Engels, *Politics of Resentment*, 112.
55. Ibid., 152.
56. Pryal, "Reframing Sanity," 161.
57. Ibid.
58. Ibid., 167.
59. LaPierre, "NRA Press Conference."
60. Early, *Crazy*.
61. Metzel and MacLeish, "Mental Illness, Mass Shootings," 241.
62. Cook and Goss, *Gun Debate*, 72.
63. One exception is Roy, *No Right to Remain Silent*.
64. *Appendix to Report on the Shootings*, 216.
65. Lysiask, *Newtown*, 231–32.
66. Quoted in ibid., 231.
67. Ibid., 60.
68. *Appendix to Report on the Shootings*, 217.
69. Virginia Tech Review Panel, *Report*, 35.
70. Langman, "Seung Hui Cho's 'Manifesto.'"
71. Larkin, "Columbine Legacy," 1314.
72. Gibbs and Roche, "Columbine Tapes."
73. Ibid.
74. Mize, "Americans' Top Fears."
75. Collier, "Death of Gun Control," 109.
76. Ibid., 116.
77. Klebold, *Mother's Reckoning*, 277.
78. Cook and Goss, *Gun Debate*, 58–59; Siegel and Rothman, "Firearm Ownership."
79. Cook and Goss, *Gun Debate*, 62.
80. Engels, *Politics of Resentment*, 3.

CHAPTER 2

1. Obama, "Gun Violence."
2. Quoted in Pappas, "NRA Leader Criticizes Obama."
3. LaPierre, "Stand and Fight."
4. Draper, "Inside the Power."
5. Obama, "Gun Violence."
6. LaPierre quoted in Pappas, "NRA Leader Criticizes Obama."
7. Farrell, "Weight of Rhetoric," 475.
8. Ibid., 486.
9. Spitzer, *Politics of Gun Control*, 8.
10. Hofstadter, "America as a Gun Culture."
11. Parker, Menasce, Horowitz, Igielnik, Oliphant, and Brown, "America's Complex Relationship."

12. Cook and Goss, *Gun Debate*, 4.
13. Ibid., 160.
14. Ibid., 159.
15. Spitzer, *Politics of Gun Control*, 8.
16. Ibid.
17. Haag, *Gunning of America*, xxi.
18. Spitzer, *Politics of Gun Control*, 11–12.
19. Quoted in ibid., 11.
20. Winkler, *Gunfight*, 165.
21. Haag, *Gunning of America*, xviii.
22. Cook and Goss, *Gun Debate*, 161.
23. Ridder, "Still-Grieving Colorado."
24. "Protestors Encircle NRA Convention Site."
25. Ridder, "Still-Grieving Colorado."
26. Quoted in Doss, *Memorial Mania*, 110.
27. Heston, *Courage to Be Free*, 228.
28. Ibid., 229.
29. Ibid., 232.
30. Ibid., 233.
31. Ibid., 232.
32. Ibid.
33. Raymond, *From My Cold Dead Hands*, 252.
34. Evensen, "Heston, Charlton."
35. Feldman, *Ricochet*, 243.
36. Heston, *Courage to Be Free*, 283.
37. Ibid., 188.
38. Ibid., 190.
39. Ibid., 192.
40. Ibid., 190.
41. Ibid., 192.
42. Ibid., 179.
43. LaPierre, *Essential Second Amendment*, vii.
44. LaPierre, "NRA Sweepstakes."
45. Lepore, *Whites of Their Eyes*, 16.
46. Ibid.
47. Engels, *Politics of Resentment*, 132.
48. Lepore, *Whites of Their Eyes*, 95.
49. Burstein, *Democracy's Muse*, 147.
50. Ibid.
51. Jefferson, "To James Madison."
52. Gerald Wetlaufer ("Rhetoric and Its Denial," 1555) makes a related point about the rhetoric of America's legal system: "Law *is* rhetoric but the particular rhetoric embraced by the law operates through the systematic *denial* that it is rhetoric." His point is even more fitting for invocations of the law that happen outside legal settings.
53. This strategy represents a form of rhetorical closure—"communication that attempts to stop further communication" (Rood, "Rhetorical Closure," 314).
54. Harpine, "Illusion of Tradition," 161.
55. Waldman, *Second Amendment*, xiv.
56. Quoted in Pappas, "NRA Leader Criticizes Obama."
57. LaPierre, "Stand and Fight."
58. Quoted in Pappas, "NRA Leader Criticizes Obama."

59. Carter, *Gun Control Movement*, 28.

60. Scalia further explained, "Although we do not undertake an exhaustive historical analysis today of the full scope of the Second Amendment, nothing in our opinion should be taken to cast doubt on longstanding prohibitions on the possession of firearms by felons and the mentally ill, or laws forbidding the carrying of firearms in sensitive places such as schools and government buildings, or laws imposing conditions and qualifications on the commercial sale of arms" (District of Columbia v. Heller, 54–55).

61. Winkler, *Gunfight*, 210–11.

62. Ibid., 211.

63. Ibid., 212.

64. Raymond, *From My Cold Dead Hands*, 250.

65. Davidson, *Under Fire*, 30.

66. Raymond, *From My Cold Dead Hands*, 250.

67. Davidson, *Under Fire*, 31.

68. Raymond, *From My Cold Dead Hands*, 250.

69. Davidson, *Under Fire*, 35.

70. Ibid., 36.

71. Quoted in ibid.

72. Ibid.

73. Winkler, *Gunfight*, 65.

74. Ibid., 68.

75. Achenbach, Higham, and Horwitz, "Mighty Gun Lobby."

76. Feldman, *Ricochet*, 171.

77. Heston, *Courage to Be Free*, 286.

78. Feldman, *Ricochet*, 171.

79. Winkler, *Gunfight*, 67–68.

80. Quoted in Achenbach, Higham, and Horwitz, "Mighty Gun Lobby."

81. "In Gun Control Debate."

82. Hochschild, *Strangers in Their Own Land*, 71.

83. LaPierre, "Stand and Fight."

84. Ibid.

85. Heston, *Courage to Be Free*, 283.

86. Ibid., 172.

87. Ibid., 170.

88. Ibid., 182.

89. Ibid., 279.

90. Ibid., 172.

91. Ibid., 188.

92. Ibid., 187.

93. See, for instance, Melzer, *Gun Crusaders*.

94. Heston, *Courage to Be Free*, 186.

95. Pappas, "NRA Leader Criticizes Obama."

96. Hochschild's *Strangers in Their Own Land* offers an excellent analysis of this narrative—or what she calls a "deep story." See especially pages 135–51.

97. See Fisher, "Narration"; Lewis, "Telling America's Story."

98. Collins, "Second Amendment as Demanding Subject," 744.

99. LaPierre quoted in Pappas, "NRA Leader Criticizes Obama."

100. Engels, *Politics of Resentment*.

101. Speaking of identity formation generally, Richard B. Gregg ("Rhetoric of Protest," 82) highlights that identities are created by "identifying against an other," by identifying as unlike or opposed to "them."

102. Quoted in LaPierre, *The Essential Second Amendment Guide*, vi.
103. LaPierre, "Stand and Fight."
104. Collins, "Rights Talk," 88.

CHAPTER 3

1. See Goss, *Disarmed*, 108–12; Hinton, *From the War on Poverty*; Spitzer, *Politics of Gun Control*, 124.
2. See Toulmin, *The Uses of Argument*; Keith and Beard, "Toulmin's Rhetorical Logic."
3. Loraux, *Invention of Athens*.
4. Campbell and Jamieson, *Presidents Creating the Presidency*, 73–103.
5. Thucydides, "Pericles' Funeral Oration."
6. Wills, *Lincoln at Gettysburg*, 263.
7. Bush, "Address to Joint Session of Congress."
8. Morris, *Remembering the AIDS Quilt*.
9. Gore, "Columbine Memorial Address."
10. Obama, "Gun Violence."
11. Obama, "Navy Yard Shooting."
12. White House, "Now Is the Time," 1.
13. Engels, *Politics of Resentment*, 3.
14. Jamieson and Campbell, "Rhetorical Hybrids," 148.
15. Verdery, *Political Lives of Dead Bodies*, 28–29.
16. Frank, "Facing Moloch," 665.
17. Obama, "Reducing Gun Violence—Hartford, CT."
18. Frank, "Facing Moloch," 666.
19. Campbell and Jamieson, *Presidents Creating the Presidency*, 80.
20. Butler, *Precarious Life*, 32.
21. Ibid., 20.
22. Mack and McCann, in "'Strictly an Act of Street Violence,'" raise similar questions. Examining media coverage and statements from public officials after a 2013 shooting in New Orleans, they note that "public discourse characterized the shooting as an episode of 'street violence' that did not warrant sustained national attention." They offer the term *affective divestment* to refer to "rhetorical maneuvers that signal a pushing away from certain bodies by intimate publics—an estrangement at the symbolic level that has naturalized or rationalized the neglect of certain forms of suffering" (334).
23. For instance, reporters who examined the FBI's data from 2006–2012 concluded that mass shootings accounted for "less than 1% of all gun-related homicides." In this case, a mass shooting referred to an incident in which four or more people were killed (Kepple, Loehrke, Hoyer, and Overberg, "Mass Shootings Toll").
24. Farrell, "Weight of Rhetoric."
25. Rood, "Racial Politics of Gun Violence."
26. Wise, "Race, Class, Violence and Denial." See also Hoerl, "Monstrous Youth in Suburbia"; Willis-Chun, "Tales of Tragedy"; Calafell, *Monstrosity, Performance, and Race*, 34–53.
27. Lafraniere, Porat, and Armendariz, "Drumbeat of Multiple Shootings."
28. O'Keefe and Rucker, "Gun-Control Overhaul."
29. "In Gun Control Debate."
30. Silver, "Gun Vote and 2014."
31. Goss, *Disarmed*, 7.

32. Obama, "Statement by the President."
33. "In Gun Control Debate."
34. Obama, "Statement by the President."
35. See, for instance, Spitzer, *Politics of Gun Control*, 113.
36. Obama, "Statement by the President."
37. Obama, "Navy Yard Shooting."
38. Obama, "Honorable Reverend Clementa Pinckney."
39. Sullivan, "Human Being."
40. Obama, "Honorable Reverend Clementa Pinckney."
41. LaPierre, "NRA Press Conference."
42. Stewart, Smith, and Denton, *Persuasion and Social Movements*, 96.
43. Aristotle, *On Rhetoric*, 222.
44. Perelman and Olbrechts-Tyteca, *New Rhetoric*, 115–20.
45. O'Gorman, "Aristotle's Phantasia," 27.
46. Kennerly, "Getting Carried Away," 269. See also Hawhee, "Looking into Aristotle's Eyes."
47. Kennerly, "Getting Carried Away," 269–70.
48. Zelizer, "Reading the Past," 226.
49. Bush, "President Bush Offers Condolences."
50. Obama, "Sandy Hook Interfaith Prayer Vigil."
51. Obama, "Shooting in Newtown, CT."
52. Perelman and Olbrechts-Tyteca, *New Rhetoric*, 116.
53. Obama, "Navy Yard Shooting."
54. Obama, "Fort Hood Memorial Service."
55. Obama, "Shootings at Umpqua Community College."
56. Obama, "Fallen Dallas Police Officers."
57. Sontag, *Regarding the Pain of Others*, 115.
58. Obama, "Reducing Gun Violence—Hartford, CT."
59. Obama, "Shooting in Newtown, CT."
60. Murphy, Xu, and Kochanek, "Deaths," 11.
61. Davey, "Divide in Chicago."
62. Slevin, "Chicago Grapples with Gun Violence."
63. Ward Room Staff, "Murder Capital in 2012."
64. Bostock, Carter, and Quealy, "Chicago Divided by Killings."
65. Obama, "State of the Union."
66. Lakoff, *Whose Freedom?*
67. Kennerly, "Getting Carried Away," 287.
68. Obama, "Sandy Hook Interfaith Prayer Vigil."
69. Obama, "Gun Violence."
70. Obama, "Reducing Gun Violence—Denver, Colorado."
71. This fits with what Goss (*Disarmed*) describes as the "child-protection frame" (62).
72. Rood, "Rhetorical Closure," 330.
73. Obama, "President on Gun Safety."
74. Obama, "Navy Yard Shooting."
75. Obama, "Gun Violence."
76. "State Gun Laws Enacted."
77. Stuckey, "Effects of Presidential Rhetoric," 294.
78. LaPierre, "NRA Press Conference."
79. Heston, *Courage to Be Free*, 232.
80. Obama, "Statement by the President."

81. Obama, "Shootings at Umpqua Community College."
82. Obama, "Mass Shooting in Orlando."
83. Duerringer, in "Dis-honoring the Dead," also identifies this dynamic at work in the post–Sandy Hook gun debate: "Rather than arguing about whether any of the proposed measures regulating assault weapons would actually help prevent similar tragedies, many pro-gun commentators sought to simply disqualify these rhetors, claiming that their efforts were indecorous responses to the tragedy" (90).
84. Rood, "Rhetorical Closure," 329.
85. LaPierre, "NRA Press Conference."
86. Obama, "Gun Violence."
87. Ibid.
88. Obama, "Sandy Hook Interfaith Prayer Vigil."
89. Carlson, *Citizen-Protectors*, 10.
90. Obama, "Navy Yard Shooting."
91. Obama, "Gun Violence."
92. Spitzer, *Politics of Gun Control*, 123.
93. Lanham, *Economics of Attention*, xii.

CHAPTER 4

1. Lopez, "Trial of Dylann Roof."
2. Gutierrez and Silva, "Charleston Massacre Survivor."
3. "Dylann Roof's Racist Manifesto."
4. Ellis, Botelho, and Payne, "Charleston Church Shooter."
5. Hanna and Ellis, "Confederate Flag's Half-Century."
6. Obama, "Shooting in Charleston, South Carolina."
7. Dyson, *Black Presidency*, 239.
8. *Time* Staff, "Donald Trump's Presidential Announcement Speech."
9. Anderson, *White Rage*, 100.
10. This filtering process resembles Kenneth Burke's insight that all language use—whether intended to persuade or not—shapes how we perceive reality. Describing what he calls "terministic screens," Burke explains that "even if any given terminology is a *reflection* of reality, by its very nature as a terminology it must be a *selection* of reality; and to this extent it must function also as a *deflection* of reality" (*Language as Symbolic Action*, 45).
11. "Dylann Roof's Racist Manifesto."
12. "No Federal Civil Rights Charges."
13. "Dylann Roof's Racist Manifesto."
14. Lunceford, "Armed Victims," 338.
15. Winkler, *Gunfight*, xviii.
16. Waldman, *Second Amendment*, 70.
17. Quoted in ibid.
18. Ibid.
19. Ibid., 70–71.
20. Ibid., 71.
21. Winkler, *Gunfight*, xviii.
22. Waldman, *Second Amendment*, 72.
23. Cook and Goss, *Gun Debate*, 166.
24. Cobb, *This Nonviolent Stuff*.
25. Quoted in Winkler, *Gunfight*, 238.

26. Wise (*White like Me*) makes a similar argument:

> With the emergence of the Tea Party movement, the nation has been treated to images of thousands of mostly white, ultra-conservative activists surrounding lawmakers and screaming at them to vote against health care reform legislation, carrying guns to rallies just to show they can, or spouting off about the potential need for secession or even revolution. Needless to say, if black or Latino activists (or Arab Americans or Muslim activists angered by racial and religious profiling, post 9/11) were to surround lawmakers and scream at them like petulant children, one can only imagine how it would be perceived by the public. They would be seen as insurrectionaries, as terrorists, as thugs; but when older whites do it, they are viewed as patriots exercising their First Amendment rights. (vii)

27. Winkler, *Gunfight*, 245.
28. Quoted in ibid.
29. The 1968 act, however, was largely reversed by the 1986 Firearm Owners' Protection Act.
30. Hinton, *From the War on Poverty*, 14.
31. Johnson, "Remarks upon Signing."
32. Stabile, *White Victims, Black Villains*, 3.
33. Delgado and Stefancic, *Critical Race Theory*, 127–28.
34. Hunter ("Dead Men Talking"), for instance, examines eighteenth-century execution and crime narratives. Also see McCann, *Mark of Criminality*.
35. Hinton, *From the War on Poverty*, 7.
36. Ibid., 12.
37. Ibid., 2.
38. Ibid., 5.
39. Giffords and Kelly, *Enough*, 128.
40. Frank, "Bill Clinton's Crime Bill."
41. Fingerhut, "5 Facts."
42. Ibid.
43. For more on race and the NRA, see Melzer, *Gun Crusaders*, 77–78, 152–66.
44. LaPierre, "NRA Press Conference."
45. Ibid.
46. "Crime in the United States."
47. LaPierre, "Stand and Fight."
48. Ibid.
49. "Why Own a Gun?"
50. Waldman, *Second Amendment*, 168.
51. Butler, *Precarious Life*, 44.
52. Smith and Cooper, "Homicide in the U.S.," 1.
53. Riddell, Harper, Cerdá, and Kaufman, "Comparison of Rates," 712.
54. Dyson, *Black Presidency*, 93–97.
55. Obama, "Trayvon Martin."
56. Ibid.
57. See https://blacklivesmatter.com/about/herstory/.
58. Obama, "Economy for the Middle Class."
59. Ibid.
60. Ibid.
61. Quoted in Dyson, *Black Presidency*, 172.
62. Ibid., 173.

63. This heading borrows from Wise, "Blinded by the White."

64. Nakayama and Krizek, "Whiteness," 291.

65. Shome, "'Global Motherhood,'" 391.

66. Alcoff, *Future of Whiteness*, 154.

67. Cullen, *Columbine*.

68. Wise, "Blinded by the White."

69. Ibid.

70. Willis-Chun, "Tales of Tragedy," 50–51. See also Hoerl, "Monstrous Youth in Suburbia."

71. Clinton, "Columbine HS Shooting (1999)."

72. Calafell, *Monstrosity, Performance, and Race*, 46.

73. See, for instance, Roy, *No Right to Remain Silent*.

74. Kellner, "Media Spectacle," 34.

75. Quoted in ibid.

76. Ibid., 35.

77. Ibid., 35–36.

78. Hong, "Koreans Aren't to Blame."

79. Veal, "South Korea's Collective Guilt."

80. Hong, "Koreans Aren't to Blame."

81. Kimmel, *Angry White Men*, back cover.

82. "Suicide Statistics."

83. hooks, *We Real Cool*, 49.

84. Butler, "Shooters of Color."

85. Bennett, "White Terrorism."

86. LaPierre, "NRA Press Conference."

87. Carlson, *Citizen-Protectors*, 68.

88. Fox, "How US Gun Culture Compares."

89. DeLong and Braunger, "Breaking Down the Dashcam."

90. Jacobo and Francis, "Robbery Suspect."

91. Lunceford, "Armed Victims," 337.

92. Carlson, *Citizen-Protectors*, 133.

93. Quoted in Lunceford, "Armed Victims," 337.

94. Dyson, *Black Presidency*, 109.

95. Hinton, *From the War on Poverty*.

96. Obama, "Honorable Reverend Clementa Pinckney."

97. Ford, "Who Commits Mass Shootings?"

98. Two sources in particular stand out for beginning this work: Carlson, *Citizen-Protectors*, and Melzer, *Gun Crusaders*.

99. Crenshaw, "Demarginalizing the Intersection."

CHAPTER 5

1. For two scholarly forums about this shooting, see Sloop and Morris, "Forum"; "Fingers on Our Pulse."

2. Data calculated from 2012–2016, Centers for Disease Control, *WISQARS Fatal Injury Reports*, accessed September 1, 2018, https://webappa.cdc.gov/sasweb/ncipc/mortrate.html.

3. Data calculated from 2010–2014, Centers for Disease Control, *WISQARS Nonfatal Injury Reports*, accessed September 1, 2018, https://webappa.cdc.gov/sasweb/ncipc/nfirates2001.html.

4. Oliphant, "Bipartisan Support."

5. Parker, Menasce, Horowitz, Igielnik, Oliphant, and Brown, "America's Complex Relationship."

6. Drake, "Mass Shootings."

7. Parker, Menasce, Horowitz, Igielnik, Oliphant, and Brown, "America's Complex Relationship."

8. Oliphant, "Bipartisan Support."

9. Parker, Menasce, Horowitz, Igielnik, Oliphant, and Brown, "America's Complex Relationship."

10. Oliphant, "Bipartisan Support."

11. Lipka and Gramlich, "5 Facts About Abortion."

12. Zarefsky, "Democratic Rhetoric," 117.

13. Obama, "Fallen Dallas Police Officers."

14. Ibid.

15. Winter, Miklaszewski, Blankstein, and Chuck, "Dallas Suspect Was Upset."

16. Obama, "Remarks by President Obama."

17. Obama, "Fallen Dallas Police Officers."

18. Ibid.

19. Ibid.

20. Ibid.

21. Ibid.

22. Ibid.

23. Cloud, *Control and Consolation*, 3.

24. Obama, "Fallen Dallas Police Officers."

25. Ibid.

26. Referenced in "The Speech of President Obama's Life."

27. Ibid.

28. "Obama's Entire Dallas Police Memorial."

29. "OK for Obama to Mention?"

30. "How Gap Between Police, Black Community."

31. McGee, "'Ideograph'" and "Fragmentation of Contemporary Culture."

32. Aristotle, *Rhetoric and Poetics*, 25.

33. For instance, Lilliana Mason, in *Uncivil Agreement*, notes that in 2013, "81 percent of Republicans personally supported a law expanding background checks," yet "only 57 of Republicans supported the Senate passing a background check bill." Although it is possible that Republicans disagreed with the specifics of the bill, she concludes that Republicans rejected the bill because it "would have been a victory for Democrats." This example is part of her book's larger argument outlining how American partisanship often depends on competing identities and group affiliations, not disagreements about issues or policies (54).

34. Burke, *Rhetoric of Motives*, 20–29.

35. Roberts-Miller, "'Aid and Comfort to the Enemy.'"

36. Greene, *Moral Tribes*.

37. "Partisan Divide."

38. Doherty, "Key Takeaways."

39. Gutmann and Thompson, *Spirit of Compromise*.

40. Putnam, *Bowling Alone*.

41. Bishop, *Big Sort*.

42. Jamieson and Capella, *Echo Chamber*.

43. Pariser, *Filter Bubble*.

44. Chandler, "Feeling Stuck."

45. Atwill, "Changing the Puzzle," 25.

46. Special thanks are due to Robert Asen, since I have borrowed some of the language from his review here.

47. Rood, "Rhetorical Closure," 313.

48. Ibid., 331.

49. Allen, *Talking to Strangers*, 17.

50. Elbow, *Writing Without Teachers*, 149.

51. Gregg, "Rhetoric of Protest," 82.

52. Corbett and Eberly, *Elements of Reasoning*, 17.

53. Hogan, Andrews, Andrews, and Williams, *Public Speaking*, 13.

54. Ceccarelli, "Manufactured Scientific Controversy."

55. Ibid.; Lipstadt, *Denying the Holocaust*.

56. Haidt, *Righteous Mind*, 61.

57. Ratcliffe, *Rhetorical Listening*, 33.

58. Obama, "Honorable Reverend Clementa Pinckney."

59. Hogan and Rood, "Rhetorical Studies," 364.

60. Obama, "Navy Yard Shooting."

61. Ibid.

EPILOGUE

1. O'Gorman, *Iconoclastic Imagination*, 7.

2. Fox, "How US Gun Culture Compares." See also Lankford, "Mass Shooters Unique?," 178.

3. Grinshteyn and Hemenway, "Violent Death Rates," 266.

4. Ibid., 271. Also see Gabor, *Confronting Gun Violence in America*, 39–50.

5. Astor, "Florida Gun Bill."

6. Wattles, "More Than a Dozen Businesses."

7. CNN Staff, "Florida Student Emma Gonzalez" (all quotations from video, not transcript).

8. Ibid.

9. See https://marchforourlives.com/.

10. Kirby, "#WalkUpNotOut."

11. Cheung, "Sexist, Racist Implications."

12. Quoted in ibid.

13. Willingham, "Donations to the NRA."

14. LaPierre, "Join NRA's March."

15. Chang, "Attack on the 2nd Amendment."

16. Durando, "March for Our Lives."

17. LaPierre, "Join NRA's March."

18. Beck, "March for Our Lives Speech."

19. Cheryl Glenn's *Unspoken* deserves credit for helping me recognize the rhetorical power of silence.

20. Nirappil, "Story Behind 11-Year-Old Naomi Wadler."

21. Now This, "Everyone Needs to Hear."

22. Price, "Trump's Video Game Summit."

23. Editorial Staff of the *Eagle Eye*, "Our Manifesto."

BIBLIOGRAPHY

Achenbach, Joel, Scott Higham, and Sari Horwitz. "How NRA's True Believers Converted a Marksmanship Group into a Mighty Gun Lobby." *Washington Post*, January 12, 2013. https://www.washingtonpost.com/politics/how-nras-true-believers-converted-a-marksmanship-group-into-a-mighty-gun-lobby/2013/01/12/51c62288-59b9-11e2-88d0-c4cf65c3ad15_story.html?utm_term=.f1cc5b50733c.

Akers, Monte, Nathan Akers, and Roger Friedman. *Tower Sniper: The Terror of America's First Active Shooter on Campus*. Houston: Hardy, 2016.

Alcoff, Linda Martín. *The Future of Whiteness*. Malden, MA: Polity, 2015.

Allen, Danielle S. *Talking to Strangers: Anxieties of Citizenship Since "Brown v. Board of Education."* Chicago: University of Chicago Press, 2004.

Amsden, Brian. "Dimensions of Temporality in President Obama's Tucson Memorial Address." *Rhetoric & Public Affairs* 17, no. 3 (2014): 455–76.

Anderson, Carol. *White Rage: The Unspoken Truth of Our Racial Divide*. New York: Bloomsbury, 2016.

Appendix to Report on the Shootings at Sandy Hook Elementary School and 36 Yogananda Street, Newtown, Connecticut, Office of the Connecticut State Attorney, Judicial District of Danbury, November 25, 2013. https://schoolshooters.info/sites/default/files/Appendix_to_Sandy_Hook_Official_Report.pdf.

Aristotle. *On Rhetoric: A Theory of Civic Discourse*. 2nd ed. Translated by George A. Kennedy. New York: Oxford University Press, 2007.

———. *The Rhetoric and Poetics of Aristotle*. Translated by W. Rhys Roberts and Ingram Bywater. New York: Modern Library, 1984.

Asen, Robert. *Democracy, Deliberation, and Education*. University Park: Pennsylvania State University Press, 2015.

———. *Invoking the Invisible Hand: Social Security and the Privatization Debates*. East Lansing: Michigan State University Press, 2009.

Astor, Maggie. "Florida Gun Bill: What's In It, and What Isn't." *New York Times*, March 8, 2018. https://www.nytimes.com/2018/03/08/us/florida-gun-bill.html.

Atwill, Janet M. "Changing the Puzzle." Contribution to "Octalog II: The (Continuing) Politics of Historiography." *Rhetoric Review* 16, no. 1 (1997): 23–25.

Baum, Dan. *Gun Guys: A Road Trip*. New York: Vintage, 2013.

Beck, Laura. "Here's Emma Gonzalez's Gut-Wrenching March for Our Lives Speech in Full." *Cosmopolitan*, March 24, 2018. https://www.cosmopolitan.com/politics/a19482963/emma-gonzalez-march-for-our-lives-speech-transcript/.

Bennett, Brit. "White Terrorism Is as Old as America." *New York Times*, June 19, 2015. http://www.nytimes.com/2015/06/19/magazine/white-terrorism-is-as-old-as-america.html?_r=0.

"The Bill of Rights: A Transcription." *National Archives*. https://www.archives.gov/founding-docs/bill-of-rights-transcript.

Birkland, Thomas A. "Focusing Events, Mobilization, and Agenda Setting." *Journal of Public Policy* 18, no. 1 (1998): 53–74.

Bishop, Bill. *The Big Sort: Why the Clustering of Like-Minded America Is Tearing Us Apart*. Boston: Mariner, 2008.

Blair, Carole, Greg Dickinson, and Brian L. Ott. "Introduction: Rhetoric/Memory/Place." In *Places of Public Memory: The Rhetoric of Museums and Memorials*, edited by Greg Dickinson, Carole Blair, and Brian L. Ott, 1–54. Tuscaloosa: University of Alabama Press, 2010.

Blight, David. *Race and Reunion: The Civil War in American Memory*. Cambridge: Harvard University Press, 2001.

Bodnar, John. *Remaking America: Public Memory, Commemoration, and Patriotism in the Twentieth Century*. Princeton: Princeton University Press, 1992.

Booth, Wayne. *The Rhetoric of Rhetoric: The Quest for Effective Communication*. Malden, MA: Blackwell, 2004.

Bostock, Mike, Shan Carter, and Kevin Quealy. "A Chicago Divided by Killings." *New York Times*, January 3, 2013. http://www.nytimes.com/interactive/2013/01/02/us/chicago-killings.html?ref=us&_r=0.

Brooke, James. "A 'Suicide Mission': Authorities Say Killers Also Used Bombs—at Least 20 Injured." *New York Times*, April 21, 1999, A1.

Brown, Brooks, and Rob Merritt. *No Easy Answers: The Truth Behind Death at Columbine*. New York: Lantern, 2002.

Brown, Peter Harry, and Daniel G. Abel. *Outgunned: Up Against the NRA*. New York: Free Press, 2003.

Browne, Stephen H. "Reading, Rhetoric, and the Texture of Public Memory." *Quarterly Journal of Speech* 81, no. 2 (1995): 237–50.

Burke, Kenneth. *Language as Symbolic Action: Essays on Life, Literature, and Method*. Berkeley: University of California Press, 1966.

———. *A Rhetoric of Motives*. Berkeley: University of California Press, 1950/1969.

Burstein, Andrew. *Democracy's Muse: How Thomas Jefferson Became an FDR Liberal, a Reagan Republican, and a Tea Party Fanatic, All the While Being Dead*. Charlottesville: University of Virginia Press, 2015.

Bush, George W. "Address to Joint Session of Congress Following 9/11 Attacks." *American Rhetoric*, September 20, 2001. http://www.americanrhetoric.com/speeches/gwbush911jointsessionspeech.htm.

———. "President Bush Offers Condolences at Virginia Tech Memorial Convocation." *The White House*, April 17, 2007. http://georgewbushwhitehouse.archives.gov/news/releases/2007/04/20070417-1.html.

———. "President's Radio Address." *The White House*, April 20, 2007. http://georgewbush-whitehouse.archives.gov/news/releases/2007/04/20070420-2.html.

Butler, Anthea. "Shooters of Color Are Called 'Terrorists' and 'Thugs.' Why Are White Shooters Called 'Mentally Ill?'" *Washington Post*, June 18, 2015. https://www.washingtonpost.com/posteverything/wp/2015/06/18/call-the-charleston-church-shooting-what-it-is-terrorism/.

Butler, Judith. *Precarious Life: The Powers of Mourning and Violence*. London: Verso, 2004.

Calafell, Bernadette Marie. *Monstrosity, Performance, and Race in Contemporary Culture*. New York: Peter Lang, 2015.

Campbell, Karlyn Kohrs, and Kathleen Hall Jamieson. *Presidents Creating the Presidency: Deeds Done in Words*. Chicago: University of Chicago Press, 2008.

Carlson, Jennifer. *Citizen-Protectors: The Everyday Politics of Guns in an Age of Decline*. New York: Oxford University Press, 2015.

Carruthers, Mary. "How to Make a Composition: Memory-Craft in Antiquity and in the Middle Ages." In *Memory: Histories, Theories, Debates*, edited by Susannah Radstone and Bill Schwarz, 15–29. New York: Fordham University Press, 2010.

Carter, Gregg Lee. *The Gun Control Movement*. New York: Twayne, 1997.

Casey, Edward S. "Public Memory in Place and Time." In *Framing Public Memory*, edited by Kendall R. Phillips, 17–44. Tuscaloosa: University of Alabama Press, 2004.

———. *Remembering: A Phenomenological Study*. 2nd ed. Bloomington: Indiana University Press, 2000.

Ceccarelli, Leah. "Manufactured Scientific Controversy: Science, Rhetoric, and Public Debate." *Rhetoric & Public Affairs* 14, no. 2 (2011): 195–228.

Chandler, Michael Alison. "Feeling Stuck in Your Social Media Bubble?" *Washington Post*, April 18, 2017. https://www.washingtonpost.com/news/inspired-life/wp/2017/04/18/feeling-stuck-in-your-social-media-bubble-heres-the-newest-of-in-a-growing-class-of-apps-designed-to-help/?utm_term=.8513c546259c.

Chang, Alvin. "How Fox News Turned the March for Our Lives into an Attack on the 2nd Amendment." *Vox*, March 26, 2018. https://www.vox.com/2018/3/26/17163680/fox-news-gun-march-for-our-lives-data.

Cheung, Kylie. "The Sexist, Racist Implications of the 'Walk Up, Not Out' Movement." *Salon*, March 25, 2018. https://www.salon.com/2018/03/25/the-sexist-racist-implications-of-the-walk-up-not-out-movement_partner/.

Clark, Ford. *The Open Square*. Greenwich, CT: Fawcett, 1962.

Clinton, Bill. "President Clinton's Remarks Regarding Columbine HS Shooting (1999)." *YouTube*, April 20, 1999. https://www.youtube.com/watch?v=sQX8KNXP14w.

———. "Remarks to the Columbine High School Community in Littleton." *The American Presidency Project*, May 20, 1999. http://www.presidency.ucsb.edu/ws/?pid=57605.

Clinton, Hillary Rodham. *It Takes a Village: And Other Lessons Children Teach Us*. New York: Simon and Schuster, 1996.

———. "Reporter Q&A Regarding Youth Violence." *Clinton Library*, April 29, 1999. http://www.clintonlibrary.gov/.

Cloud, Dana L. *Control and Consolation in American Culture and Politics: Rhetorics of Therapy*. Thousand Oaks, CA: Sage, 1998.

CNN Library. "Mass Killings at U.S. Schools." *CNN*, December 14, 2012. http://www.cnn.com/2012/12/14/us/school-shootings/.

CNN Staff. "Florida Student Emma Gonzalez to Lawmakers and Gun Advocates: 'We Call BS.'" *CNN*, February 17, 2018. https://www.cnn.com/2018/02/17/us/florida-student-emma-gonzalez-speech/index.html.

Cobb, Charles E., Jr. *This Nonviolent Stuff'll Get You Killed: How Guns Made the Civil Rights Movement Possible*. New York: Basic, 2014.

Collier, Charles W. "The Death of Gun Control: An American Tragedy." *Critical Inquiry* 41, no. 1 (2014): 102–31.

Collins, Laura J. "Rights Talk and Political Dispositions." *Rhetoric & Public Affairs* 19, no. 1 (2016): 83–90.

———. "The Second Amendment as Demanding Subject: Figuring the Marginalized Subject in Demands for an Unbridled Second Amendment." *Rhetoric & Public Affairs* 17, no. 4 (2014): 737–56.

"'Columbine' Author on Newtown Massacre." *CBS News*, December 18, 2012. http://www.cbsnews.com/videos/columbine-author-on-newtown-massacre/.

Condit, Celeste Michelle. *Decoding Abortion Rhetoric: Communicating Social Change*. Urbana: University of Illinois Press, 1990.

Cook, Philip J., and Kristin A. Goss. *The Gun Debate: What Everyone Needs to Know*. New York: Oxford University Press, 2014.

Corbett, Edward P. J., and Rosa A. Eberly. *The Elements of Reasoning*. 2nd ed. Boston: Allyn and Bacon, 2000.

Crenshaw, Kimberle. "Demarginalizing the Intersection of Race and Sex: A Black Feminist Critique of Antidiscrimination Doctrine, Feminist Theory and Antiracist Politics." *University of Chicago Legal Forum* 1 (1989): 139–67.

"Crime in the United States 2011: Expanded Homicide Data." *FBI: UCR.* https://ucr.fbi.gov/crime-in-the-u.s/2011/crime-in-the-u.s.-2011/offenses-known-to-law-enforcement/expanded/expanded-homicide-data.

Cullen, Dave. *Columbine.* New York: Twelve, 2009.

Davey, Monica. "In a Soaring Homicide Rate, a Divide in Chicago." *New York Times,* January 2, 2013. http://www.nytimes.com/2013/01/03/us/a-soaring-homicide-rate-a-divide-in-chicago.html.

Davidson, Osha Gray. *Under Fire: The NRA and the Battle for Gun Control.* New York: Holt, 1993.

DeBrabander, Firmin. *Do Guns Make Us Free?* New Haven: Yale University Press, 2015.

Delgado, Richard, and Jean Stefancic. *Critical Race Theory: An Introduction.* New York: New York University Press, 2012.

DeLong, Matt, and Dave Braunger. "Breaking Down the Dashcam: The Philando Castile Shooting Timeline." *Star Tribune,* June 21, 2017. http://www.startribune.com/castile-shooting-timeline/429678313/.

District of Columbia v. Heller, 554 U.S. 570 (2008).

Doherty, Carroll. "Key Takeaways on Americans' Growing Partisan Divide over Political Values." *Pew Research Center,* October 5, 2017. http://www.pewresearch.org/fact-tank/2017/10/05/takeaways-on-americans-growing-partisan-divide-over-political-values/.

Doss, Erika. *Memorial Mania: Public Feeling in America.* Chicago: University of Chicago Press, 2010.

Drake, Bruce. "Mass Shootings Rivet National Attention, but Are Small Share of Gun Violence." *Pew Research Center,* September 17, 2013. http://www.pewresearch.org/fact-tank/2013/09/17/mass-shootings-rivet-national-attention-but-are-a-small-share-of-gun-violence/.

Draper, Robert. "Inside the Power of the N.R.A." *New York Times Magazine,* December 12, 2013. http://www.nytimes.com/2013/12/15/magazine/inside-the-power-of-the-nra.html.

Duerringer, Christopher M. "Dis-honoring the Dead: Negotiating Decorum in the Shadow of Sandy Hook." *Western Journal of Communication* 80, no. 1 (2016): 79–99.

Durando, Jessica. "March for Our Lives Could Be the Biggest Single-Day Protest in D.C.'s History." *USA Today,* March 24, 2018. https://www.usatoday.com/story/news/nation/2018/03/24/march-our-lives-could-become-biggest-single-day-protest-d-c-nations-history/455675002/.

Dyson, Michael Eric. *The Black Presidency: Barack Obama and the Politics of Race in America.* Boston: Houghton Mifflin Harcourt, 2016.

Early, Pete. *Crazy: A Father's Search Through America's Mental Health Madness.* New York: Berkley, 2006.

Eaton, William J. "Ford, Carter, Reagan Push for Gun Ban." *Los Angeles Times,* May 5, 1994. http://articles.latimes.com/1994-05-05/news/mn-54185_1_assault-weapons-ban.

Eberly, Rosa A. "Acknowledgments." In *Towers of Rhetoric: Memory and Reinvention.* Intermezzo, 2018. http://intermezzo.enculturation.net/05-eberly/eberly-acknowledgements.html.

———. "Deliver Ourselves from 'Evil.'" *Rhetoric & Public Affairs* 6, no. 3 (2003): 551–53.

Ede, Lisa, Cheryl Glenn, and Andrea Lunsford. "Border Crossings: Intersections of Rhetoric and Feminism." *Rhetorica* 13, no. 4 (1995): 401–41.

Editorial Staff of the *Eagle Eye*. "Our Manifesto to Fix America's Gun Laws." *Guardian*, March 23, 2018. https://www.theguardian.com/us-news/commentisfree/2018/mar/23/parkland-students-manifesto-americas-gun-laws.

Elbow, Peter. *Writing Without Teachers*. New York: Oxford University Press, 1998.

Ellis, Ralph, Greg Botelho, and Ed Payne. "Charleston Church Shooter Hears Victim's Kin Say, 'I Forgive You.'" *CNN*, June 19, 2015. http://www.cnn.com/2015/06/19/us/charleston-church-shooting-main/.

Engels, Jeremy. *The Politics of Resentment: A Genealogy*. University Park: Pennsylvania State University Press, 2015.

Erickson, William H. *The Report of Governor Bill Owens' Columbine Review Commission*. Columbine Review Commission, May 2001. https://schoolshooters.info/sites/default/files/Columbine%20-%20Governor's%20Commission%20Report.pdf.

Evensen, Bruce J. "Heston, Charlton." *American National Biography Online*, March 2011. http://www.anb.org/articles/18/18-03826.html.

Farrell, Thomas B. "The Weight of Rhetoric: Studies in Cultural Delirium." *Philosophy & Rhetoric* 41, no. 4 (2008): 467–87.

Feldman, Richard. *Ricochet: Confessions of a Gun Lobbyist*. Hoboken, NJ: Wiley and Sons, 2008.

Fingerhut, Hannah. "5 Facts About Guns in the United States." *Pew Research Center*, January 5, 2016. http://www.pewresearch.org/fact-tank/2016/01/05/5-facts-about-guns-in-the-united-states/.

"Fingers on Our Pulse: Engaging Orlando's Aftermath and Futurity." *QED* 3, no. 3 (2016): 95–173.

Fisher, Walter R. "Narration as a Human Communication Paradigm: The Case of Public Moral Argument." *Communication Monographs* 51, no. 1 (1984): 1–22.

Ford, Dana. "Who Commits Mass Shootings?" *CNN*, July 24, 2015. https://www.cnn.com/2015/06/27/us/mass-shootings/.

Foucault, Michel. *History of Madness*. Translated by Jonathan Murphy and Jean Khalfa. New York: Routledge, 2006.

Fowler, Katherine A., Linda L. Dahlberg, Tadesse Haileyesus, and Joseph L. Annest. "Firearm Injuries in the United States." *Preventive Medicine* 79 (2015): 5–14.

Fox, Kara. "How US Gun Culture Compares with the World in 5 Charts." *CNN*, October 4, 2017. http://www.cnn.com/2017/10/03/americas/us-gun-statistics/index.html.

Frank, David A. "Facing Moloch: Barack Obama's National Eulogies and Gun Violence." *Rhetoric & Public Affairs* 17, no. 4 (2014): 653–78.

Frank, Thomas. "Bill Clinton's Crime Bill Destroyed Lives, and There's No Point in Denying It." *Guardian*, April 15, 2016. http://www.theguardian.com/commentisfree/2016/apr/15/bill-clinton-crime-bill-hillary-black-lives-thomas-frank.

Fraser, Nancy. "Rethinking the Public Sphere: A Contribution to the Critique of Actually Existing Democracy." In *Habermas and the Public Sphere*, edited by Craig Calhoun, 109–42. Cambridge: MIT Press, 1992.

Gabor, Thomas. *Confronting Gun Violence in America*. New York: Palgrave, 2016.

Gastil, John. *Political Communication and Deliberation*. Thousand Oaks, CA: Sage, 2008.

Gibbs, Nancy, and Timothy Roche. "The Columbine Tapes." *Time*, December 20, 1999. http://content.time.com/time/magazine/article/0,9171,992873,00.html.

Giffords, Gabrielle, and Mark Kelly. *Enough: Our Fight to Keep America Safe from Gun Violence*. New York: Scribner, 2014.

Glenn, Cheryl. *Unspoken: A Rhetoric of Silence*. Carbondale: Southern Illinois University Press, 2004.

Goodman, Walter. "With Abundance of Confusion and Few Facts, Nonstop Coverage." *New York Times*, April 21, 1999, A16.

Gore, Al. "Columbine Memorial Address." *C-SPAN*, April 25, 1999. http://www.c-span.org/video/?c4090707/al-gore-columbine-memorial-service.

Gore, Tipper. "Protect Children from the Culture of Violence." *St. Petersburg Times*, March 15, 1988.

Goss, Kristin A. *Disarmed: The Missing Movement for Gun Control in America*. Princeton: Princeton University Press, 2006.

Greene, Joshua. *Moral Tribes: Emotion, Reason, and the Gap Between Us and Them*. New York: Penguin, 2013.

Greenhouse, Linda. *Just a Journalist: On the Press, Life, and the Spaces Between*. Cambridge: Harvard University Press, 2017.

Gregg, Richard B. "The Ego-Function of the Rhetoric of Protest." *Philosophy & Rhetoric* 4, no. 2 (1971): 71–91.

Grinshteyn, Erin, and David Hemenway. "Violent Death Rates: The US Compared with Other High-Income OECD Countries, 2010." *American Journal of Medicine* 129, no. 3 (2016): 266–73.

Gunn, Joshua. "Tears of Refusal: Crying with Collins (and Lundberg), with Reference to Pee-wee Herman." *Rhetoric & Public Affairs* 18, no. 2 (2015): 347–58.

"Gunned Down." *PBS Frontline*, January 6, 2015. http://video.pbs.org/video/2365397152/.

"Gun Spree at Columbine High." *New York Times*, April 21, 1999, A22.

Gutierrez, Gabe, and Daniella Silva. "Charleston Massacre Survivor Says Suspect Dylann Roof Opened Fire as Victims Stood to Pray." *NBC News*, December 14, 2016. https://www.nbcnews.com/storyline/charleston-church-shooting/charleston-massacre-survivor-says-suspect-dylann-roof-opened-fire-victims-n695911.

Gutmann, Amy, and Dennis Thompson. *The Spirit of Compromise: Why Governing Demands It and Campaigning Undermines It*. Princeton: Princeton University Press, 2012.

———. *Why Deliberative Democracy?* Princeton: Princeton University Press, 2004.

Haag, Pamela. *The Gunning of America: Business and the Making of American Gun Culture*. New York: Basic, 2016.

Haidt, Jonathan. *The Righteous Mind: Why Good People Are Divided by Politics and Religion*. New York: Vintage, 2012.

Halbwachs, Maurice. *On Collective Memory*. Edited and translated by Lewis A. Coser. Chicago: University of Chicago Press, 1992.

Hanna, Jason, and Ralph Ellis. "Confederate Flag's Half-Century at South Carolina Capitol Ends." *CNN*, July 10, 2015. http://www.cnn.com/2015/07/10/us/south-carolina-confederate-battle-flag/.

Harpine, William D. "The Illusion of Tradition: Spurious Quotation and the Gun Control Debate." *Argumentation and Advocacy* 52, no. 3 (2016): 151–64.

Hawhee, Debra. "Kairotic Encounters." In *Perspectives on Rhetorical Invention*, edited by Janet M. Atwill and Janice M. Lauer, 16–35. Knoxville: University of Tennessee Press, 2002.

———. "Looking into Aristotle's Eyes: Toward a Theory of Rhetorical Vision." *Advances in the History of Rhetoric* 14, no. 2 (2011): 139–65.

Hayden, Sara. "Family Metaphors and the Nation: Promoting a Politics of Care Through the Million Mom March." *Quarterly Journal of Speech* 89, no. 3 (2003): 196–215.

Hemenway, David. *Private Guns, Public Health*. Ann Arbor: University of Michigan Press, 2006.

"Here's What Appears to Be Dylann Roof's Racist Manifesto." *Mother Jones*, June 20, 2015. http://www.motherjones.com/politics/2015/06/alleged-charleston-shooter-dylann-roof-manifesto-racist.

Heston, Charlton. *The Courage to Be Free*. Kansas City: Saudade Press, 2000.

Hinton, Elizabeth. *From the War on Poverty to the War on Crime: The Making of Mass Incarceration in America*. Cambridge: Harvard University Press, 2016.

Hlavacik, Mark. *Assigning Blame: The Rhetoric of Education Reform*. Cambridge: Harvard Education Press, 2016.

Hochschild, Arlie Russell. *Strangers in Their Own Land: Anger and Mourning on the American Right*. New York: New Press, 2016.

Hoerl, Kristen. "Monstrous Youth in Suburbia: Disruption and Recovery of the American Dream." *Southern Communication Journal* 67, no. 3 (2002): 259–75.

Hoerl, Kristen E., Dana L. Cloud, and Sharon E. Jarvis. "Deranged Loners and Demented Outsiders? Therapeutic News Frames of Presidential Assassination Attempts, 1973–2001." *Communication, Culture, and Critique* 2, no. 1 (2009): 83–109.

Hofstadter, Richard. "America as a Gun Culture." *American Heritage* 21, no. 6 (1970). https://www.americanheritage.com/content/america-gun-culture.

Hogan, J. Michael. *The Nuclear Freeze Campaign: Rhetoric and Foreign Policy in the Telepolitical Age*. East Lansing: Michigan State University Press, 1994.

Hogan, J. Michael, Patricia Hayes Andrews, James R. Andrews, and Glen Williams. *Public Speaking and Civic Engagement*. 4th ed. Boston: Pearson, 2017.

Hogan, J. Michael, and Craig Rood. "Rhetorical Studies and the Gun Debate: A Public Policy Perspective." *Rhetoric & Public Affairs* 18, no. 2 (2015): 359–72.

Hollihan, Thomas A., and Francesca Marie Smith, eds. "Special Issue on Civility." *Rhetoric & Public Affairs* 17, no. 4 (2014): 577–736.

Holloway, Diane. "40 Years Later, KTBC Retells the Tale of UT's Tragic Day." *Austin American-Statesman*, July 27, 2006. https://www.mystatesman.com/news/special-reports/years-later-ktbc-retells-the-tale-tragic-day/uE8jPFinegOZAav9MNU87K/.

Hong, Adrian. "Koreans Aren't to Blame." *Washington Post*, April 20, 2007. http://www.washingtonpost.com/wp-dyn/content/article/2007/04/19/AR2007041902942.html.

hooks, bell. *We Real Cool: Black Men and Masculinity*. New York: Routledge, 2004.

"How Gap Between Police, Black Community Worsened Under Obama." *Fox News*, July 12, 2016. https://video.foxnews.com/v/5033078068001/?#sp=show-clips.

Hunter, Donna Denise. "Dead Men Talking: Africans and the Law in New England's Eighteenth-Century Execution Sermons and Crime Narratives." PhD diss., University of California, Berkeley, 2000.

Hunter, James Davison. *Culture Wars: The Struggle to Define America*. New York: Basic, 1991.

"In Gun Control Debate, Several Options Draw Majority Support: Gun Rights Proponents More Politically Active." *Pew Research Center*, January 14, 2013. http://www.people-press.org/2013/01/14/in-gun-control-debate-several-options-draw-majority-support/.

Ivie, Robert L. "Rhetorical Deliberation and Democratic Politics in the Here and Now." *Rhetoric & Public Affairs* 5, no. 2 (2002): 277–85.

Jacobo, Julia, and Enjoli Francis. "Cops May Have Thought Philando Castile Was a Robbery Suspect, Noting 'Wide-Set Nose,' Dispatch Audio Indicates." *ABC News*, July 11, 2016. http://abcnews.go.com/US/cops-thought-philando-castile-robbery-suspect-dispatch-audio/story?id=40439957.

Jamieson, Kathleen Hall, and Karlyn Kohrs Campbell. "Rhetorical Hybrids: Fusions of Generic Elements." *Quarterly Journal of Speech* 68, no. 2 (1982): 146–57.

Jamieson, Kathleen Hall, and Joseph N. Cappella. *Echo Chamber: Rush Limbaugh and the Conservative Media Establishment*. New York: Oxford University Press, 2008.

Jefferson, Thomas. "To James Madison, Paris, Sep. 6, 1789." *American History: From Revolution to Reconstructions and Beyond*. Accessed November 29, 2017. http://www.let.rug.nl/usa/presidents/thomas-jefferson/letters-of-thomas-jefferson/jefl81.php.

Johnson, Lyndon B. "Remarks upon Signing the Gun Control Act of 1968." *The American Presidency Project*, October 22, 1968. https://www.presidency.ucsb.edu/documents/remarks-upon-signing-the-gun-control-act-1968.

———. "Statement by the President on the Need for Firearms Control Legislation." *The American Presidency Project*, August 2, 1966. http://www.presidency.ucsb.edu/ws/index.php?pid=27753.

Kahan, Dan M. "The Gun Control Debate: A Culture-Theory Manifesto." *Washington and Lee Law Review* 60, no. 1 (2003): 3–12.

Keith, William, and David Beard. "Toulmin's Rhetorical Logic: What's the Warrant for Warrants?" *Philosophy & Rhetoric* 41, no. 1 (2008): 22–50.

Kellner, Douglas. *Guys and Guns Amok: Domestic Terrorism and School Shootings from the Oklahoma City Bombing to the Virginia Tech Massacre*. Boulder, CO: Paradigm, 2008.

———. "Media Spectacle and the 'Massacre at Virginia Tech.'" In *There Is a Gunman on Campus: Tragedy and Terror at Virginia Tech*, edited by Ben Agger and Timothy W. Luke, 29–54. Lanham, MD: Rowman and Littlefield, 2008.

Kennerly, Michele. "Getting Carried Away: How Rhetorical Transport Gets Judgment Going." *Rhetoric Society Quarterly* 40, no. 3 (2010): 269–91.

Kepple, Kevin A., Janet Loehrke, Meghan Hoyer, and Paul Overberg. "Mass Shootings Toll Exceeds 900 in Past Seven Years." *USA Today*, December 2, 2013. http://www.usatoday.com/story/news/nation/2013/02/21/mass-shootings-domestic-violence-nra/1937041/.

"Killer's Manifesto: 'You Forced Me into a Corner.'" *CNN*, April 18, 2007. http://www.cnn.com/2007/US/04/18/vtech.shooting/index.html?eref=onion.

Kimmel, Michael. *Angry White Men: American Masculinity at the End of an Era*. New York: Nation, 2013.

King, Stephen. *Guns*. Kindle edition. Bangor, ME: Philtrum Press, 2013.

Kirby, Jen. "#WalkUpNotOut: A Walkout Alternative That Asked Students to Be Nicer to Each Other." *Vox*, March 14, 2018. https://www.vox.com/2018/3/14/17119674/national-school-walkout-walkupnotout-alternative.

Klebold, Sue. *A Mother's Reckoning: Living in the Aftermath of Tragedy*. New York: Crown, 2016.

Kleck, Gary. *Point Blank: Guns and Violence in America*. New Brunswick, NJ: Transaction, 2009.

Kochanek, Kenneth D., Sherry L. Murphy, Jiaquan Xu, and Betzaida Tejada-Vera. "Deaths: Final Data for 2014." *National Vital Statistics Reports* 65, no. 4 (2016): 1–122. https://www.cdc.gov/nchs/data/nvsr/nvsr65/nvsr65_04.pdf.

Krouse, William J., and Daniel Richardson. "Mass Murder with Firearms: Incidents and Victims, 1999–2013." *Congressional Research Service*, July 30, 2015. https://fas.org/sgp/crs/misc/R44126.pdf.

"KTBC News UT Tower Shooting Special Report." *YouTube*, August 1, 2016. https://www.youtube.com/watch?v=bBtrFS-C1ug.

Kurtz, Jeffrey B. "Civility, American Style." *Relevant Rhetoric* 3 (2012): 1–23.

Lafraniere, Sharon, Daniela Porat, and Agustin Armendariz. "A Drumbeat of Multiple Shootings, but America Isn't Listening." *New York Times*, May 22, 2016. http://www.nytimes.com/2016/05/23/us/americas-overlooked-gun-violence.html?_r=0.

Lakoff, George. *Whose Freedom? The Battle over America's Most Important Idea*. New York: Picador, 2006.

Landau, Jamie, and Bethany Keeley-Jonker. "Conductor of Public Feelings: An Affective-Emotional Rhetorical Analysis of Obama's National Eulogy in Tucson." *Quarterly Journal of Speech* 104, no. 2 (2018): 166–88.

Langman, Peter. "Seung Hui Cho's 'Manifesto.'" *School Shooters*, July 29, 2014. https://schoolshooters.info/sites/default/files/cho_manifesto_1.1.pdf.

———. *Why Kids Kill: Inside the Minds of School Shooters*. New York: Palgrave, 2008.

Lanham, Richard A. *The Economics of Attention: Style and Substance in the Age of Information*. Chicago: University of Chicago Press, 2006.

Lankford, Adam. "Are America's Public Mass Shooters Unique? A Comparative Analysis of Offenders in the United States and Other Countries." *International Journal of Comparative and Applied Criminal Justice* 40, no. 2 (2016): 171–83.

LaPierre, Wayne. "Announcing an All-New NRA Sweepstakes." Promotional material, February/March 2017.

———. *The Essential Second Amendment Guide*. Fairfax, VA: Boru, 2007.

———. "Join NRA's March for Freedom." NRA email, March 17, 2018.

———. "NRA Press Conference, December 21, 2012." *New York Times*, December 21, 2012. http://www.nytimes.com/interactive/2012/12/21/us/nra-news-conference-transcript.html.

———. "Stand and Fight." *Daily Caller*, February 13, 2013. http://dailycaller.com/2013/02/13/stand-and-fight/.

Larkin, Ralph W. "The Columbine Legacy: Rampage Shootings as Political Acts." *American Behavioral Scientist* 52, no. 9 (2009): 1309–26.

———. *Comprehending Columbine*. Philadelphia: Temple University Press, 2007.

Lavergne, Gary M. *A Sniper in the Tower: The Charles Whitman Murders*. Denton: University of North Texas Press, 1997.

Lepore, Jill. *The Whites of Their Eyes: The Tea Party's Revolution and the Battle over American History*. Princeton: Princeton University Press, 2010.

Lewis, William F. "Telling America's Story: Narrative Form and the Reagan Presidency." *Quarterly Journal of Speech* 73, no. 3 (1987): 280–302.

Lipka, Michael, and John Gramlich. "5 Facts About Abortion." *Pew Research Center*, January 26, 2017. http://www.pewresearch.org/fact-tank/2017/01/26/5-facts-about-abortion/.

Lipstadt, Deborah. *Denying the Holocaust: The Growing Assault on Truth and Memory*. New York: Penguin, 1994.

Longo, Nicholas V., Idit Manosevitch, and Timothy J. Shaffer. Introduction to *Deliberative Pedagogy: Teaching and Learning for Democratic Engagement*, edited by Timothy J. Shaffer, Nicholas V. Longo, Idit Manosevitch, and Maxine S. Thomas, xix–xxxv. East Lansing: Michigan State University Press, 2017.

Lopez, German. "America's Unique Gun Violence Problem, Explained in 17 Maps and Charts." *Vox*, April 20, 2018. https://www.vox.com/policy-and-politics/2017/10/2/16399418/us-gun-violence-statistics-maps-charts.

———. "The Trial of Dylann Roof for the Charleston Church Shooting, Explained." *Vox*, January 10, 2017. https://www.vox.com/identities/2016/12/7/13868662/dylann-roof-trial-verdict-charleston-church-shooting.

Loraux, Nicole. *The Invention of Athens: The Funeral Oration in the Classical City*. Translated by Alan Sheridan. New York: Zone, 2006.

Lunceford, Brett. "Armed Victims: The Ego Function of Second Amendment Rhetoric." *Rhetoric & Public Affairs* 18, no. 2 (2015): 333–45.

———. "On the Rhetoric of Second Amendment Remedies." *Journal of Contemporary Rhetoric* 1 (2011): 31–39.

Lysiak, Matthew. *Newtown: An American Tragedy*. New York: Gallery, 2013.

Mack, Ashley Noel, and Bryan J. McCann. "'Strictly an Act of Street Violence': Intimate Publicity and Affective Divestment in the New Orleans Mother's Day Shooting." *Communication and Critical/Cultural Studies* 14, no. 4 (2017): 334–50.

Mason, Lilliana. *Uncivil Agreement: How Politics Became Our Identity*. Chicago: University of Chicago Press, 2018.

Matthews, Chris. "Virginia Tech Shooter Cho Seung-Hui's Description by Roommate." *YouTube*, September 19, 2007. https://www.youtube.com/watch?v=kwS4GKIDcBU.

McCann, Bryan J. *The Mark of Criminality: Rhetoric, Race, and Gangsta Rap in the War-on-Crime Era*. Tuscaloosa: University of Alabama Press, 2017.

McGee, Michael Calvin. "The 'Ideograph': A Link Between Rhetoric and Ideology." *Quarterly Journal of Speech* 66, no. 1 (1980): 1–16.

———. "Text, Context, and the Fragmentation of Contemporary Culture." *Western Journal of Speech Communication* 54, no. 3 (1990): 274–89.

Melzer, Scott. *Gun Crusaders: The NRA's Culture War*. New York: New York University Press, 2009.

Metzl, Jonathan M., and Kenneth T. MacLeish. "Mental Illness, Mass Shootings, and the Politics of American Firearms." *American Journal of Public Health* 105, no. 2 (2015): 240–49.

Meyers, Bess R. "Barack Obama, 'Remarks by the President at a Memorial Service for the Victims of the Shooting in Tucson, Arizona' (12 January 2011)." *Voices of Democracy* 13 (2018): 24–36.

Mize, Laura. "Americans' Top Fears Relate to Everyday Life." *UF Health Communications*, February 26, 2015. http://news.health.ufl.edu/2015/24113/multimedia/health-in-a-heartbeat/americans-top-fears-relate-to-everyday-life/.

Mohr, Charles. "U.S. Bans Imports of Assault Rifles in Shift by Bush." *New York Times*, March 15, 1989. https://www.nytimes.com/1989/03/15/us/us-bans-imports-of-assault-rifles-in-shift-by-bush.html.

Morris, Charles E., III, ed. *Remembering the AIDS Quilt*. East Lansing: Michigan State University Press, 2011.

Murphy, Sherry, Jiaquan Xu, and Kenneth D. Kochanek. "Deaths: Final Data for 2010." *National Vital Statistics Reports* 61, no. 4 (2013): 1–118. http://www.cdc.gov/nchs/data/nvsr/nvsr61/nvsr61_04.pdf.

Murphy, Sherry L., Jiaquan Xu, Kenneth D. Kochanek, Sally C. Curtin, and Elizabeth Arias. "Deaths: Final Data for 2015." *National Vital Statistics Reports* 66, no. 6 (2017): 1–75. https://www.cdc.gov/nchs/data/nvsr/nvsr66/nvsr66_06.pdf.

Mutz, Diana C. *Hearing the Other Side: Deliberative Versus Participatory Democracy*. Cambridge: Cambridge University Press, 2006.

Nakayama, Thomas K., and Robert L. Krizek. "Whiteness: A Strategic Rhetoric." *Quarterly Journal of Speech* 81, no. 3 (1995): 291–309.

Newman, Katherine S. *Rampage: The Social Roots of School Shootings*. New York: Basic, 2004.

Nichols, Chris. "How Is a 'Mass Shooting' Defined?" *Politifact California*, October 4, 2017. https://www.politifact.com/california/article/2017/oct/04/mass-shooting-what-does-it-mean/.

Nimmo, Beth, and Darrell Scott. *Rachel's Tears: The Spiritual Journal of Columbine Martyr Rachel Scott*. Nashville: Nelson, 2008.

Nirappil, Fenit. "The Story Behind 11-year-old Naomi Wadler and Her March for Our Lives Speech." *Washington Post*, March 25, 2018. https://www.washingtonpost.com/local/education/the-story-behind-11-year-old-naomi-wadler-and-her-march-for-our-lives-speech/2018/03/25/3a6dccdc-3058-11e8-8abc-22a366b72f2d_story.html?noredirect=on&utm_term=.0cffaeef543d.

"No Federal Civil Rights Charges in Trayvon Martin Case." *CBS News*, February 24, 2015. http://www.cbsnews.com/news/department-of-justice-no-civil-rights-charges-trayvon-martin-case/.

Now This. "Everyone Needs to Hear This Chicago Native Explain How City, State, and Federal Governments Are Enabling Gun Violence #MarchForOurLives." *Twitter*, March 24, 2018. https://twitter.com/nowthisnews/status/977597877592711170.

Obama, Barack. "Remarks by President Obama, President Tusk of the European Council, and President Juncker of the European Commission After U.S.-EU Meeting." *The White House*, July 8, 2016. https://obamawhitehouse.archives.gov/the-press-office/2016/07/08/remarks-president-obama-president-tusk-european-council-and-president.

———. "Remarks by the President and the Vice President on Gun Violence." *The White House*, January 16, 2013. https://obamawhitehouse.archives.gov/the-press-office/2013/01/16/remarks-president-and-vice-president-gun-violence.

———. "Remarks by the President at Fort Hood Memorial Service." *The White House*, April 9, 2014. https://obamawhitehouse.archives.gov/the-press-office/2014/04/09/remarks-president-fort-hood-memorial-service.

———. "Remarks by the President at Memorial Service for the Fallen Dallas Police Officers." *The White House*, July 12, 2016. https://obamawhitehouse.archives.gov/the-press-office/2016/07/12/remarks-president-memorial-service-fallen-dallas-police-officers.

———. "Remarks by the President at Sandy Hook Interfaith Prayer Vigil." *The White House*, December 16, 2012. https://obamawhitehouse.archives.gov/the-press-office/2012/12/16/remarks-president-sandy-hook-interfaith-prayer-vigil.

———. "Remarks by the President at the Memorial Service for Victims of the Navy Yard Shooting." *The White House*, September 22, 2013. https://obamawhitehouse.archives.gov/the-press-office/2013/09/22/remarks-president-memorial-service-victims-navy-yard-shooting.

———. "Remarks by the President in a Press Conference." *The White House*, December 19, 2012. https://obamawhitehouse.archives.gov/the-press-office/2012/12/19/remarks-president-press-conference.

———. "Remarks by the President in Eulogy for the Honorable Reverend Clementa Pinckney." *The White House*, June 26, 2015. https://obamawhitehouse.archives.gov/the-press-office/2015/06/26/remarks-president-eulogy-honorable-reverend-clementa-pinckney.

———. "Remarks by the President on Gun Safety." *The White House*, March 28, 2013. https://obamawhitehouse.archives.gov/the-press-office/2013/03/28/remarks-president-gun-safety.

———. "Remarks by the President on Mass Shooting in Orlando." *The White House*, June 12, 2016. https://obamawhitehouse.archives.gov/the-press-office/2016/06/12/remarks-president-mass-shooting-orlando.

———. "Remarks by the President on Reducing Gun Violence—Denver, Colorado." *The White House*, April 3, 2013. https://obamawhitehouse.archives.gov/photos-and-video/video/2013/04/03/president-obama-speaks-reducing-gun-violence#transcript.

———. "Remarks by the President on Reducing Gun Violence—Hartford, CT." *The White House*, April 8, 2013. https://obamawhitehouse.archives.gov/the-press-office/2013/04/08/remarks-president-reducing-gun-violence-hartford-ct.

———. "Remarks by the President on Strengthening the Economy for the Middle Class." *The White House*, February 15, 2013. https://obamawhitehouse.archives.gov/the-press-office/2013/02/15/remarks-president-strengthening-economy-middle-class.

———. "Remarks by the President on the State of the Union." *The White House*, February 12, 2013. https://obamawhitehouse.archives.gov/the-press-office/2013/02/12/remarks-president-state-union-address.

———. "Remarks by the President on Trayvon Martin." *The White House*, July 19, 2013. https://obamawhitehouse.archives.gov/the-press-office/2013/07/19/remarks-president-trayvon-martin.

———. "Statement by the President." *The White House*, April 17, 2013. https://obamawhitehouse.archives.gov/the-press-office/2013/04/17/statement-president.

———. "Statement by the President on the School Shooting in Newtown, CT." *The White House*, December 14, 2012. https://obamawhitehouse.archives.gov/the-press-office/2012/12/14/statement-president-school-shooting-newtown-ct.

———. "Statement by the President on the Shootings at Umpqua Community College, Roseburg, Oregon." *The White House*, October 1, 2015. https://obamawhitehouse.archives.gov/the-press-office/2015/10/01/statement-president-shootings-umpqua-community-college-roseburg-oregon.

———. "Statement by the President on the Shooting in Charleston, South Carolina." *The White House*, June 18, 2015. https://obamawhitehouse.archives.gov/the-press-office/2015/06/18/statement-president-shooting-charleston-south-carolina.

"Obama's Entire Dallas Police Memorial Speech." *YouTube*, July 12, 2016. https://www.youtube.com/watch?v=xQPBPB8UDyQ.

Office of the Press Secretary. "Press Briefing by Dana Perino." *The White House*, April 16, 2007. http://georgewbush-whitehouse.archives.gov/news/releases/2007/04/20070416-1.html.

———. "Press Briefing by Dana Perino." *The White House*, April 18, 2007. http://georgewbush-whitehouse.archives.gov/news/releases/2007/04/20070418-3.html.

———. "Press Briefing by Dana Perino." *The White House*, April 19, 2007. http://georgewbush-whitehouse.archives.gov/news/releases/2007/04/20070419-1.html.

O'Gorman, Ned. "Aristotle's Phantasia in the Rhetoric: Lexis, Appearance, and the Epideictic Function of Discourse." *Philosophy & Rhetoric* 38, no. 1 (2005): 16–40.

———. *The Iconoclastic Imagination: Image, Catastrophe, and Economy in America from the Kennedy Assassination to September 11*. Chicago: University of Chicago Press, 2016.

O'Keefe, Ed, and Phillip Rucker. "Gun-Control Overhaul Is Defeated in Senate." *Washington Post*, April 17, 2013. https://www.washingtonpost.com/politics/gun-control-overhaul-is-defeated-in-senate/2013/04/17/57eb028a-a77c-11e2-b029-8fb7e977ef71_story.html?utm_term=.59443c63817f.

"OK for Obama to Mention Black Lives Matter at Memorial?" *Fox News*, July 12, 2016. http://video.foxnews.com/v/5032700531001/?#sp=show-clips.

Oliphant, Baxter. "Bipartisan Support for Some Gun Proposals, Stark Partisan Divisions on Many Others." *Pew Research Center*, June 23, 2017. http://www.pewresearch.org/fact-tank/2017/06/23/bipartisan-support-for-some-gun-proposals-stark-partisan-divisions-on-many-others/.

Pappas, Alex. "NRA Leader Criticizes Obama for Attacks on 'Absolutism.'" *Daily Caller*, January 22, 2013. http://dailycaller.com/2013/01/22/nra-leader-criticizes-obama-for-attacks-on-absolutism/.

Pariser, Eli. *The Filter Bubble: How the New Personalized Web Is Changing What We Read and How We Think*. New York: Penguin, 2011.

Parker, Kim, Juliana Menasce Horowitz, Ruth Igielnik, Baxter Oliphant, and Anna Brown. "America's Complex Relationship with Guns." *Pew Research Center*,

June 22, 2017. http://www.pewsocialtrends.org/2017/06/22/americas-complex-relationship-with-guns/.

"The Partisan Divide on Political Values Grows Even Wider." *Pew Research Center*, October 5, 2017. http://www.people-press.org/2017/10/05/1-partisan-divides-over-political-values-widen/.

Perelman, Chaïm, and Lucie Olbrechts-Tyteca. *The New Rhetoric: A Treatise on Argumentation*. Translated by John Wilkinson and Purcell Weaver. Notre Dame: University of Notre Dame Press, 1969.

Phillips, Kendall R., ed. *Framing Public Memory*. Tuscaloosa: University of Alabama Press, 2004.

Price, Dawnthea. "Trump's Video Game Summit Looks like a Farce Before It's Even Happened (Update: It Was a Farce)." *Slate*, March 8, 2018. https://slate.com/technology/2018/03/trumps-video-game-summit-is-a-farce.html.

"Protestors Encircle NRA Convention Site." *CNN*, May 1, 1999. http://www.cnn.com/US/9905/01/nra.protest.01/index.html?_s=PM:US.

Pryal, Katie Rose Guest. "Reframing Sanity: Scapegoating the Mentally Ill in the Case of Jared Loughner." In *Re/Framing Identifications*, edited by Michelle Ballif, 159–68. Long Grove, IL: Waveland Press, 2014.

Putnam, Robert D. *Bowling Alone: The Collapse and Revival of American Community*. New York: Simon and Schuster Paperbacks, 2000.

Ratcliffe, Krista. "The Current State of Composition Scholar/Teachers: Is Rhetoric Gone or Just Hiding Out?" *Enculturation* 5, no. 1 (2013). http://enculturation.net/5_1/ratcliffe.html.

———. *Rhetorical Listening: Identification, Gender, Whiteness*. Carbondale: Southern Illinois University Press, 2005.

Raymond, Emilie. *From My Cold Dead Hands: Charlton Heston and American Politics*. Lexington: University of Kentucky Press, 2006.

Reagan, Ronald. "Remarks at the Annual Members Banquet of the National Rifle Association in Phoenix, Arizona." *The American Presidency Project*, May 6, 1983. https://www.presidency.ucsb.edu/documents/remarks-the-annual-members-banquet-the-national-rifle-association-phoenix-arizona.

———. "Why I'm for the Brady Bill." *New York Times*, March 29, 1991.

Ricoeur, Paul. *Memory, History, Forgetting*. Translated by Kathleen Blamey and David Pellauer. Chicago: University of Chicago Press, 2004.

Riddell, Corinne A., Sam Harper, Magdalena Cerdá, and Jay S. Kaufman. "Comparison of Rates of Firearm and Nonfirearm Homicide and Suicide in Black and White Non-Hispanic Men, by U.S. State." *Annals of Internal Medicine* 168, no. 10 (2018): 712–20.

Ridder, Knight. "Still-Grieving Colorado Turns Out to Protest NRA Meeting." *Baltimore Sun*, May 2, 1999. http://articles.baltimoresun.com/1999-05-02/news/9905020166_1_charlton-heston-nra-president-charlton-columbine-victims.

Roberts-Miller, Patricia. "Dissent as 'Aid and Comfort to the Enemy': The Rhetorical Power of Naïve Realism and Ingroup Identity." *Rhetoric Society Quarterly* 39, no. 2 (2009): 170–88.

Rood, Craig. "'Our Tears Are Not Enough': The Warrant of the Dead in the Rhetoric of Gun Control." *Quarterly Journal of Speech* 104, no. 1 (2018): 47–70.

———. "The Racial Politics of Gun Violence: A Brief Rhetorical History." In *Was Blind but Now I See: Rhetoric, Race, Religion, and the Charleston Shooting*, edited by Sean Patrick O'Rourke and Melody Lehn. Lanham, MD: Lexington, forthcoming.

———. "Rhetorical Closure." *Rhetoric Society Quarterly* 47, no. 4 (2017): 313–34.

Roy, Lucinda. *No Right to Remain Silent: What We've Learned from the Tragedy at Virginia Tech*. New York: Three Rivers Press, 2009.

Schwartz, Barry. *Abraham Lincoln in the Post-heroic Era: History and Memory in Late Twentieth-Century America*. Chicago: University of Chicago Press, 2008.

Selby, W. Gardner. "Steve Adler Wrong That First U.S. 'Mass Shooting' Occurred in Austin." *Politifact*, June 23, 2016. http://www.politifact.com/texas/statements/2016/jun/23/steve-adler/steve-adler-wrong-first-us-mass-shooting-occurred-/.

Shome, Raka. "'Global Motherhood': The Transnational Intimacies of White Femininity." *Critical Studies in Media Communication* 28, no. 5 (2011): 388–406.

Siegel, Michael B., and Emily F. Rothman. "Firearm Ownership and the Murder of Women in the United States: Evidence That the State-Level Firearm Ownership Rate Is Associated with the Nonstranger Femicide Rate." *Violence and Gender* 3, no. 1 (2016): 20–26.

Silver, Nate. "The Gun Vote and 2014: Will There Be an Electoral Price?" *FiveThirtyEight*, April 23, 2013. http://fivethirtyeight.blogs.nytimes.com/2013/04/23/the-gun-vote-and-2014-will-there-be-an-electoral-price/.

Slevin, Peter. "Chicago Grapples with Gun Violence; Murder Tolls Soars." *Washington Post*, December 21, 2012. https://www.washingtonpost.com/national/chicago-grapples-with-gun-violence-murder-toll-soars/2012/12/20/b16601fe-4a1e-11e2-ad54-580638ede391_story.html?utm_term=.1abdfdee7045.

Sloop, John M., and Charles E. Morris III, eds. "Forum: Feeling the Pulse After Orlando." *Communication and Critical/Cultural Studies* 14, no. 2 (2017): 176–202.

Smith, Erica L., and Alexia Cooper. "Homicide in the U.S. Known to Law Enforcement, 2011." *U.S. Department of Justice*, December 2013. http://www.bjs.gov/content/pub/pdf/hus11.pdf.

Smith, Francesca Marie, and Thomas A. Hollihan. "'Out of Chaos Breathes Creation': Human Agency, Mental Illness, and Conservative Arguments Locating Responsibility for the Tucson Massacre." *Rhetoric & Public Affairs* 17, no. 4 (2014): 585–618.

Sontag, Susan. *Regarding the Pain of Others*. New York: Picador, 2003.

"The Speech of President Obama's Life." *MSNBC*, July 13, 2016. http://www.msnbc.com/morning-joe/watch/the-speech-of-president-obama-s-life-724220995901?playlist=associated&v=a.

Spitzer, Robert J. *The Politics of Gun Control*. 5th ed. New York: Routledge, 2012.

Stabile, Carol A. *White Victims, Black Villains: Gender, Race, and Crime News in US Culture*. New York: Routledge, 2006.

"State Gun Laws Enacted in the Year After Newtown." *New York Times*, December 10, 2013. http://www.nytimes.com/interactive/2013/12/10/us/state-gun-laws-enacted-in-the-year-since-newtown.html?_r=0.

Stewart, Charles J., Craig Allen Smith, and Robert E. Denton Jr. *Persuasion and Social Movements*. 5th ed. Long Grove, IL: Waveland Press, 2007.

Strain, Christopher B. *Reload: Rethinking Violence in American Life*. Nashville: Vanderbilt University Press, 2009.

Stuckey, Mary E. "Jimmy Carter, Human Rights, and the Instrumental Effects of Presidential Rhetoric." In *The Handbook of Rhetoric and Public Address*, edited by Shawn J. Parry-Giles and J. Michael Hogan, 293–312. Malden, MA: Wiley-Blackwell, 2010.

"Suicide Statistics." *American Foundation for Suicide Prevention*, 2016. Accessed November 29, 2017. https://afsp.org/about-suicide/suicide-statistics/.

Sullivan, Andrew. "I Used to Be a Human Being." *New York Magazine*, September 18, 2016. http://nymag.com/selectall/2016/09/andrew-sullivan-technology-almost-killed-me.html.

Thucydides. "Pericles' Funeral Oration." University of Minnesota Human Rights Library. Accessed November 29, 2017. http://hrlibrary.umn.edu/education/thucydides.html.

Time Staff. "Here's Donald Trump's Presidential Announcement Speech." *Time*, June 16, 2015. http://time.com/3923128/donald-trump-announcement-speech/.

Toulmin, Stephen. *The Uses of Argument*. Updated edition. New York: Cambridge University Press, 2003.

Tower. Animated documentary. Directed by Keith Mitland. Netflix, 2016.

Turner, Kathleen J., ed. *Doing Rhetorical History: Concepts and Cases*. Tuscaloosa: University of Alabama Press, 1998.

Veal, Jennifer. "South Korea's Collective Guilt." *Time*, April 18, 2007. http://content.time.com/time/nation/article/0,8599,1611964,00.html.

Verdery, Katherine. *The Political Lives of Dead Bodies: Reburial and Postsocialist Change*. New York: Columbia University Press, 1999.

Victor, Daniel. "Mass Shooters Are All Different. Except for One Thing: Most Are Men." *New York Times*, February 17, 2018. https://www.nytimes.com/2018/02/17/us/mass-murderers.html.

Virginia Tech Review Panel. *Report of the Virginia Tech Review Panel Presented to Timothy M. Kaine, Governor, Commonwealth of Virginia*, August 2007. http://www.washingtonpost.com/wp-srv/metro/documents/vatechreport.pdf.

Vivian, Bradford. *Public Forgetting: The Rhetoric and Politics of Beginning Again*. University Park: Pennsylvania State University Press, 2010.

Waldman, Michael. *The Second Amendment: A Biography*. New York: Simon and Schuster, 2014.

Ward Room Staff. "Chicago Was Nation's Murder Capital in 2012." *NBC Chicago*, September 3, 2013. http://www.nbcchicago.com/blogs/ward-room/chicago-fbi-homicide-report-224396461.html.

Wattles, Jackie. "More Than a Dozen Businesses Ran Away from the NRA. How It Went Down." *CNN Money*, February 26, 2018. http://money.cnn.com/2018/02/25/news/companies/companies-abandoning-nra-list/index.html.

Webster, Daniel W., and Jon S. Vernick, eds. *Reducing Gun Violence in America: Informing Policy with Evidence and Analysis*. Baltimore: Johns Hopkins University Press, 2013.

Wetlaufer, Gerald B. "Rhetoric and Its Denial in Legal Discourse." *Virginia Law Review* 76, no. 9 (1990): 1545–97.

White House, The. "Now Is the Time: The President's Plan to Protect Our Children and Our Communities by Reducing Gun Violence." *The White House*, January 16, 2013. https://obamawhitehouse.archives.gov/sites/default/files/docs/wh_now_is_the_time_full.pdf.

"Why Own a Gun? Protection Is Now Top Reason." *Pew Research Center*, March 12, 2013. http://www.people-press.org/2013/03/12/section-3-gun-ownership-trends-and-demographics/.

"Why? Portraits of the Killers: The Science of Teen Violence." *Newsweek*, May 3, 1999. Front cover.

Williams, Mark T., and Theresa Enos. "Vico's Triangular Invention." In *Perspectives on Rhetorical Invention*, edited by Janet M. Atwill and Janice M. Lauer, 192–211. Knoxville: University of Tennessee Press, 2002.

Willingham, A. J. "Donations to the NRA Tripled After the Parkland Shooting." *CNN*, March 28, 2018. https://www.cnn.com/2018/03/28/us/nra-donations-spike-parkland-shooting-trnd/index.html.

Willis-Chun, Cynthia. "Tales of Tragedy: Strategic Rhetoric in News Coverage of the Columbine and Virginia Tech Massacres." In *Critical Rhetorics of Race*, edited by

Michael G. Lacy and Kent A. Ono, 47–64. New York: New York University Press, 2011.

Wills, Gary. *Lincoln at Gettysburg: The Words That Remade America*. New York: Simon and Schuster, 1992.

Wilson, Harry L. *Guns, Gun Control, and Elections: The Politics and Policy of Firearms*. Lanham, MD: Rowman and Littlefield, 2007.

Winkler, Adam. *Gunfight: The Battle over the Right to Bear Arms in America*. New York: Norton, 2013.

Winter, Tom, Jim Miklaszewski, Andrew Blankstein, and Elizabeth Chuck. "Dallas Suspect Was Upset About Recent Police Shootings, 'Wanted to Kill White People.'" *NBC News*, July 8, 2016. https://www.nbcnews.com/storyline/dallas-police-ambush/dallas-suspect-was-upset-about-recent-police-shootings-wanted-kill-n605916.

Wise, Tim. "Blinded by the White: Race, Crime and Columbine High." *Tim Wise*, June 15, 1999. http://www.timwise.org/1999/06/blinded-by-the-white-race-crime-and-columbine-high/.

———. "Race, Class, Violence and Denial: Mass Murder and the Pathologies of Privilege." *Tim Wise*, December 17, 2012. http://www.timwise.org/2012/12/race-class-violence-and-denial-mass-murder-and-the-pathologies-of-privilege/.

———. *White like Me: Reflections on Race from a Privileged Son*. Berkeley, CA: Soft Skull Press, 2011.

Young, Iris Marion. "Activist Challenges to Deliberative Democracy." *Political Theory* 29, no. 5 (2001): 670–90.

Zarefsky, David. "Four Senses of Rhetorical History." In *Doing Rhetorical History: Concepts and Cases*, edited by Kathleen J. Turner, 19–32. Tuscaloosa: University of Alabama Press, 1998.

———. *President Johnson's War on Poverty: Rhetoric and History*. 2nd ed. Tuscaloosa: University of Alabama Press, 2005.

———. "Reflections on Making the Case." In *Making the Case: Advocacy and Judgment in Public Argument*, edited by Kathryn M. Olson, Michael William Pfau, Benjamin Ponder, and Kirt H. Wilson, 1–15. East Lansing: Michigan State University Press, 2012.

———. "Two Faces of Democratic Rhetoric." In *Rhetoric and Democracy: Pedagogical and Political Practices*, edited by Todd F. McDorman and David M. Timmerman, 115–37. East Lansing: Michigan State University Press, 2008.

Zelizer, Barbie. "Reading the Past Against the Grain: The Shape of Memory Studies." *Critical Studies in Mass Communication* 12, no. 2 (1995): 214–39.

Zhang, Sarah. "Why Can't the U.S. Treat Gun Violence as a Public Health Problem?" *Atlantic*, February 15, 2018. https://www.theatlantic.com/health/archive/2018/02/gun-violence-public-health/553430/.

INDEX

This index deliberately excludes the names of mass shooters. Although this choice risks dehumanizing mass shooters, I also believe that we need to resist routine cultural practices—even small ones—that elevate particular mass shooters by giving them undue attention.

Other Books in the Series

Karen Tracy, *Challenges of Ordinary Democracy: A Case Study in Deliberation and Dissent* / Volume 1

Samuel McCormick, *Letters to Power: Public Advocacy Without Public Intellectuals* / Volume 2

Christian Kock and Lisa S. Villadsen, eds., *Rhetorical Citizenship and Public Deliberation* / Volume 3

Jay P. Childers, *The Evolving Citizen: American Youth and the Changing Norms of Democratic Engagement* / Volume 4

Dave Tell, *Confessional Crises and Cultural Politics in Twentieth-Century America* / Volume 5

David Boromisza-Habashi, *Speaking Hatefully: Culture, Communication, and Political Action in Hungary* / Volume 6

Arabella Lyon, *Deliberative Acts: Democracy, Rhetoric, and Rights* / Volume 7

Lyn Carson, John Gastil, Janette Hartz-Karp, and Ron Lubensky, eds., *The Australian Citizens' Parliament and the Future of Deliberative Democracy* / Volume 8

Christa J. Olson, *Constitutive Visions: Indigeneity and Commonplaces of National Identity in Republican Ecuador* / Volume 9

Damien Smith Pfister, *Networked Media, Networked Rhetorics: Attention and Deliberation in the Early Blogosphere* / Volume 10

Katherine Elizabeth Mack, *From Apartheid to Democracy: Deliberating Truth and Reconciliation in South Africa* / Volume 11

Mary E. Stuckey, *Voting Deliberatively: FDR and the 1936 Presidential Campaign* / Volume 12

Robert Asen, *Democracy, Deliberation, and Education* / Volume 13

Shawn J. Parry-Giles and David S. Kaufer, *Memories of Lincoln and the Splintering of American Political Thought* / Volume 14

J. Michael Hogan, Jessica A. Kurr, Michael J. Bergmaier, and Jeremy D. Johnson, eds., *Speech and Debate as Civic Education* / Volume 15

Angela G. Ray and Paul Stob, eds., *Thinking Together: Lecturing, Learning, and Difference in the Long Nineteenth Century* / Volume 16

Sharon E. Jarvis and Soo-Hye Han, *Votes that Count and Voters Who Don't: How Journalists Sideline Electoral Participation (Without Even Knowing It)* / Volume 17

Belinda Stillion Southard, *How to Belong: Women's Agency in a Transnational World* / Volume 18

Melanie Loehwing, *Homeless Advocacy and the Rhetorical Construction of the Civic Home* / Volume 19

Kristy Maddux, *Practicing Citizenship: Women's Rhetoric at the 1893 Chicago World's Fair* / Volume 20